Name on the Schoolhouse

Published by the Washington State Retired Teachers Association
910-B Lakeridge Way S.W., Olympia, WA 98502
An Approved Project of the
Washington State Centennial Commission

Graphic Production provided as a public service by
The Boeing Company, Seattle

ISBN 0-9630702-0-7

"One day a Mrs. Matteson, teacher in the little valley school, wrote on the side of the building 'Zenkner Valley Schoolhouse.' Since then, this has been the name of the valley."—Austin Zenkner, quoted by Herndon Smith, in *Centralia, The First 50 Years,* published in 1942.

About the Editor

Kenneth L. Calkins was born and reared in Washington State — born in Shelton, attending public schools in Port Angeles, Shelton, and Chehalis. He has a bachelor of arts degree in journalism and a master of arts degree in communications, both from the University of Washington. He has worked as an editor, writer, and teacher for more than 40 years.

Cover photo: Stadium High School in Tacoma was originally intended to be a hotel. (Photo from Tacoma Public Library files via Pat Flynn, Community Relations, Tacoma School District)

Preface

In 1990 New Yorker writer Ian Frazier asked several New York City merchants, a policeman, and a fireman "Where did the Holland Tunnel get its name?" None knew the answer. All had businesses or were stationed within two blocks of the New York entrance to the world's first underwater tunnel for motor vehicles. A Japanese tourist Frazier talked to had read the plaque under the bronze likeness of Clifford Holland, tunnel designer and chief engineer. The plaque is at the New York end of the tunnel, which goes under the Hudson River to New Jersey. The tourist was the only person Frazier found who could answer his question.

That's not just another story of New York City indifference. It is representative of most of us. We don't know for whom our tunnels, towns, bridges, and schools are named, and we are only mildly curious. But if we want to know, for instance, where towns in Washington State got their names, there are at least two books in many libraries that can tell us: *Washington State Place Names,* by James W. Phillips, and *Place Names of Washington,* by Robert Hitchman. And now there is this book, *Name on the Schoolhouse—An Anecdotal Listing of Some Historic Names of Schools in Washington State.*

In the late 1970s, this book evolved from my own interest in a high school in Clarkston named Charles Francis Adams. I finally rediscovered the story behind the naming of that school, and the experience made me want to look into the backgrounds of other school names. After intermittent efforts over several years, I found the school name research was a job I could not do alone.

In 1987 I approached the Washington Centennial Commission. It was getting ready to celebrate the state's 100th birthday in 1989. Could a study of the origin of school names be a Centennial Project? Indeed it could if I had a non-profit organization sponsor the project. I approached Jessie Schroeder, then president of the Washington State

Retired Teachers Association (WSRTA) of which I was and am a member. She agreed to support my proposal before the WSRTA executive board. Because of her enthusiasm, and that of her successors, the Washington State Retired Teachers Association not only became the sponsor but its members became the primary researchers.

Four organizations endorsed our application to the Washington State Centennial Commission: the Washington Association of School Administrators, the Association of Washington School Principals, the Washington State School Directors Association, and the Mason County Centennial Committee. The State Centennial Commission subsequently approved the project but did not allocate commission funds for its support.

WSRTA is a genuine non-profit organization and did not have funds for printing this book. My association with The Boeing Company as a writer and an editor in the company's public relations department for 17 years in the 1950s and '60s led me to ask for the company's help in defraying printing costs. Harold Carr, vice president of public relations and an old friend and former co-worker, made the Boeing printing services available at no cost.

On another page you will find the names of the people who researched this book. My wife, Dorine Calkins, and my daughters, SuAnn Denning and Kyle Hadley, helped with editing and copyreading.

What Is a Historic School Name?

Not every Washington State resident reading this book will find a school name from his or her community. That's because we restricted our list to pre-college schools—private, parochial, and public—having distinctive names with historic connections. But even those limitations proved too expansive for our resources.

There are about 1,600 public pre-college schools in this state plus some 400 private and parochial schools. Add to that perhaps a thousand pre-college schools in this state now closed, many of them having names worthy of remembering. There also are school-related facilities such as historically named athletic and play fields, grandstands, school libraries, and buildings within a school complex.

We had to find a way to reduce this list of historic school names to a manageable size, a list of schools we could reasonably expect to identify within two or three years using volunteer researchers. In short, we had to define a historic school name.

Because schools deal with humans, they are depositories of human history. So we chose school names that dealt directly with human history which is just another way of saying human culture. However, in most cases, we did not select schools named for towns or communities or real estate developments unless the town and school were named simultaneously, or the town was named for the school, or the school is the sole remaining evidence that there ever was a town, or the school played an important role in human history irrespective of its name. We usually excluded schools named for natural landmarks such as rivers but included schools named for man-made landmarks such as roads. Place names in Washington State have been extensively researched and the results published in at least two readily available books. We did not want to duplicate that information in our text.

This book does not pretend to be a list of schools which have historic significance, although many of those listed do have such significance. But that was not a criterion for selecting which schools to list. We wanted schools whose *names* were historic. That immediately reduced our list of schools from 3,000 to about 1,000. These 1,000 schools have been named directly for real persons, historic events or entities, man-made landmarks or objects, and symbols of cultural heritage or educational philosophies.

Here are examples of schools named directly for historic events: Little Kentucky School in Lewis County is believed to have been so-named for the early settlers migrating from that state to the area served by the school. Garrison School in Walla Walla was named for the garri-

son of troopers stationed at Fort Walla Walla during the Indian Wars of the 1850s. Such school names are inherently historic.

Symbols of our cultural history include the many Indian names given to our schools. A school named Tapteal qualifies as being named for a historic cultural symbol—in this case a word from the Chinook jargon. A school named Steilacoom does not qualify because it is named for a town. The town has a historic cultural Indian name, but the school only borrowed that name.

Speaking of Indian names, we aren't completely confident of the spellings and translations of Native American words in English. The literature available and understandable to laymen on the meaning of Indian words is sparse, the spellings diverse. We sought expert help from public agencies and private individuals believed to be knowledgeable about Indian culture. They evidently have been so inundated with such requests for Indian cultural information that they respond only to the most persistent inquirers. I was not persistent enough. Relying on my credentials as a representative of the Washington State Retired Teachers Association working on a project approved by the Washington Centennial Commission, I wrote two letters of inquiry to a curator at the Burke Memorial Museum on the campus of the University of Washington. Neither was acknowledged. I wrote to a member of a state-wide Indian intertribal council, and to the great-grandson of Chief Smithkin of the Okanogan country, both of whom had indicated interest in the research project. Their responses were nonexistent. The experience was dispiriting but understandable when one keeps in mind that all our Indian words were devised by Europeans or Americans of European ancestry, or American-educated Indians attempting to mimic the sounds they heard emanating from Native American mouths. Their work is undoubtedly of uneven quality. So for interpreting Indian names cited in this book, we used what sources were readily available to us in libraries and museums, adequate for our purposes here.

Errors and Omissions

The information in this book was gathered by almost 300 volunteers from around the state. Among the most active researchers were members of the Washington State Retired Teachers Association to whom I am most grateful. They were joined by other researchers, mostly active school personnel who have an interest in school histories. These researchers got their information from local historical societies, school district files, scrapbooks, museums, old newspaper files, interviews with school personnel and area old-timers, and from the researchers' own personal experiences. In some instances, the information gathered from one source conflicted with information gathered from another source. In such cases, we used both pieces of information.

This technique almost guarantees that there will be errors of fact in our accounts of how schools got their names. However, since this is intended to be an anecdotal history, we do not find this policy to be in conflict with our purpose. The reader may decide which account seems to have the most validity.

We have omitted some schools whose names fit our definition of "historic" because we did not know about them in time to meet publication deadlines. If there is ever a second edition of this volume, we will be able to include these additional school names.

As we received information on school names, we wrote it down in paragraphs, sent copies off to the researchers who provided the information, to the public school districts of the schools mentioned in the text, to the Yakima and Spokane Roman Catholic dioceses and the Seattle Archdiocese, and, in many cases, to administrators of individual schools. They were asked to correct any errors or oversights. But in fact a number of units, schools, and districts solicited for their corrections did not respond to our queries.

If you find errors or if you know of school names meeting our definition of "historic" and not included in our listing, let me know. Write to Ken Calkins, Name on the School House, Washington State Retired Teachers Association, 910-B Lakeridge Way S.W., Olympia, WA 98502.

How These School Lists Are Organized

Pre-college schools in Washington State, whose names meet our criteria for being historic, are listed in alphabetical order according to the root word in their names. If the school has been named after a person, then it is listed by that person's surname.

For example, there is a Governor John R. Rogers School, a John R. Rogers School, and a Rogers School. All are listed under R. Schools named for persons who have titles are listed alphabetically by the surname or root word. Commodore Bainbridge School is found under B. Chief Joseph School is listed under J. However, school names beginning with St. or Fort are listed under S and F respectively.

Within groups of schools having the same name, such as Whitman, schools are listed in alphabetical order of the counties in which those schools are situated.

If you are interested in reading about the schools in your county, you will find them indexed in the back of the book.

Practical Uses for This Book

When school populations are expanding, public school boards, private school trustees, and parochial school committees often have the opportunity to name new schools. Some schools, school districts, and dioceses have policies or practices that guide school name selections from a group of "Great Americans," or from a list of saints. Others follow policies that stipulate no school will be named for a living person, or no school will be named for any person whatsoever. This accounts for so many schools and school districts being named Evergreen, Cascade, or Mountain View. Such names are usually safefrom public criticism. However, in 1990 the Issaquah School District found itself sued for naming a school Mountain View when there already was a private schoolwith that name in the vicinity. School-naming episodes have occasionally resulted in hurt feelings and injured pride. Some of those instances are related in this book.

This listing of historic names of schools should be read by every person ever involved in the naming of a school. Such people need to know how many names of ex-presidents have yet to be used on any school anywhere in the state. They need to know that too many schools have already been named Evergreen, or Lincoln, or Washington, or Garfield, or Cascade, or McKinley, or Highland, or Mountain View, or St. Joseph, knowledge that perhaps will dissuade them from adding still more schools to the list.

The school names listed in this book can be used to define what areas of endeavor have been most honored by school naming committees and those which have never been honored. For example, there are more than a hundred schools named for teachers, superintendents, and school board members. There are no schools named for anyone principally known for their work in the performing arts: acting, dancing, music, or athletics. While the performing arts encompass many of the fields that draw big salaries—one measure of public esteem—they are neglected in sharing school name honors.

As you read through the book, see if you can find the following schools: There are two school facilities named for custodian-bus drivers, and two schools named for food service personnel. There are three schools and one athletic facility named for school-aged children, and two schools named for infants. There are three schools named for a founder of the temperance and women's rights movements. There once was a high school in Seattle named for Samuel Gompers, founder of the American Federation of Labor. What name does that school now have?

You will find the answers to these questions, and to many more intriguing questions, in the following pages.

Kenneth L. Calkins
Editor
April 12, 1991

Who Wrote This Book?

The following persons contributed to *Name on the Schoolhouse*. They are the authors; I am the compiler and editor. They did not all give equally of their time and effort but how does one acknowledge their help in proportion to its volume? I could not think of a way. So instead I list them here under the name of the county in which they provided school name information.

Among these 300 authors you will find teachers, pastors, librarians, secretaries, school and school district administrators, historical society members, relatives of persons for whom schools were named, archivists, and other citizens interested in local history. In some cases, information was provided by an unnamed person at a school or school district. The Seattle Archdiocese of the Roman Catholic Church sent many unattributed pages on its schools. Information on Catholic schools came largely from the Seattle Archdiocese, which covers schools in western Washington, the Yakima Diocese for Catholic schools in central Washington, the Spokane Diocese for schools in eastern Washington, and the Sisters of Providence archives in Seattle. Additional parochial and private schools were reached directly by mail.

Pay particular attention to the nearly 60 names identified as members of the Washington State Retired Teachers Association (WSRTA). They made up the statewide network that carried out the original research. In most cases, these are the members of the research team who stayed together for more than three years. None of these researchers was paid. Their only incentive was to perform a service which would survive them and of which they could be proud.

One of these researchers was Camilla Summers, who died August 6, 1990, at age 82, without ever seeing a copy of this book. She was the author of three other books, one of them a textbook, and a recognized historian in her community of Kelso. In 1987 this former teacher was named First Citizen of Cowlitz County and Kelso Citizen of the Year. In 1990 a new waterfront park in Kelso was dedicated in her honor. The information on Kelso Schools in this book was done principally by Mrs. Summers.

Many of our contributors are old enough to be writing about history in which they participated. In many cases they did not have to interview others to get their information. It was available to them in their scrapbooks and in their memories. While I did not take a survey, I believe the oldest of our researchers was Ruth Wear, retired teacher of Sunnyside. She was 92 as I wrote this in 1991. Her age and memories and energies are the reasons schools in the lower Yakima Valley are so well covered in this book.

I have kept the letters and clippings from Camilla, Ruth, and all the other researchers. Those records will be filed carefully for the possible use of future historians.

Adams County

Ruth A. Danielson, Washington State Retired Teachers Association (WSRTA), James M. Davis, Robert Eckert, Irma Gfieler.

Asotin County

Harold Beggs, Mark A. Mitrovich, Elizabeth Verburg (WSRTA), R. P. Weatherly.

Benton County

Steve Aagaard, Catherine Ferguson, Louis Gates, Rodney P. Hahn, Mary F. Johnson, Sister Noreene O'Connor, Arden E. Smith Jr., Nina Thomas (WSRTA), Albert V. Vandenberg, Jane Yelenc (WSRTA), Helen Willard.

Chelan County

Bill Gordon, Vicki Hoffman, Albert Long, Mary Louise Schneider (WSRTA), Wilma Stellingwerf, Ethel Taylor, Norm Veach.

Clallam County

Lucille Jarmuth, Sam G. Kenzy (WSRTA), William A. Serrette, Sandra Smith.

Clark County

Garnet Allen (WSRTA), Louise Allworth, Sister Rita Bergamini, Loretta Zwolak Greene, Beverly Mae Isaacson (WSRTA), Lola Glay, Nancy Nellor, Dick Mariotti, Beth C. Reich, Clarice B. Schorzman, Sandra Stanton.

Columbia County

Sue Bell, Franklin Hanson (WSRTA), Charlotte Hutchens, Robert C. Mostek.

Cowlitz County

Sister Rita Bergamini, Denise B. Doerfler, Loretta Zwokak Greene, George Heaton, Grant Hendrickson, Helen M. Leonard (WSRTA), Linda Peck, Camilla Summers (WSRTA).

Douglas County

Edward A. Barnhart, Earle W. Jenkin, Les Lillquist (WSRTA), Mary Louise Schneider (WSRTA).

Ferry County

No contributors

Franklin County

Elizabeth Gladden (WSRTA), Larry Nyland, James Verhulp, Patricia J. Wilson.

Garfield County

R. P. Weatherly

Grant County

Brenda Follett, Ray Gilman, Gladys Hull (WSRTA), Maurice Johnson, Leslie Lillquist (WSRTA), Amy Mahoney, Lark Moore, Reuben Ruff, Marge Schoessler, George I. Werner (WSRTA).

Grays Harbor County

Bill Denholm, Ray Lorton, Donald R. Simpson, Rosalie Spellman (WSRTA), Richard Voege.

Island County

Grace Cornwell (WSRTA)

Jefferson County

Germaine Arthur, George Hicks, Marilyn S. Pedersen, Betty Pfouts, Gwen McLaughlin (WSRTA).

King County

Douglas C. Arthur, Karen Bates, Donna Batter, Velma Beck (WSRTA), Karen Beeson, Dina Benedetti, Mary Benedict, Sister Rita Bergamini, Jill Bergeson, Brigitte Bertschi, Barbara Birch, Sandy Bohman, Gloria Boyce, Frank Brouillet (WSRTA), Doris Brown, Kristine A. Brynildsen-Smith, Judy Christiansen, Evelyn Crandall (WSRTA), Sister Dolores Crosby, Barbara de Michele, Geri Fain, James Fugate, Loretta Zwolak Greene, Rich Hamlin, Dinah L. Haugum, Paul Hoerlein (WSRTA), James F. Kolessar, Gloria M. Langen, Nancy Langlow, Leslie Larsen Jr., Margit Larson (WSRTA), Terry Malinowski, Michael Mallin, Angelo Marinaro (WSRTA), Linda McCleary, Gwen McLaughlin (WSRTA), Rebecca McPharlin, Marilyn Mettlin, Wil E. Neutzmann (WSRTA), Jan Orr, Judy Parker, Joyce Quinlan (WSRTA), Burbank Rideout (WSRTA), Mary Helen Robinson, Joan Scanlon, Jackie Smith, Rick Sullivan, Christine Taylor, Ethel Telban (WSRTA), Carl E. Tingelstad, Eleanor Toews, Ellen Toole, Tom Traeger, Judith M. Wall, Delores Wivag (WSRTA).

Kitsap County

Gerald Elfendahl, Jean Fankell, Karen V. Gross, Mary Harding, Helen Hoey, Linda S. Munson, Field Ryan, Lydia M. Simonson (WSRTA), Julia Wan.

Kittitas County

Joseph L. Carter, Karen Cocheba, Lucile Johnson (WSRTA), Joe Lassoie (WSRTA), Karol Malde, Lew Moormann, Arley Vancil (WSRTA), Verna Watson (WSRTA).

Klickitat County

Ruth Danielson (WSRTA), Mary Ledbetter, Homer J.E. Townsend (WSRTA).

Lewis County

Bob Fay, Sherri Garland, Linda Godat, Elizabeth Wedin (WSRTA), Loraine Williams.

Lincoln County

Sister Rita Bergamini, Loretta Zwolak Greene, Gordon L. Wallace

Mason County

Lorna and Douglas Dayton (WSRTA), Kathy Haynes, George Willett.

Okanogan County

Rebecca Bratrude, Keith Davis (WSRTA), Irmal Jones (WSRTA), Geneva Kinzie (WSRTA), Bill Laws, Charles McKain, Samuel F. Sampson, Maribeth Segerdal.

Pacific County

No contributors

Pend Oreille County

Darlene Beacham, Helen Roos (WSRTA), James Sewell, Margaret Townsend (WSRTA), Nora Lee Winiarskia.

Pierce County

Charles Alexander, Linda E. Ames, Doris Anderson (WSRTA), Sister Rita Bergamini, Pat Flynn, Cherry A. Goudeau, Loretta Zwolak Greene, Richard Harris, Tom R. Hulst, Kathleen A. Kellogg, Robert D. Klarsch, Ernest L. Louk (WSRTA), Don Malloy, Marilyn Moorhead, Wanda O'Brien, Winnifred L. Olsen (WSRTA), Greg S. Paus, Paul B. Raymond, Jane D. Sellars, Ray Tobiason, Leslie Tollefson, Daniel C. Webber S.J., Ila Zbaraschuk.

San Juan County

John Eiland (WSRTA), Carol Gill.

Skagit County

Joan Bogensberger, Paul G. Chaplik, John E. Clark (WSRTA), Wally Funk, Leon Greene (WSRTA), Mabel Hickson (WSRTA), Carol Kirkby, Robert Knorr, Darlene Pearson, Thomas J. Pollino, Eloise M. Stendal (WSRTA), Gertrude Stendal (WSRTA), P.A. Stendal.

Skamania County

Jerry A. Harding

Snohomish County

Sister Victoria Adlum, Alice Anderson, Sister Rita Bergamini, Ralph Bilbao, Marian Burge, Grace Cornwell (WSRTA), Loretta Zwolak Greene, Richard L. Husselton, Donna McKinney, Carolyn Meagher, Larry O'Donnell, Lynda Schuler, Violet Stevens (WSRTA), Mrs. Wood of St. Pius.

Spokane County

C. William Anderson (WSRTA), Joann Armstrong, Brian L. Benzel, Steve Caires, Thelma Carlberg, C. Culp, Anne Doherty, Paul Doneen, Nancy Ferrette, Gene Fink, Dominic Frucci, Lee Isherwood, Bill Hibbard, Barbara LaDean Jones, Sister Wanda Jordan, Gale Marrs, Sally Merriwether, M.S. Morrison, Marcia K. Olson, Clarence Pence, Rodney D. Peterson, Neil Prescott (WSRTA), Barbara Pugh (WSRTA), Garry Ratliff, George Reuner, Frank Roth, Joanne Snyder, Charles G. Stocker, Thomas C. Ward, George Werner (WSRTA), Neil Williams, Seth Woodard.

Stevens County

Sister Rita Bergamini, Don Fekete, Loretta Zwolak Greene, and Wayne Pringle (WSRTA).

Thurston County

Ramona Bennett, Sister Rita Bergamini, Loretta Zwolak Greene, Harry Hawkins, Patricia Kennedy, Arnold Miller (WSRTA), Nancy Roberts, Norman R. Wisner.

Wahkiakum County

Gary W. Patterson

Walla Walla County

Yvon Barber, Sister Rita Bergamini, James Chubb, Harry Flemmer, Loretta Zwolak Greene, Franklin B. "Pete" Hanson (WSRTA), C.E. Murphy, Phil Rolfe.

Whatcom County

Michaela Boynton, Richard Clark, Lavelle Freudenberg, Howard Heppner.

Whitman County

Sister Lucille Dehen, Patsy Dunning, Edith Erickson (WSRTA), Buddy L. Gibson, James Menzies, Larry Warner.

Yakima County

Dick Baines, Sister Rita Bergamini, Sister Helen Brennan, Ellen Brzoska (WSRTA), Virginia Campbell (WSRTA), Dona Clash, Loretta Zwolak Greene, Mary E. Hagedorn (WSRTA), Ernest Hager, Fran Housel, Evelyn James, Walter Johnson, Steven R. Kaufman, S. Dale Knott, Darrel G. McCallum, Richard Miller, Everett Morgan, Pat Olsen, Ron Ott, Diane Pettit, Dorothy (Morgan Gray) Smith, Stanley V. Snow, Roy C. Snyder, Warren D. Starr, A. J. Strom, Ruth Thompson, Darlene Trautman, J. Tuman, Roy Wandling, Francis Wattenbarger, Ruth H. Wear (WSRTA), Martha B. Yallup, Vernie Young.

I wish also to acknowledge the prompt and efficient assistance received from the state office of the Washington State Retired Teachers Association: Former Executive Director Marianna Moore, her successor, Lois Sheppard, and office manager Brenda Johnson.

And to the executive board of the Washington State Retired Teachers Association, I offer thanks for board members' patience and support of this research project. Community Service Chair Adrienne Birdsell and her successors, Bob Wallenstien and Patricia Johnson, were interested and involved in this project. The research spanned the terms of office of four WSRTA presidents: Jessie Schroeder, Eloise Stendal, Jack Hill, and Cal Watness. They all were willing and helpful participants.

Many county and regional historical societies were instrumental in finding photographs for this volume as well as pointing our researchers to long-forgotten schools. In fact, many of the names you read above are those of members of historical associations.

In the preface I note the role of The Boeing Company in this project. As a community service, that company made its graphic production facilities and personnel available to print this book.

Kenneth L. Calkins
Editor

A

Abernathy School, Dungeness Valley, Sequim School District (Clallam County). This school (sometimes spelled Abernethy) is believed to be the first school in Clallam County, opened in 1861 and used for one or two years. The school was named for the Andrew Abernathy family on whose land it was placed.

Adams County Schools (Adams County). Too little is known of early rural schools in Adams County to warrant individual entries. Yet many of these schools have names which reflect the earliest families in that part of the state. Adams County, named for the second president of the United States, was formed by the territorial legislature in 1884. It had been a part of Whitman County. There were schools in what became Adams County before the county itself was in existence. The following list includes those schools whose names appear to meet our definition of a historic name. Notice the strong Germanic flavor of some of the school names: German School (later Rosenoff), Knowlton or Moeller, Willes, Paha, McQueen (later Rankin), Lemman, Couch (later Griffith), Leonard, Sutton, Williams, Schwerin or Teutonia, Comparet, Olsen, Glover, Kanzler, Scheel, Burkhart, Newland, Achzigerr, Bennett, McCall or Robinson, Schaefer or Hollenshead, Eckhardt or Packard, Weber, Howard, Hollbaut, Lauer, Menno, Kaufman, Cottingham, Wahl, Hoefel, Batum, Thompson, Seivers, Hawkins or Tipton, Schmidt or Moody, Billington, Booker, Kagele, Klemmer, Bradford, Hoskin, Schafer, Scheller, Knottingham, Lantz, Geissler, Morgan, Gering, McMannanon, Allert, Schrag, Presnell, Ralston, Fletcher, Harder-McCall. H.R. Williams, one-time vice president of the Milwaukee Line (Milwaukee, St. Paul, and Pacific Railroad), personally named 32 railroad sidings and stations along the Milwaukee right of way. Ralston School listed above, for example, came from Mr. Williams who named the wheat-shipping station after the Ralston Purina company.

Charles Francis Adams High School, 401 Chestnut, Clarkston School District (Asotin County). Completed in 1923 and named for Charles Francis Adams II, president in the late 19th Century of the Union Pacific Railroad. Adams was of the Massachusetts family that produced two U.S. presidents. He was the brother of Henry Adams, the son of Congressman (and one-time vice-presidential candidate) Charles Francis Adams, the grandson of John Quincy Adams (sixth president of the United States), great grandson of John Adams (second president of the United States). Charles Francis Adams II was the leading financial sponsor in 1895 of the development of Jawbone Flat, then a waterless desert in Washington State near Lewiston, Idaho. An irrigation canal tapping Asotin Creek turned the arid land into valuable property, part of which became the city of Clarkston.

This is the older, original portion of the Charles Francis Adams High School of Clarkston, Asotin County. (Photo from R.P. Weatherly, Asotin)

Adams Elementary School, 6129 26th Ave. N.W., Seattle School District (King County). The school, opened in 1910, is believed to have been named for John Adams, second president of the United States, as were many schools in the first quarter of the 20th Century. School District archives do not disclose the origin of this school's name. One speculation is that the school was named for a real estate developer named Adams.

Representative of schoolhouses built during the Great Depression, this is Aster Elementary School of Colville, built in 1938 primarily with federal Works Progress Administration funds. (Photo from Wayne Pringle, Stevens County Retired Teachers Association).

Adams Elementary School, E. 14707 Eighth Ave., Veradale, Central Valley School District (Spokane County). The school, opened in 1958, borders on the Adams Road, believed to have been named for Russell Adams, an early valley settler. Many roads in the valley were named in the 1890s and early 1900s for pioneer settlers.

Adams Elementary School, E. 2909 37th Ave., Spokane School District (Spokane County). The school was opened in 1902, named for Charles Adams, a local owner of 14.5 acres of land in the vicinity of the school who probably donated the school site. Adams Elementary was acquired by the Spokane School District through consolidation in 1908.

Adams Elementary School, Pullman (old District 59 in Whitman County). Whitman County has had more than 180 school districts within its borders. The first one was established in 1872 and the last in 1918. The first consolidation of two or more districts into one took place about 1910, a practice that accelerated during the Depression years of the 1930s. Dates when all these schools opened and closed are not known to contemporary school administrators. Adams School was named by the principal, a former first grade teacher, because it was a name first graders could soon learn to spell. The school later was renamed Edison and is now a commercial building called Adams Mall.

Adams Elementary School, 723 S. Eighth St., Yakima School District (Yakima County). The original building was opened in 1907 as Fairview School. After a remodeling in 1911, the school was renamed Adams for John Quincy Adams, sixth president of the U.S. A new building was constructed in 1937 and additions made in 1955, 1960, 1965, 1970, and 1977. The old building was not destroyed until 1960. The remaining building is still called Adams, following a long-time policy in Yakima for naming schools after presidents. This school, however, is the only one in the state named for John Quincy Adams.

Jane Addams Junior High School, North 113th and 34th Avenue North, Seattle School District (King County). Opened in 1949 in the Shoreline School District, Jane Addams School was acquired by the Seattle School District in 1954 when an area north of Seattle was annexed to the city. The school was closed at a date not available from the Seattle School District. The school was named for Jane Addams, an American social worker who, in 1889, co-founded Hull House, a settlement house which became a center for social reform. In 1931 Addams shared the Nobel Peace Prize. The Shoreline School District has named several of its schools for Nobel Peace Prize recipients.

John Ahl School, N. 36840 Highway 101, Lilliwaup (Mason County). John Alfred Ahl was born in Sweden March 6, 1855. He migrated to New York at age 26 and almost immediately headed west, stopping in 1882 in the Hood Canal area of Washington Territory. He homesteaded near Eldon. Partly through his efforts, a school was built in Eldon in 1889. He served on its board until his death in 1920. In 1926 land for a new school was given to the Eldon School District No. 16 by Mrs. Allie Ahl, John's second wife and his widow. In 1927 a new school built on that land was named for pioneer John Ahl. The school operated until 1944 when Eldon School District was consolidated with Lilliwaup and Hoodsport School Districts. In 1990 the Ahl School was a residence, the home of John and Corda Watkins.

Ainslee School, near Olequa Creek, one mile south of Winlock (Lewis County). Named for the president of the Ainslee Lumber Company in 1889. A post office of the same name was located at the railroad siding in 1887. Neither school nor community now exist. At one time the lumber company employed more than 100 men.

Louisa May Alcott Elementary School, 4213 228th N.E., Redmond, Lake Washington School District (King County). Opened in 1986 and named for the New England writer, author of *Little Women* and *Little Men* among other immensely popular novels. She was the daughter of Bronson Alcott, a leading educational reformer in Concord, Massachusetts.

Alcott School, E. 4714 Eighth Ave., Spokane School District (Spokane County). Opened in 1914 and named for Louisa May Alcott, popular American fiction writer of the 19th Century. The building was closed as a school in 1972 and in 1990 was being used as the school district's instructional media center.

Alfalfa School, Granger (Yakima County). In 1884 the Northern Pacific Railroad extended its line from Spokane into the lower Yakima Valley. A station was built on Toppenish Creek and named for the abundant hay crop that grew on the rich bottom land of the Satus. A post office was established at Alfalfa in 1903, and it is believed the school was built the same year. The school was badly damaged by wind in 1906, and students were moved to temporary quarters during repairs. The school was closed in 1928, and the building later became the Alfalfa Grange Hall.

Allen Elementary School, Methow Valley School District, Twisp (Okanogan County). No response from this school district.

Allen School, 6615 Dayton Ave. N., Seattle School District (King County). Opened in 1902, the school was named for John B. Allen, the first U.S. Senator from the state of Washington. It is no longer listed in the state directory of active schools. John Beard Allen was born in

Crawfordsville, Indiana, in 1845. As an adult he became a lawyer and moved to Walla Walla in 1887. As Senator Allen he was instrumental in acquiring the Navy Yard sited at Bremerton, the construction of Fort Lawton, and of the Lake Washington Ship Canal.

Alpha-Omega School, Unaffiliated traditional Christian, 32nd and Hancock Streets, Port Townsend, (Jefferson County). Founded by Ruth Hickenbottom after a family tragedy which left her with a deep mistrust of child care facilities available to most families. The school had 33 students in 1989, Grades 1-8, and was planning to expand to high school. The school's name comes from the beginning and the end of the Greek alphabet and is a phrase associated with Christian worship.

Sarah J. Anderson Elementary School, 2215 N.E. 104th in the Vancouver School District (Clark County). In 1954, when a new elementary school was needed in the Hazel Dell area, the name of Sarah Jane Anderson was given to the new school opened in 1955. Mrs. Anderson and her husband, William Reese Anderson, were the first permanent residents of the Hazel Dell area. In 1883 Sarah Jane donated the land for the first school—Hazel Dell Elementary.

Anderson Building, 18603 Bothell Way N.E., Bothell, Northshore School District (King County). Built in 1931 and named Bothell Junior High, this school was renamed in 1956 after Wilbur A. Anderson, who served as the school's principal from 1931 to 1936. Anderson retired in 1956 after 25 years of service in Northshore Schools.

Grant C. Angle School, Ninth and Franklin Streets, Shelton School District (Mason County). Opened in 1953, the school was named for the founder of the Shelton Mason County Journal at the suggestion of the Shelton Chamber of Commerce. At first the building was used for both junior- and senior-high-age students. In 1990 it was a middle school serving sixth, seventh, and eighth grades. Grant Angle, born in Chinese Camp, California, in 1868, came to Shelton in 1886 and became the youngest newspaper editor in the Washington Territory at age 19.

When he died in 1951 at age 83, he was the oldest active newspaper editor in Washington State. He had an eighth grade education and served an apprenticeship as a printer at 14 in Portland, Oregon.

Annie Wright School (See Wright.)

Apollo Elementary School, 15025 S.E. 117th, Renton (mailing address: 565 N.W. Holly St., Issaquah), Issaquah School District (King County). In 1990 this was a primary school serving kindergarten through second grade. The school was named in 1970 soon after the Apollo spacecraft landing on the moon. Another justification for the name is that Apollo was one of the most important of the Greek Olympian gods. He was especially concerned with prophecy, medicine, music, poetry, law, philosophy, the arts, purification, youth, and beauty.

Argonne Junior High School, E. 8823 Trent, Spokane, West Valley School District (Spokane County). Built in 1924 as West Valley Union High School. No information forthcoming on the origin of the name.

Armstrong School, county school west of Yakima near Tampico on lower Ahtanum Road (Yakima County). This one-room school (later expanded to two rooms) was built in 1905 or 1906 on land donated by farmer Jared H. Armstrong, a Pennsylvanian who came west with a wagon train in 1865. One of the last independent one-school districts in the state, Armstrong School became a part of Yakima County's West Valley School District in 1957.

Artz-Fox Elementary School, Mabton School District (Yakima County). Two separate classroom buildings were constructed on the same site. The Fox Building was completed in 1955 and dedicated that year to Mary E. Fox, a beloved teacher for 36 years. She was 72 when the school was named for her, and she did not retire until she was 78. She died in 1969 at the age of 86. The Artz Building was completed in 1962 and named for Louis M. Artz, at that time still active as a school custodian and bus driver. He served in those capacities from 1934 until his retirement in 1965. Since completion of the Artz Building, the school has been known as the Artz-Fox Elementary School. In 1990 a new building was constructed to replace the two earlier structures. However, the Artz-Fox name was retained.

Assumption School (Assumption of the Blessed Virgin Mary), Roman Catholic, W. 3400 Weile Ave., Spokane Diocese (Spokane County). This school was founded by the Dominican Sisters of Kettle Falls in 1958. In 1990 it offered a preschool through Grade 8 program.

Assumption Elementary School, 2066 E. Alder, Walla Walla (Walla Walla County). Opened in 1955 and named for the nearby parish. As with the school above, this school was named for the assumption into heaven of Mary, mother of Jesus.

Aster Elementary School, 225 S. Hofstetter, Colville School District (Stevens County). Built in 1938 with Works Progress Administration federal funds and local funds, this school was known as New Primary Building until 1952. That year J.C. Harrifan, publisher of the local newspaper, "named" the school Aster, presumably with school board concurrence. Since the Colville School District had a tradition of naming schools for historic persons, Aster School has been identified as having been named for John Jacob Astor, American entrepreneur who in 1811 financed the establishment of the Pacific Fur Company site at Fort Astoria at the mouth of the Columbia River. A street that runs to the school grounds is named Astor. No explanation has been found for the apparent misspelling of Mr. Astor's name as it is applied to this school.

Audubon Elementary School, 3045 180th Ave. N.E., Redmond, Lake Washington School District (King County). Opened in 1966 and named for John James Audubon, Santo Domingo-born (now Haiti) artist who did his most extensive work in the United States of America. His reputation rests on his drawings and paintings for *The Birds of America* (1827-1838).

Audubon Elementary School, W. 2020 Carlisle Ave. Spokane School District (Spokane County). This school, opened in 1909, was named for John James Audubon who lived from 1785 to 1851. The *Concise Columbia Encyclopedia* states that Audubon's "drawings and paintings remain among the great achievements of American intellectual history." The Spokane school was named for Audubon because of its proximity to Audubon Park, a subdivision in the city. A new building replaced the old structure in 1979.

Azwell School District No. 70 (Chelan County). Azwell School was named in 1918 by Leonard L. Harn, manager of the A.Z. Wells Orchards. About the time the school was being organized, Harn applied for a local post office named Wells. The government informed Harn there were already too many post offices named Wells so he added the A and Z to the beginning of the word for both the school district and the post office. The school construction was completed in 1919 and was in use until the 1940s when the district was consolidated with Pateros School District. The building was empty for several years, and then, when the schoolyard was needed for orchard, the school was either torn down or moved. Alfred Z. Wells, for whom the district and post office were named, moved to Wenatchee in 1902 and opened a hardware store with his nephew, Alfred Morris. They also planted an apple orchard alongside the Columbia River about 50 miles north of Wenatchee. In 1914 they dissolved the partnership, with Mr. Wells taking the orchard and Mr. Morris the hardware store. Mr. Wells died in 1950.

Barge School of Yakima was eventually merged with Lincoln School in a new structure named Barge-Lincoln. (Photo from Ron Ott, Yakima, via Virginia Campbell, Yakima Retired Teachers Association)

B

Bagley Downs Elementary School, 4100 Plomondon St., Vancouver School District (Clark County). This is the original name of what in 1946 became the Lewis and Clark Elementary School (named for Meriwether Lewis and William Clark, explorers of the Pacific Northwest in the early 1800s). Bagley Downs Elementary School was built in 1943 and named for the Bagley family who had owned the property and operated a race track there. The name-change from Bagley Downs to Lewis and Clark was prompted by some citizens' objections to a school named for a race track. After the emergence of Clark Junior College in Vancouver, the word "Clark" was dropped from the elementary school's name to avoid possible confusion between the two schools. In 1953 Lewis became a junior high, and in 1986 Lewis Junior High was closed when the district went to a middle school graded organization. The building was being used in 1989 for book storage and classes offered by the Vancouver Parks and Recreation Department. It was once again known by the name Bagley Downs.

Bagley Elementary School, 7821 Stone Ave. N., Seattle School District (King County). Bagley was opened in 1905; a second Bagley building was constructed in 1907. The third Bagley building, facing Stone Avenue and just east of the site of the old school, was constructed in 1929. The school was named for The Reverend Mr. Daniel Bagley, Seattle pioneer Methodist-Protestant Church preacher, one of the founders of the University of Washington, whose spirit is said still to haunt the Capitol Hill area of Seattle. Daniel was the father of Clarence Bagley, eminent historian.

Bagshaw Field, adjacent to North Middle School, 2514 Rainier, Everett School District (Snohomish County). This athletic field was named in the 1920s for Enoch Bagshaw (1884-1930), legendary Everett High School football coach. Bagshaw Field was the home field for Everett High School until the construction of Everett Memorial Stadium in 1947. Bagshaw coached at Everett High from 1909 through the 1920 season. On January 1, 1921, his Everett football team defeated the East Technical High School team of Cleveland, Ohio, for what was then regarded as the national high school football championship. From Everett, Bagshaw went to the University of Washington where as head football coach he led the Huskies on their first trip to the Rose Bowl.

Lillian Bailey Elementary School, 219 Park St., Metaline Falls, Selkirk School District (Pend Oreille County). On a fall day in 1910 in Metaline Falls, the town's first school opened its doors to some 20 children of various ages in the first seven grades. Welcoming them was the newly hired teacher, Mrs. Lillian Bailey. Mrs. Bailey was the teacher there for the next 38 years. She had been a teacher since she was 19 in 1895 near her home town of Evart, Michigan. On October 1, 1958, some 63 years later, a new school in Metaline Falls was named in her honor. Mrs. Bailey, then 82, was in attendance at the ceremony. In 1948, her last year of teaching, she had 49 fourth graders in her class. Mrs. Bailey died in 1973 at the age of 97. Before her death, she set up a trust fund to aid student scholars at Selkirk High School with college expenses.

Commodore Bainbridge Middle School, 9530 N.E. High School Rd., Bainbridge Island School District (Kitsap County). Parts of what was then called Captain Bainbridge Elementary School were in use in the 1949-1950 school year. The school later promoted Captain Bainbridge to Commodore Bainbridge. It traces its name to Commodore William Bainbridge, who commanded the frigate *Constitution,* also known as

"Old Ironsides," in the War of 1812. The *Constitution* and her sister frigates "destroyed a half dozen of the proud warships of the British line..." in the battles for supremacy on the high seas, according to Harold Underwood Faulkner, historian.

Bainbridge Island Schools (Kitsap County). Some early schools on Bainbridge Island have historic names under the definition used in this book. However, little is known of the origin of their names. Seabold School, a one-room school started in 1883 and closed in 1923, still existed on the same site in 1991. Moran School for boys was open in Manitou Park during the 1920s. There have been at least 36 other schools on Bainbridge Island named for communities or geographic landmarks.

Bainter School, one and one-half miles southwest of Wapato (Yakima County). Built in 1900. Origin of the name has been lost.

Baker Junior High School, 8320 S. "I" St., Tacoma School District (Pierce County). Baker opened in 1954. The school was named for John S. Baker, long-time Tacoma businessman who was 93 when the school was named and died some six months later. Baker, who came to Tacoma in 1881 at the age of 20, worked as a railroad clerk, grocer, banker, and real estate investor. In 1889 his fellow citizens sent him to the first Washington State legislature as a senator.

Baker School District No. 62, Banner School District No. 37, Beauridell School District No. 23, Belmont School District No. 22, Belshaw School District No. 24, Bryant School District No. 67 (Whitman County). These were all school districts established between 1880 and 1918 in Whitman County to support small rural schools. Research has failed to uncover the origin of the names of these schools. All are gone now.

Balboa Elementary School, W. 3010 Holyoke Ave., Spokane School District (Spokane County). Balboa Elementary School was named in 1960 for Vasco Nunez de Balboa, Spanish-born explorer of much of Central America claiming it for Spain. Balboa was the first European

to see the Pacific Ocean from "the new world" after crossing the isthmus of Panama in 1513. He seized command from the appointed leader of the party and later was accused of treason and beheaded. The school in Spokane was named for Balboa because the neighborhood it serves is known as the Pacific Heights Addition.

Baldwin School (Columbia County). The Alex Baldwin family donated the land for this school in 1871 with the understanding that the school district would pay the fee for recording the deed. The school was built by the men and women whose children would be attending the grade school. A new building was erected by the school district in 1924. A few years later the school was consolidated with Columbia School District No. 1. The Baldwin school was later used as a residence.

John Ball Elementary School, N. Richland, Richland School District (Benton County). The school opened February 16, 1948, and was named for John Ball, a member of Dr. John McLoughlin's party after he established Fort Vancouver for the Hudson's Bay Company in the 1820s. John Ball organized and taught the first school north of the Columbia River in the Oregon Territory. The John Ball School of Richland opened to serve the children of those working on the Hanford nuclear project. It consisted of 12 Quonset huts end to end with a center hallway an eighth of a mile long. The school was erected in weeks in an area without sidewalks or paved roads. Dust sometimes built up to more than a foot deep outside and an inch or so inside the school. The standing joke among teachers trying to conduct two shifts of classes each day was "And they said John Ball was a pioneer." The school was closed in 1955 when enrollment declined. The Quonset huts were hauled away, and some of them surely survive as useful structures in the Richland area.

Ballard High School, 1418 N.W. 65th, Seattle School District (King County). Built in 1916 and named for the former city of Ballard, which was annexed by Seattle near the turn of the century. Ballard, in turn, was named for Captain William Ballard.

Ballard School District No. 9 (Kittitas County). This one-room school was operating in 1909 and was named for Miles Clinton Ballard, a farmer who may have provided the land for the school. The school is now closed, but the building was still being used as a Grange Hall and community meeting hall in 1990.

Helen Baller Elementary School, 1954 N.E. Garfield, Camas School District (Clark County). Baller was opened in 1948. The school was named for its designer, Helen Baller, who also served the district as a teacher, principal, and primary supervisor over her long career in Camas. Many of her years of service were spent at Oak Park and Central Schools.

Ballou Junior High School, 9916 136th St. E., Puyallup School District (Pierce County). Built in 1970 and named for Frank Ballou, a supporter of youth activities in the Puyallup area and a respected county agriculture agent, now deceased.

Bancroft Elementary School, N. 1515 Monroe, Spokane School District (Spokane County). One of the oldest schools in Spokane, Bancroft was built in 1886 at a cost of $543. Locally it was referred to as the Northside School until 1890. It was then named for Hubert Howe Bancroft, San Francisco businessman and book collector. In 1891 a new building was constructed. In 1930 the school housed classes for visually-impaired pupils. Closed as an elementary school in 1981, by 1990 it housed several special programs and a district alternative high school.

Barge-Lincoln Elementary School, 219 E. "I" St., Yakima School District (Yakima County). Barge-Lincoln is a merger of two schools. One was named for Abraham Lincoln, 16th president of the United States. Lincoln School in Yakima opened in 1907, replacing a high school that burned. The other school, Barge Elementary School, opened in 1905 on North Naches Avenue between "E" and "F" Streets. The school was named for Benjamin T. Barge, local real estate salesman, developer, deacon of the Baptist Church, president of the school

board, former teacher, former superintendent of schools, and former superintendent of Ellensburg Normal School (now Central Washington University). Mr. Barge was born February 2, 1834, to John Milton Barge and Flora Nash Barge of Massachusetts. Mr. Barge died on February 10, 1926, and is buried in Yakima. The school was named for him when the school board received a petition signed by 300 students. Barge School was closed at the end of the 1959 school year and torn down. A newer building, built on East "I" Street in 1955, was later given the names of the two schools it replaced: Barge-Lincoln.

Barnes Elementary School, 401 Barnes St., Kelso School District (Cowlitz County). Named in 1924 either for the street on which it is located or for Frank G. Barnes, state senator from Cowlitz County for 42 years, for whom the street is named.

L.H. Bates Vocational-Technical Institute, 1101 S. Yakima, Tacoma School District (Pierce County). Bates was opened in 1941 as a vocational training school and named in 1969 for LaVerne Hazen Bates, who was hired away from the Spokane School District in 1944 to become director of vocational training for Tacoma schools. Mr. Bates was instrumental in persuading the legislature that vocational education was an integral part of basic education and deserved state financial support. He also helped establish a day program in vocational training for servicemen returning from World War 2.

Alexander Graham Bell Elementary School, 11212 N.E. 112th, Kirkland, Lake Washington School District (King County). Bell opened in 1967. The school was named for the Scottish-born, Canadian-reared, American teacher of the deaf and inventor of the telephone. Dr. Bell also experimented in his laboratory in Nova Scotia with hydrofoil boats and aircraft design improvements.

Bellarmine Preparatory School, Roman Catholic, 2300 S. Washington St., Tacoma, Seattle Archdiocese (Pierce County). Bellarmine was named for St. Robert Bellarmine. The school, which opened for classes in 1928 as a boys' school, is one of 47 Jesuit high schools in

America. Robert Bellarmine was an Italian priest who lived between 1542 and 1621 and was named Cardinal in recognition of his great scholarship. Bellarmine School became co-educational in 1974.

Belma School, country school near Grandview (Yakima County). Built in 1896, this two-story, four-room structure saw mostly Grades 1-8 and an occasional high schooler. The school was moved from near the river at the turn of the century up to a nearby road. Both the road and the school were named Belma, a Spanish word for rose. The song "My Beautiful Rose" was popular at the time and is believed to have had an influence on the naming of the school. In 1940 the school was closed and the students divided among Grandview, Mabton, and Sunnyside schools. A farmer by the name of Charvet bought the Belma School and land in 1941 and tore the building down.

Bemiss Elementary School, E. 2323 Bridgeport Ave., Spokane School District (Spokane County). Built in 1909 as the Hays Park School, it was renamed in 1915 for David Bemiss, the first superintendent of Spokane Public Schools. Mr. Bemiss held two degrees from the University of Toronto, was a member of the Washington Council of Education, and one-time member of the state board of education. He is buried in a local Spokane cemetery. In 1912 eight classrooms were added to the school. In 1949 a gymnasium and lunchroom were added.

Bennett Elementary School, 17900 N.E. 16th St., Bellevue School District (King County). Bennett was built in 1970 in the Lake Washington School District and annexed into the Bellevue District in 1976. The school is named for Richard F. Bennett, Irish-born illustrator and author of children's books, who grew up on a farm, part of which is now the school's site.

R.E. Bennett Elementary School, 233 S.W. Market, Chehalis School District (Lewis County). Bennett opened in 1927 as a junior high school, the second junior high in the state of Washington, according to Ray Gunderson, the principal in 1989. The school was named for the Chehalis

superintendent of schools serving from 1924 to 1936, who died at his desk at age 61. After the 1949 earthquake, which destroyed the Chehalis High School, Bennett School became the high school for a few years until a new one could be built.

Samuel Benn School, East Third Street between North "F" and North "G" Streets, Aberdeen School District (Grays Harbor County). Opened as an elementary school in 1917, this school was named for the founder of Aberdeen. Mr. Benn was instrumental in laying out the current city and served as its first mayor. He later served on the school board. This school was built on part of the Benn homestead site. In 1945 the school was razed, but the Samuel Benn name is still attached to the high school gym.

Samuel Benn Gymnasium, Fifth and "G" Streets, Aberdeen School District (Grays Harbor County). The Samuel Benn Gymnasium was named at its opening in 1964 for the founder of Aberdeen. The ground on which the gym stands was once part of the Benn homestead.

Corinne Berg Music Building, Bainbridge High School, Bainbridge Island School District (Kitsap County). Opened in 1990 and named for a long-time teacher and professional organist. In addition to her musical activities, Mrs. Berg worked in several community roles. She organized the Bainbridge Island School District resource volunteer program in 1968 and was a founder of Bainbridge Performing Arts and Bainbridge Helpline House, an ecumenical social service agency for mental health services, a food bank, and referral agency for medical services. Mrs. Berg died of cancer at 62 in 1990.

Harry Bergh Field, 10601 N.E. 132nd, Kirkland, Lake Washington School District (King County). This Juanita High School athletic field was named in 1985 for Coach Harry Bergh who was struck down at an early age by cancer.

Berney Elementary School, Pleasant Street and School Avenue, Walla Walla School District (Walla Walla County). Berney was dedicated in 1904. Ulysses H.

Berney, for whom the school was named, gave the dedicatory address. Mr. Berney, chairman of the then Walla Walla County School District No. 5, gave the school its bell and the land for an athletic field. Mrs. Berney was a member of the first Berney Parent-Teacher Association and devoted many years to the furthering of children's education. The Berney School succeeded the old Seeber School nearby and was often interchangeably called the Seeber School. Records do not disclose for whom the Seeber School was named.

Bertschi School, Unaffiliated, 2227 10th Ave. E., Seattle (King County). Bertschi is a private school named for its director-founder Brigette Bertschi. In 1990 it offered a preschool and Grades 1-5.

Bethany School, corner of Stover and Bethany Roads, Grandview (Yakima County). Built in 1904 as District 81 (the 81st school to be built in Yakima County), Bethany School may have been named for the road which likely was named for a pioneer family. In 1911 the school building was moved to Woodworth and Bethany Roads. It is not known what year the school was closed.

Bethel High School, 22215 38th Ave. E. and **Bethel Junior High,** 22201 38th Ave. E., both in Spanaway and in the Bethel School District (Pierce County). These schools as well as the school district were named for Ruth Bethel. In the late 1920s Ruth Bethel, mother of a toddler and pregnant, was deserted by her husband, a fate not uncommon during the Great Depression. To support her family she attended Bellingham Normal School and became a teacher in 1930. She taught in the Roy School District of rural Pierce County, eventually becoming principal of Roy High School and then superintendent of the Roy School District. When the county superintendent of schools entered military service during World War 2, Mrs. Bethel became acting superintendent, later deputy superintendent. Upon the superintendent's resignation in 1946, Mrs. Bethel became Pierce County school superintendent. One of her tasks was to consolidate some rural districts, one of them encompassing her old Roy School District, Spanaway, Kapowsin, Elk Plain, and Rocky Ridge. The new district was formed in 1949 and named for Mrs. Bethel. The high school was named Bethel in 1952, the junior high in 1958. Mrs. Bethel retired from education in 1963.

Bethlehem Lutheran School, Missouri Synod, 1409 S. Garfield St., Kennewick (Benton County). The original school was built in 1911 at the corner of Third Avenue and Benton Street. In 1954 a new building was erected at 1409 S. Garfield, serving kindergarten through eighth grade. The school's name comes from the historic birthplace of Jesus Christ.

Edward F. Betz Elementary School, 317 N. Seventh St., Cheney School District (Spokane County). Betz Elementary opened in 1956. The school was named for Edward Betz, local banker, farmer, and school board member for more than 30 years.

Billington School, Othello (Adams County). Formed in 1902, a rural school east of Othello and named for a family of early settlers.

Birney Elementary School, 1202 S. 76th, Tacoma School District (Pierce County). Birney opened in 1962. The school was named for Alice McClellan Birney, one of the founders and first president of the National Congress of Mothers in 1897. A few years later the name of the organization was changed to the National Congress of Parents and Teachers. Mrs. Birney had studied for a career in medicine but left school for financial reasons and went into the advertising business. Her skills in that field helped the Congress of Parents and Teachers attain nationwide recognition.

Bishop School District No. 96 (Whitman County). Another of the early rural schools in Whitman County. This one was established in 1878 and named for John and Dell Bishop who furnished the land for the schoolhouse.

Bishop School District No. 149 (Whitman County). Another Bishop School, perhaps named for another branch of the same family cited above. In 1895 J.E. Bishop was given permission to move the Leitchville District school to the site of a new school district.

Bishop School District No. 96 of Whitman County. (Photo from Edith Erickson, Whitman County Retired Teachers Association)

Blaine Elementary School, 2550 34th Ave. W., Seattle School District (King County). Blaine was opened in 1952 as a junior high school. It was named for Catherine Blaine, who, almost 100 years earlier, had opened the first school in Seattle. David and Catherine Blaine were missionaries for the Methodist-Episcopal Church and arrived at Alki, the first Seattle settlement, not long after the original Denny party. In fact, they stayed with the Dennys until their own house was built. On their trip from the East around Cape Horn at the southern tip of South America, David Blaine wrote sermons while his new bride planned her duties to her new community. Among those plans was the beginning of a contract school.

Blair Elementary School, 1000 Fairchild St., Fairchild Air Force Base, Medical Lake School District (Spokane County). Blair Elementary School opened in the spring of 1952, one year after the Spokane Air Force Base was renamed Fairchild Air Force Base in honor of General Muir S. Fairchild, a native of Bellingham. The school serves the children of military personnel and was named for William E. Blair, an Air Force pilot from Spokane, who died on September 30, 1949, when his B-25 medium bomber developed an engine fire over Chatanooga, Tennessee. Captain Blair, after directing his crew to bail out, stayed with the plane to maneuver it away from the more congested areas of the city. He rode the plane to the outer edges of the city. By that time it was too late for him to escape.

Blake Elementary School, E. 13313 Broadway, Spokane, Central Valley School District (Spokane County). Blake opened in 1963. Blake School is bordered by Blake Road, named for a valley pioneer family.

Captain Johnston Blakely Elementary School, 4704 Blakely Ave. N.E., Bainbridge Island School District (Kitsap County). Blakely was built in 1965. The school's namesake was an Irish-born sea captain who was best-known as the skipper of the American sloop *Wasp* during the War of 1812. Captain Blakely and his crew were lost at sea in the approaches to the English Channel in October, 1814. The captain also gave his name to Port Blakely, site of the world's largest sawmill during the period 1860 to 1900.

Blanchet High School, Roman Catholic, 8200 Wallingford N., Seattle Archdiocese (King County). Blanchet was Seattle's first co-educational Catholic high school when it opened in 1954. The school is named for Augustine Magloire Alexander Blanchet, French Canadian priest born in 1797. Father Blanchet was named Bishop of Walla Walla in 1846, Bishop of the Diocese of "Nesqually" (now the Seattle Archdiocese) in 1850.

Bruce Blevins Gymnasium, 1610 Blaine St., Port Townsend School District (Jefferson County). Built in 1943, the gymnasium was named for Bruce Blevins when he retired in 1957 after having coached all sports for 28 years. He remained as athletic director and teacher for several more years. Eventually he retired to Arizona where he died in 1987. Mr. Blevins was a much-admired youth leader. He was an athlete and graduate of the University of Puget Sound in Tacoma where his name is listed in that school's Athletic Hall of Fame.

Blough School, rural school up through eighth grade, on Hanford Highway (Yakima County). It is not known at this time when Blough School was started. The school was named for Joe Blough who contributed the land for the school. Dorothy (Morgan) Grey taught the last term of school there. When she resigned at the end of the 1925-1926 school year, the school was closed.

Booker School, Othello (Adams County). Another early rural Adams County school. This school is believed to have opened in 1902. It no longer exists.

Bordeaux Elementary School, 250 University Ave., Shelton School District (Mason County). The original building of the Bordeaux school was opened in 1928 and torn down in 1969. A new building was erected in 1956. The school is named for two brothers from Quebec — Thomas and Joseph Bordeaux — who organized the Mason County Logging Company in the 1890s. They donated the land on which the school now sits.

Louisa Boren School, 5950 Delridge Way S.W., Seattle School District (King County). Boren was opened as a middle school in 1963. It is no longer used as a middle school but, in 1990, housed some administrative offices, the American Indian Heritage High School, and other specialized educational services. The school was named for Louisa Boren, one of the original Denny party Seattle settlers, stepdaughter to John Denny. Miss Boren, 24 when she arrived in Seattle, had been a teacher in Illinois. She became the first white woman to be married in Seattle. Her groom was her stepbrother David Denny. Louisa Boren Denny died August 31, 1916, at the age of 89. During her lifetime she was active in the women's suffrage movement and, with her husband, donated land for the city's first park.

Bowdish Junior High School, S. 2109 Skipworth, Spokane, Central Valley School District (Spokane County). Bowdish was opened in 1959. The school is named for a bordering road which in turn was named for a pioneer valley family. The name originally was pronounced boe dish but over the years has been changed to bow (rhymes with wow) dish.

Boze Elementary School, 1140 E. 65th, Tacoma School District (Pierce County). Boze was opened in 1969. The school is named for James L. Boze, insurance executive and the senior school board member (19 years of service) when the school was built in 1969. He retired from the board in 1983 after 32 years of service.

Bradshaw School, Lateral B and Jones Road, Wapato School District (Yakima County). Bradshaw was an elementary school named for the family on whose land it was built. In 1920 the structure contained both a two-room school and teacher's cottage. It was closed in 1938 and is now a private residence.

Bramall Family School, Unaffiliated, 1142 22nd Pl. N.E., Lake Stevens (Snohomish County). The school did not respond to 1989 inquiry. No longer listed in Washington Education Directory.

Breidablik Elementary School, Waghorn Road, Poulsbo, North Kitsap School District (Kitsap County). "Breidablik" is a Norwegian word meaning "broadview." The first Breidablik School existed in 1893 in what was then Breidablik District 35. That school no longer exists. However, a new school of the same name opened in September, 1990. The name chosen by the school board was on a list of names suggested by a citizen's committee. In Norse mythology Breidablik is the name of the home of Baldur, the Nordic god of love and beauty.

Brighton School, 4425 S. Holly St., Seattle School District (King County). Brighton was acquired by annexation in 1907. The original structure was damaged by fire in 1946. The Seattle School District did not respond to an inquiry about the origin of the name.

Brim School (Lewis County). This school was established March 15, 1882, on land owned by Jim and Walter Brim, farmers and members of the school board.

Brink School District 184 (Whitman County). This country school, established in 1918 and consolidated with other school districts in Whitman County in 1940, was named for Otto Brink, a local farmer and likely the man who owned the land on which the schoolhouse was built. The school also was called Little Alkali, probably a reference to the quality of the farm soil.

Brinnon Elementary and Junior High School, Schoolhouse Road, Brinnon School District (Jefferson County). Ewell P. Brinnon, an early settler on the Duckabush and Dosewallips Rivers in territorial times, gave the land for the school, a low, almost level place just up the Dosewallips River road. He also gave land for a cemetery above the school. Brinnon and his Native American wife, Kate, were always willing to share their good fortune with other settlers wiped out in the Depression of 1893. Mr. Brinnon lived in a house on the Duckabush River until his death in 1895. The town of Brinnon also was named for him.

Broadbent School, Morton (Lewis County). Dates not known at this writing. Named for a Broadbent family in the area.

Broadview-Thomson Elementary School, 13052 Greenwood Ave. N., Seattle School District (King County). The old Broadview school at 12515 Greenwood Ave. N. was acquired by annexation of part of the Shoreline School District in 1954 and later merged with the Thomson School at the Thomson site. Thomson, built in 1963, was named for R.H. Thomson, visionary and controversial Seattle city engineer from 1892 to 1913 who leveled many of Seattle's hills. He also planned the city's

This is the Brim School of Lewis County in about 1903. (Photo from Lewis County Historical Museum via Elizabeth Wedin, Lewis County Retired Teachers Association)

water supply from the Cedar River watershed, was instrumental in the construction of the Hiram Chittenden boat locks in Ballard and the Lake Washington ship canal, and played a prominent role in the development of Seattle City Light and the Duwamish waterway. It was Thomson who, for easier docking, aligned Seattle's piers with the mouth of the waterway rather than at right angles to the shoreline. His largest project, however, was the removal of Denny Hill, an earth-moving project started in 1898 and completed in 1930.

Broadway Elementary School, 1410 Eighth Ave. at Broadway, Longview School District (Cowlitz County). Named in 1946 for the street on which it was situated, the school was closed in 1981 for lack of enrollment. For awhile it was used as a clinic of the Monticello Hospital. When that hospital was absorbed by St. John's Hospital, Broadway School was rented to Head Start and a Montessori school for awhile. In 1989 it was being used for special classes for handicapped and classes for "at risk" preschoolers.

Broadway High School, corner of Broadway and East Pine, Seattle School District (King County). Built of stone in 1902, this school originally was called Seattle High School then Washington High School. It was so commonly known as the high school on Broadway that in 1908 the school board made the name official. The high

Built as Seattle High School in 1902, later named Washington High School and, in 1908, Broadway High School, part of this building is now incorporated into Seattle Central Community College. (Photo from Don Peterson, Seattle Central Community College)

school was closed in 1946 and the buildings used by Edison Technical School. In 1966 the buildings and site became a part of Seattle Central Community College, which absorbed the functions of Edison Technical School.

Brookdale Elementary School, 611 S. 132nd St., Tacoma, Franklin Pierce School District (Pierce County). The school was built in 1957 and enlarged in 1962. Depending on which source is used, the school either was named for a brook that ran through the property or for a pioneer family in the Parkland area. Mr. Brookdale (first name not given) was, by one account, a partner in the Parkland Land Company, which platted the original Parkland Townsite.

Frank "Buster" Brouillet Elementary School, 17207 94th Ave., Puyallup School District (Pierce County). Opened in September, 1990, with an enrollment of 600, this school is named for Dr. Frank Brouillet, former state superintendent of public instruction, former legislator, teacher, and Puyallup schoolboy. In 1990 he was president of Pierce College in Tacoma.

Leland P. Brown Elementary School, 2000 26th Ave. N.W., Olympia School District (Thurston County). The school was named in 1963 for a retired superintendent of Olympia schools. Leland P. Brown spent 38 of his 40 years in education in the Olympia School District as Latin teacher, high school principal, journalism teacher, and athletic coach and, from 1931 until 1957, as superintendent of schools. The L.P. Brown Elementary School opened in 1965.

Browne Elementary School, N. 5134 Driscoll Blvd., Spokane School District (Spokane County). Browne opened in 1910 as Boulevard Park School. In 1915 the school was renamed for John J. Browne, early Spokane pioneer and member of the Spokane School Board for 15 years. J.J. Browne, an attorney, arrived in Spokane Falls in 1897. Through his law practice and business pursuits he had become the state's first millionaire by 1889. Twice he was a delegate to the National Democratic Convention from the state of Washington. He also was a delegate to the state constitutional convention in 1889.

Brumbaugh Elementary School, W. 563 Golden Pheasant Rd., Shelton, Elson School District (Mason County). Clermont Stewart Brumbaugh taught at Shelton's first school in 1884 and served as Mason County superintendent of schools from 1888 to 1894. He returned to farming and donated land for a school site in 1897. The school was used until 1914 and, after extensive remodeling, is now used as a private residence.

Bryant Elementary School, 3311 N.E. 60th St., Seattle School District (King County). Bryant was opened in 1918. The school was named for William Cullen Bryant, American poet and editor of the New York *Evening Post* from the early to mid 1800s.

Bryant School, N. 910 Ash St., Spokane School District (Spokane County). Opened in 1891 and named for William Cullen Bryant. In 1957 a new school replaced the original building. In 1973-74 Bryant became a special education school for both developmentally disabled and gifted students.

Bryant Elementary School, 717 Grant Ave. S., Tacoma School District (Pierce County). The first Bryant building dates back to 1891 at 814 S. Ainsworth. The present building was occupied in 1962. It was named for the famous author of *Thanatopsis*—William Cullen Bryant (1794-1878), elected to the American Hall of Fame in 1910. Many schools have been named for those persons elevated to the American Hall of Fame.

Bundy School, Bundy Hollow (Columbia County). The school was located on the Bundy homestead. Two generations of Bundy children attended the school. It was named in 1870 when the first building was completed. A larger school was soon needed as the population of the area grew. In addition to the instruction of children, the school was used as a funeral chapel, magic lantern theater, polling place, auditorium for debates and spelling bees, and community church. The school was closed when the district merged with Columbia School District No. 1 in 1929.

Burbank School for Boys, 8400 S.E. 24th, Mercer Island, Seattle School District (King County). In 1890 Major and Mrs. Cicero Newell opened a contract school for boys and girls in need of parental care. It was a kind of combination orphanage, vocational, and reform school for live-in students. The school was situated at East Union and 35th Avenue in Seattle. Major Newell became the city schools' truant officer. He also was under a per-pupil-served contract with the county and received a few dollars from local merchants for keeping homeless children off the streets and out of their stores. On April 10, 1901, the Seattle School Board decided to purchase land for construction of a truant school on Mercer Island. The board action required the passage of a truant school bill by the state legislature, an act accomplished in 1903. The designation of the truant school was eventually changed from "industrial school" to "parental school" to soften the harshness of its image as a Victorian workhouse. William Rand, a school staff member, became the school's superintendent in 1906. He arranged to acquire more acreage for expansion of the school. He was superintendent, by one account, for 38 years. The boys were heavily engaged in agriculture, producing crops which paid for much of the school's operating cost. By 1914 girls at the Mercer Island school had been transferred to a parental school of their own. In 1931 the name Luther Burbank was given to the boys' parental school. The school was named for the famous American plant breeder who improved on the commercial value of fruits, vegetables, and flowers. In 1957 the state of Washington agreed to accept responsibility for the operation of parental schools. Luther Burbank was closed as a Seattle public school and is now the site of Luther Burbank King County Park.

Burnt Ridge School, Onalaska area (Lewis County). The region was called Burnt Ridge because Indians had burned the area to make pasture for grazing their stock.

The school was up Burnt Ridge Road from its junction with Jorgensen Road. In 1989 a home sat on the foundation of the old school.

Burrowes School, Palo Alto Road, Blyn School District No. 11 (Clallam County). Opened August 23, 1887, on land donated by the James Burrowes family to serve the Burrowes children and other children in the immediate area. In 1921 the school was consolidated with the Sequim School District.

Burton Elementary School, 14015 N.E. 28th St., Vancouver, Evergreen School District (Clark County). Opened in 1970, the school retains the name of a small rural school in the same area that was one of the original schools which consolidated in 1945 to form the Evergreen School District. For whom the school originally was named was not determined at the time of this writing.

The Bush School, Independent, 405 36th Ave. E., Seattle (King County). This independent private school offering kindergarten through Grade 12 classes was founded in 1924 by Helen Taylor Bush in the playroom of her Denny Blaine Park home. Mrs. Bush was noted for "progressive" educational curriculum and soon had expanded to new quarters. The Helen Bush School became an elementary school for girls. The upper grades are co-educational and called the Parkside School.

Bush School District No. 7 (Thurston County). Bush School District was formed on July 2, 1896, and eventually was consolidated with the Tumwater School District on March 20, 1937. It is believed to have served all grade levels. The school was named for George Washington Bush, a pioneer settler of the area for whom Bush Prairie also is named. Mr. Bush was of mixed black and white parentage and was therefore barred by the Negro Law of the period from settling in the Oregon country south of the Columbia. He was not legally allowed north of the Columbia either, but the sheriff was not required to cross the river to enforce laws so the Bush party was in reality quite immune to the Negro Law. Bush's fellow emigrants found him to be a hospitable, generous man and accepted him and his family quite readily. For nearly all the year of 1844 the parties stayed near Fort Vancouver before striking out to the north. Bush settled in what is now Thurston County south of Tumwater. As a Negro he could not file a Donation Claim. Nevertheless he farmed the land there for 10 years, and, in 1855, Congress passed a special resolution giving him title to the land.

Butler Acres Elementary School, 1609 Burcham St., Kelso School District (Cowlitz County). In 1906 D.W. Butler, his wife Alice, and a widow named Mary E. Rewey, registered an area of land in Cowlitz County as Butler Acres. On May 10, 1934, some of this land was reserved as non-residential. In 1956 a school was built on part of the Butler Acres plat.

This is likely the 1912 Catlin School in Kelso. The horse teams apparently are being used to clear land, probably for construction of buildings or a playfield. (Photo from Cowlitz County Historical Museum)

C

Wade Calavan Elementary School, 1202 Wood Ave., Sumner School District (Pierce County). The school was constructed in 1925 but did not receive the Calavan name until after Mr. Calavan's death. Mr. Calavan was an early superintendent of schools in Sumner and a very popular man. He was responsible for the planning and construction of the school that eventually bore his name. The school was closed in 1972 and now houses the district's administrative offices.

Callow School, W. 5341 Highway 108, Callow School District (Mason County). Edward J. Callow was born May 29, 1842, on the Isle of Man. His family migrated to the U.S. and settled in Wisconsin in 1856. As an adult Callow became a pilot on the Great Lakes and the Mississippi River. He married Hannah Mary Lewis in 1868 and, with their first two children, arrived in 1871 at the Kamilche Valley of Mason County where he took up a homestead. In 1898 he donated one acre of land for a schoolhouse. The school and the school district were named for both Callows, husband and wife. The school functioned until 1951 when it was consolidated into the Kamilche School District. The Callow schoolhouse was sold and torn down and a private residence built on its foundation. In 1989 the teacher's cottage still stood but was in a deteriorated condition.

John Campbell Elementary School, North First Street, Selah School District (Yakima County). Named for former Superintendent of Schools John Campbell shortly after his death in 1946. The school board wanted to recognize Mr. Campbell for his 13 years of leadership and for his successful efforts in getting voter approval of the bond issue needed to build the school.

Campi Satellite Preschool, 1121 33rd Ave., Seattle School District (King County). No information available.

Capehorn-Skye Elementary School, Mile Post 9.80L, State Highway 140, Washougal School District (Clark County). No information available.

Carl Cozier School (See Cozier.)

Carmichael Junior High School, 620 Thayer, Richland School District (Benton County). In 1949 the Richland School Board named a new school, then under construction, after John Gray, a pioneer settler of the area. The school was being built on land once owned by S.P. Carmichael, who had been superintendent from 1923 to 1938 of the Hanford School District, a district since merged into Richland. His widow, county superintendent of schools at the time the new Richland school was under construction, "raised such an unholy fuss," according to a contemporary, that the new school was renamed Carmichael.

George Washington Carver Middle School, 2514 Rainier, Everett School District (Snohomish County). When this school was built in 1925 it was named North Junior High. For some 10 years, beginning in 1970, the school's name was changed to Carver, honoring a famous black agricultural chemist who did his research at Tuskegee Institute, Alabama, in the 1920s and '30s. Dr. George Washington Carver was born in 1864 and died in 1943. The Carver School was demolished in 1980 and the replacement school, opened in 1981, reverted to the old name—North.

Cashup School District No. 29 (Whitman County). Another of the early rural schools in Whitman County that were consolidated into larger districts by 1938. This school was named for a storekeeper and hotel-keeper known as Cashup Davis who always had hard money to make a deal.

Cassalery School, Jamestown Road junction with Sequim Dungeness Road, Sequim (Clallam County). Named after the Cassalery family on whose land the school was placed in 1871. The father of the Cassalerys was an Italian immigrant. The school was consolidated with the Sequim School District in 1913.

Cataldo Catholic School, Roman Catholic, W. 455 18th Ave., Spokane Diocese, Grades K-8 (Spokane County). Cataldo is a consolidation of three parish schools: Our Lady of Lourdes, established in 1888; St. Augustine, established in 1915; and Sacred Heart, established in 1921. The merged school was named Cataldo in 1972 after Father Joseph Cataldo, a Jesuit priest who had come to the territory in 1860 to work among the Indians and settlers. He is considered to be the founder of Catholic education in the Inland Northwest. Father Cataldo also had a hand in the founding of Gonzaga College in Spokane.

Calavan School in Sumner was being used in 1991 to house the district's administrative offices. (Photo from Ernest Louk, Pierce County Retired Teachers Association)

Cathcart Elementary School, 8201 188th S.E., Snohomish School District (Snohomish County). Opened in 1960, the school was named for Isaac Cathcart, local pioneer, who was a leader in developing the rich farm land. He was instrumental in the location of a Northern Pacific rail center in the area. The first Cathcart School was built in 1921. On November 8, 1972, Cathcart School District No. 109 was dissolved and annexed to Snohomish School District No. 201.

Catlin Elementary School, 404 W. Long St., Kelso School District (Cowlitz County). The first Catlin School was built in 1878 on land donated by Seth Catlin in Freeport. A later Catlin School was built at the present site in 1912, torn down some years later, and a new building erected nearby in 1945. The school was named for the pioneer Catlin family. Seth Catlin brought his family to the Cowlitz country in 1849 where he participated in both the Cowlitz Landing and the Monticello Conventions. West Kelso, where the Catlin School is located, was once the town of Catlin, so-named by Seth's son, Adam, in 1889.

Cave School District No. 101 (Whitman County). One of 180 rural district schools in Whitman County from 1882 to 1918. This one was named for J.W. Cave, the first member of the Cave School Board.

Washington State Centennial Elementary School, 24323 E. 54th Ave., Graham, Bethel School District (Pierce County). Opened September 5, 1989, Centennial Elementary School was named to commemorate the Washington State Centennial year, the 100th anniversary of the state of Washington.

Centennial Elementary School, 3100 Martin Rd., Mount Vernon School District (Skagit County). Students' and citizens' suggestions were solicited by the superintendent and school board. The board selected "Centennial" to honor the 100th anniversary of statehood. The school was built and opened in 1989, the year of the Centennial Celebration in Washington State.

Centennial Elementary School, 2637 45th Ave. S.E., Olympia School District (Thurston County). In 1988 students, staff, parents, and other citizens of Olympia submitted 18 names for consideration for the new elementary school then under construction. From that list the school board selected Centennial to honor Washington's admission to the Union as the 42nd state. The school opened in January, 1989, replacing McKinley Elementary School.

Central Avenue Elementary School, 4505 E. 104th St., Tacoma, Franklin Pierce School District (Pierce County). Central Avenue School is all that is left of the name "Central Avenue." The street still exists but under a different name: Bingham Avenue. It still dead-ends at the school as it always has. The current main building of the school was finished in 1923.

Challenger Elementary School, 52500 Klahanie Blvd., Issaquah School District (King County). This school was opened in the fall of 1988. The name is a tribute to the astronauts who perished in the Challenger space flight tragedy in January, 1986. The name also connotes the significance of the challenges of learning. The Issaquah District has several schools whose names are associated with the U.S. space program.

Challenger High School, 18002 "B" St., Spanaway, Bethel School District (Pierce County). The school was named Bethel Alternative School when it opened in 1974. It was renamed Challenger after the Challenger space shuttle in 1988. It was that space shuttle that took Commander Dick Scobee, teacher-astronaut Christa McAuliffe, and others to their deaths on January 28, 1986. The Bethel School District has several schools whose names are associated with the U.S. space program. Challenger High is a part of the Bethel District's "Extended Learning Family"—a unit of the Schools for the 21st Century Project.

Challenger Elementary School, 9600 Holly Dr., Mukilteo School District (Snohomish County). This is one of several schools in the Mukilteo District whose names are associated with the U.S. space program. No further information was made available.

Chambers Elementary School, 9101 56th Ave. W., Tacoma, University Place School District (Pierce County). The school was named in 1971 (opened in 1972) for Judge Thomas McCutchen Chambers, a Kentuckian who migrated west to the Oregon country in 1845. Judge Chambers operated the first Pierce County grist mill on

what is now Chambers Creek near Steilacoom. He was responsible for establishing and naming Fort Steilacoom. On November 15 each year the students of Chambers School celebrate Judge Chambers' birthday.

Chestnut School District No. 116 (Whitman County). Named for J.Y. Chestnut who donated the land for a school site in the early part of the 20th Century.

Chief Joseph Junior High School (See Joseph.)

Childs Elementary School, 2000 S. 18th St., Yakima School District (Yakima County). Ruth E. Childs (1885-1960) taught at Jefferson School outside Yakima. In 1937 she started a PTA and a free hot lunch program at Jefferson. She also got the PTA members to knit mittens for some students. She is remembered as one of Yakima's finest teachers who met any emergency with courage and spirit. An elementary school built in 1952 was named in honor of Ruth Childs. When the Childs School was torn down and the Martin Luther King School built, there was an organized effort to have Ruth Childs remembered by some school structure. Thus the library in the Martin Luther King School displays a plaque that once was mounted at the Ruth Childs School, and the room is known as the Ruth Childs Library.

Chinook Middle School, 4301 N.E. Eighth, Lacey, North Thurston School District (Thurston County). No information available on this school. However, Chinook was the name of a tribe of Native Americans who lived along the Columbia River near its mouth before the whites came and in the early days of European exploration. That location put tribe members in frequent contact with other tribes and later with whites. The Chinook language became rich with words from other Indian languages and with English, French, and Russian words. It became the base language for a mutually understood tongue among many tribes in the Northwest west of the Cascade Mountains. After the influx of trappers and traders, portions of the Chinook language became known as the Chinook jargon, the language of trade among Indians and whites.

Chinook Middle School, 18650 42nd Ave. S., Seattle, Highline School District (King County). Opened in 1958 as a junior high school, this Chinook Middle School, like the one in the North Thurston School District, took its name from the Indian tribe and language. The word Chinook also was used as the name of a warm wind that blew into the Willamette Valley from the coast regions north of the Columbia River. Chinook has come to mean any warm, rain-bearing wind.

Christensen Elementary School, 10232 Barnes Lane, Tacoma, Franklin Pierce School District (Pierce County). Built in 1956, the school was named for Andrew C. Christensen Sr., a Norwegian immigrant who served on the Midland School Board from 1935 to 1955. Midland was a predecessor district to the Franklin Pierce School District.

Christ the King Roman Catholic School in Richland was established in 1954. (Photo from Diocese of Yakima Education Center)

Christ the King Academy, Traditional Christian, 705 N.E. Lincoln Rd., Poulsbo (Kitsap County). No information available.

Christ the King Lutheran School, 8059 Chico Way N.W., Bremerton (Kitsap County). No information available.

Christ the King Grade School, Roman Catholic, 1122 Long Ave., Richland, Yakima Diocese, Grades K-8 (Benton County). Established in 1954 and staffed at that

time by the Sisters of the Holy Names of Jesus and Mary. The founding pastor was Father William Sweeney.

Christ the King School, Roman Catholic, 415 N. 117th St., Seattle (King County). Established in 1939.

Chrysalis School, Unaffiliated, 14241 Woodinville-Duvall Rd., Woodinville (King County). No information available.

Cicero School, three miles south of Darrington (Snohomish County). Cicero School was named by Stephen Cicero in 1906. Cicero and his family arrived in the Darrington area in 1889. He opened a store which he ran for many years. The school was later consolidated with the Darrington School District.

Clara E. Rogers School (See Rogers.)

Clark Elementary School, 500 Second Ave. N.E., Issaquah School District (King County). Built in 1951, this school was named for George M. Clark, superintendent of schools in Issaquah from 1916 to 1930. In 1990 the school housed the district alternative elementary program—The Learning Community—also called TLC, for kindergarten through Grade 5.

Clark High School, Hartford (Snohomish County). In 1909 David Hanks was principal of the White School on the shore of Lake Stevens. He taught the seventh and eighth grades and offered high school classes after regular school hours to a class of 11 students. This was the first high school in the Lake Stevens area. By 1911 and 1912, a Mr. Clark (first name unrecorded) was teaching in rooms over the post office in Hartford, taking over some of the high school classes after the grammar school had dismissed each day. In 1913 and again in 1915 a school bond levy passed to raise $20,000 for a high school building. The election was held a second time because the auditor had voided the first election on grounds that there was not enough property value in the district to support such a large amount of revenue. Mr. Clark, who by then was school superintendent, and a Mr. St. John, were the faculty for the new high school, which became known as the Clark High School.

Cleveland High School, 5511 15th S., Seattle School District (King County). Started in 1925 at the old Georgetown School and moved to its present site to a new junior-senior high school building in 1927, Cleveland High School's proposed name was Wilson. School board member Dr. Caspar Sharples, prominent Republican, objected to naming the school for Woodrow Wilson not because Wilson was a Democrat but because Wilson had not yet been established as having been a good president. Dr. Sharples suggested the school be named for Grover Cleveland, another dead Democrat with no following at that time and a reputation for conservative government. Dr. Sharples' recommendation was adopted by the board. It wasn't until 1954 that Seattle had a Wilson School, a junior high acquired by annexation of part of the Shoreline School District.

Cleveland Elementary School, 1401 Cleveland Ave., Mount Vernon School District (Skagit County). Opened in 1937, closed in 1970, and later sold to the Skagit County government. Since 1986 and as of 1990 the old school, named for former President Grover Cleveland, was being used as a senior citizens' center.

Coe Elementary School, 2433 Sixth Ave. W., Seattle School District (King County). Opened in 1907, Coe School was named for Dr. Frantz H. Coe, a prominent physician who had served on the school board from 1901 to 1904 and whose wife also was active in school and community affairs.

Collins Elementary School, 4608 128th St. E., Tacoma, Franklin Pierce School District (Pierce County). The Collins School District served Parkland area children from 1902 until consolidation in 1949. The first Collins School was held in an old cook shack in 1907. The current school was built in 1935. The school was named for the Collins family which settled in the area in the late 19th Century.

Collins School District No. 42 (Whitman County). This early country school was named for L.H. Collins, who donated the school land.

The first Coe School opened in Seattle in 1907. In 1991, the school was still in operation. (Photo from Seattle Public Schools Archives)

Colman Elementary School, 1515 24th Ave. S., Seattle School District (King County). In 1910 the Seattle School Board authorized a new school at 24th Avenue South and Atlantic Street to be named in honor of pioneer Laurence J. Colman. Colman, a native of Scotland, came to Seattle in 1869, an engineer who soon directed the building of many early sawmills in the Seattle area. Water for Seattle was pumped from Lake Washington to a tank at the top of one of the city's hills. When the main pump failed to perform efficiently, engineers were brought in from the East to find and correct the problem. When they were unable to do so, Colman worked for 36 hours straight until he got all pumps working to capacity, thereby saving the city and the lumber mills from a water shortage. Construction of freeway ramps in the 1970s isolated the Colman School from ready access and diminished its attendance area. The school is no longer used in the regular education program. It was forcibly occupied in the mid-1980s by black activists who proclaimed the old school a center for Afro-American cultural and social history. In 1990 a new Colman Elementary School was in the works, site unannounced.

Colockum School, 8301 Colockum Rd., Malaga, Wenatchee School District (Chelan County). The first settlers to that part of the Columbia River which is now the site of Wenatchee came over the mountains from the Kittitas Valley between 1883 and 1887. They used the Colockum Pass, in existence from 1873 on. Before long the pass area had become sufficiently settled to require a school. The first structure used as a school, situated 16 miles before the beginning of Colockum Pass, was built in 1896 or 1897 and used until 1916. At that time a new structure was built close to the old school. The older building was moved and used as a dwelling until destroyed by fire some years later. The second school was used until 1933 when it was consolidated with the Malaga School District. Malaga has now consolidated with the Wenatchee School District. By 1989 the former Middle Colockum School was being used as a family home. The word Colockum is believed to be Indian and represents the sound of wild geese.

Columbia Valley Gardens Elementary School, 2724 30th, Longview School District (Cowlitz County). The planned city of Longview was built in the 1920s on a flood plain of the Columbia River. Dikes were built around the city to protect it from spring floods. On the west side of the city this man-made valley is called Columbia Valley, whose fertile soil supports many local gardens. Hence the name of a school built in the area in 1925.

Columbus School, Harrah Drain Road, rural school district (Yakima County). The school was built early in this century by citizens of the area and named for Christopher Columbus, Genoan sailor who explored the New World under the Spanish flag in the 15th Century, believed by most people to be the first European to land on New World soil. The school was later torn down and replaced by a new building named Victory School after the World War 1 armistice of 1918.

Colvin School District No. 29 (Thurston County). This school was organized on June 4, 1896, to serve rural children in Thurston County near Tenino. It was consolidated with Tenino School District on June 2, 1942. The school was built on land homesteaded by Ignacious Colvin in the early 1800s. The Colvin family home is on the Historical Register.

Commodore Bainbridge Middle School (See Bainbridge.)

This is the old Columbia Valley Gardens School in Longview. There is a new school on this site. (Photo from Cowlitz County Historical Museum, via Helen Leonard, Lower Columbia Retired Teachers Association)

Comstock Elementary School, W. 620 33rd Ave., Spokane School District (Spokane County). Opened in 1956 and closed in 1972. Named for James Comstock, early Spokane entrepreneur, city councilman, and mayor. Comstock began a dry goods store with partners J.E. Paterson, J.L. Paine, and E.A. Shadle the day before the great Spokane fire. The store survived and later became the Crescent, one of Spokane's finest department stores. The Comstock family donated Comstock Park and pool and land for a school. When the school closed in 1972 after failure of a tax levy at the polls, it was found that the original deed limited the use of the land and building to the education of Spokane children. The Comstock building was moved to school land at 63rd Avenue in 1977. A new structure was built around the former Comstock School and the combined plant named Mullan Road Elementary School.

Concord Elementary School, 723 S. Concord St., Seattle School District (King County). Opened in 1913. No information provided but it would appear this school was named for the street on which it is situated.

Cooper Elementary School, 4408 Delridge Way S.W., Seattle School District (King County). The Youngstown School in the Humphrey Settlement south of Seattle opened in 1905 to serve the children of steel mill and sawmill workers. In 1908 the school was annexed to the Seattle School District and a five-room frame building built on the Youngstown School site. By 1917 a larger school was needed for the families of this expanding industrial area. A brick building was erected. In 1929 the school was renamed Cooper Elementary for Frank B. Cooper, superintendent of schools in Seattle from 1901 to 1922.

Cooper Elementary School, N. 3200 Ferrall St., Spokane School District (Spokane County). Opened in 1908 and named for James Fennimore Cooper (1789-1851), first major American novelist. His *Leatherstocking Tales* were noted for their idealization of the

American Indian. The present schoolhouse dates from 1979.

Covington Junior High School, 11200 N.E. Rosewood Rd., Vancouver, Evergreen School District (Clark County). Opened in 1960 and named for Richard Covington and his wife, Ann, who were brought from England by Dr. John McLoughlin, chief factor at Fort Vancouver from 1825 into the 1840s, to teach school. John Ball, another teacher brought to the Oregon Territory by Dr. McLoughlin, also has a school named for him. Mr. Ball preceded the Caringtons to Fort Vancouver. Mr. Covington loved music and brought with him a piano, violin, and guitar. Mrs. Covington was an accomplished musician also. After teaching at the Fort several years, the Covingtons in 1848 took up a homestead at Fourth Plain near the present Orchards community where they operated a boarding school with six pupils. The census of 1850 gives the schools in Clark County as two, one of them being the Covingtons'. In about 1920, the original Covington log home, which had been the first boarding school in this area, was dismantled log by log, each log numbered and moved to Vancouver at 4201 Main Street where it was reassembled. It is the oldest existing school building in Clark County, perhaps in the state. The building is now used as a community meeting place and for social occasions. It is managed by the Vancouver Women's Club.

Coweeman Junior High School, 2000 Allen St., Kelso School District (Cowlitz County). Built in 1960. Coweeman is an Anglacized Cowlitz Indian word—ko-wee-na—meaning "short man," believed to be a reference to a very short Indian who lived on the bank of the river given the name Coweeman. The river had formerly been named for Anton Gobar, a herdsman for the Hudson's Bay Company, who pastured stock nearby. Parsing out the Anglacized word Coweeman gives us "cow" (a reference to Anton Gobar?), "wee man" (a reference to the short Indian?), and results in suspect word etymology. But since all Indian words represented in writing are European attempts to capture the Indian word's sound,

The first school in Kelso started in 1887 in the residence of Peter W. Crawford. It was a private subscription school. (Photo from Cowlitz County Historical Museum)

Coweeman is not more nor less authentic than most printed Indian words.

Cowley Elementary School, Clarke and Maple Streets, Spokane School District (Spokane County). Opened in 1917, closed in 1930, this two-room brick building was built close to Spokane River in Peaceful Valley. It was named after H.T. Cowley, an early missionary and teacher to the Nez Perce Indians. He opened the first school in Spokane Falls in 1875 at his home, Sixth and Division Streets, where Cowley Park is situated at this writing. The school was closed in 1930 but reopened in 1940 as part of Franklin D. Roosevelt's New Deal economic recovery program. The building was used for National Youth Administration classes. In 1964 the school and land were sold to a developer, but the building was still on the site as of 1990.

Cozier Elementary School, 1330 Lincoln St., Bellingham School District (Whatcom County). Built in 1951 and occupied in 1952, the school was named for Carl Cozier, a school board member very active in the early days of the community.

Crabtree School District No. 110 (Whitman County). This early country school was named for M.V. Crabtree, who donated the school site.

Crawford House School, Crawford and First Avenue North, Kelso School District (Cowlitz County). The Crawford House School, a subscription grade school started in the fall of 1887 in the former family home of Peter W. Crawford, opened with 20 pupils. Rosa Brooks, a graduate of the Annie Wright School in Tacoma, was the teacher. She was the granddaughter of Victor Wallace, a prominent Cowlitz County pioneer. In two years the enrollment outgrew the Crawford House and led to the formation of the first public school in the area in 1889. Peter Crawford had immigrated to the area from Kelso, Scotland, in 1847 as a team driver over the Oregon Trail. He hired on as a surveyor in Washington Territory and took out a Donation Land Claim near the Cowlitz River. When he left the area, he platted his farm into the city of Kelso, named for his hometown in Scotland, and gave his house over to be used as a school.

Curtis Junior High School and Curtis Senior High School, 8901 40th St. W, and 8425 40th St. W., respectively, Tacoma, University Place School District (Pierce County). Both schools were named for George C. Curtis, teacher and principal in the district from 1927 to 1957 and superintendent of the district from 1957 to 1972. The PTA circulated a petition that the junior high, opened in 1957, be named for Mr. Curtis. No other name was considered by the school board. The PTA petition was included among other documents placed in the school's cornerstone. The senior high was built in 1959 when a 10th grade was added to the University Place program. Mr. Curtis, a native of Washington State, attended school in Gig Harbor. One of his teachers was Lucy Goodman for whom a Gig Harbor school is named.

Cushman Elementary School, 4330 N. Visscher St., Tacoma School District (Pierce County). Opened in 1909, this school was named for Francis W. Cushman, then a Congressman from Tacoma who was instrumental in getting title to federal land at Point Defiance for a city park. In 1911 a new school was built on the Cushman School site and the name was changed to Point Defiance School to avoid confusion with the Cushman Industrial School for Indians on Indian reservation land in Tacoma. That Indian school later took the name Chief Leschi, an Indian leader during the Washington Territory Indian Wars of the 1850s.

Damman School was built in 1890. In 1991 it had an enrollment of 41 pupils. (Photo from Verna Watson, Kittitas County Retired Teachers Association)

D

Damman School, Manastash and Damman Roads (Kittitas County). This one-room country school has been in continuous use since 1890. In 1916 the building was remodeled and a gymnasium added. The first six grades were still being taught in this school in 1990, according to an official tour guide of Ellensburg published by the Chamber of Commerce. The school was named for Merrit M. Damman, not identified. Original records cited by the Ellensburg *Daily Record* indicate the school was built on skids on the Snowden property and moved on January 23, 1893, to property owned by Matthew Damman. Perhaps the Merrit Damman listed in the Chamber of Commerce brochure went by the middle name Matthew. A surviving member of the Damman family, Marvin Damman, who attended the Damman School in 1923 and 1924, thinks his grandmother was the first teacher in the school. He had always thought the school was named for her. Some 150 ex-students came to Ellensburg to celebrate the school's 100th anniversary in 1990. It is believed that Damman is the oldest continuously operated school in the state.

Edna E. Davis School, across from Irving School at W. 1716 Seventh Ave., Spokane School District (Spokane County). Edna E. Davis began teaching deaf students in Spokane in 1922, moving to portable buildings at Irving Elementary School in 1934. In 1952 Davis was named principal of what was then called the Spokane Day School for the Deaf. In 1954 when a new building for deaf students was added to the Irving complex, the parents requested that it be named for the school's principal, Edna E. Davis. In 1974 the program was moved to the Madison School when the Irving School was closed.

Davis Elementary School, 31 S.E. Ash St., College Place School District (Walla Walla County). Named in 1931 in honor of William J. Davis, a teacher and principal in College Place schools for 30 years—1902 to 1932. The auditorium and athletic field nearby also are named for Mr. Davis, who was instrumental in consolidating the old Whitman School District with the College Place School District.

Davis High School, 212 S. Sixth Ave., Yakima School District (Yakima County). Angus C. Davis was superintendent of the Yakima School District from 1913 to 1947. In 1957 the Yakima School Board renamed the newly remodeled North Yakima High School, built in 1908, for A.C. Davis, the former superintendent. Davis was born in 1880 in Polo, Illinois, and educated in Denison University in Ohio and Chicago University in Illinois. He taught school in Texas, Oregon, and Spokane before arriving in Yakima.

Day-Orca Elementary School, 3921 Linden Ave. N., Seattle School District (King County). In 1891 the Seattle School District was given what is probably still the most generous donation it has ever received: a block of 20 lots, valued at the time at $10,000. The gift was from B.F. and Frances Day. Mr. Day was an early member of the Seattle School Board. In accepting the land, the board passed a set of resolutions pledging the erection of a brick school building on this site "to cost no less than $25,000" and to be called the B.F. Day School. That school opened in 1892 to welcome 185 students. The second name— Orca—which does not appear in a 1955 list of Seattle schools, is not explained in an official school district history book in the Seattle School District archives. The district headquarters offices did not answer questions about its schools' names.

Decatur High School, 2800 S.W. 320th, Federal Way School District (King County). Opened in 1976, Decatur High School began an unofficial tradition in the Federal Way School District of naming high schools for famous American historical figures. Stephen Decatur (1779-1820) was an American naval officer. During the war against Tripoli in 1804, he led a daring raid into the Tripoli harbor to burn the captured American frigate Philadelphia. In the War of 1812, Decatur commanded the *United States* and captured the British frigate *Macedonian*. Decatur was mortally wounded in a duel with James Barron in 1820.

Decatur Elementary School, 7711 43rd Ave., Seattle School District (King County). Because it drew many children from families of men in the U.S. Navy at the time it was completed, Stephen Decatur School was named in honor of the American naval officer who was the hero of the Tripoli War and the War of 1812. Decatur Elementary School opened in September 1961. The school was built on land that had once been the playground area of the Shearwater Housing Project, government homes for Navy personnel and families associated with Sand Point Naval Air Station.

DeLancey-Houghton Elementary School, Fourth and Canna, Soap Lake School District (Grant County). Opened in 1947 and named for two local businessmen who had served more than 20 years each on the school board. F. Duer DeLancey was a Soap Lake merchant. Ralph E. Houghton was manager of the Potlatch Lumber Yard in Soap Lake. The school was named the year these men died unexpectedly of natural causes.

DeLong Elementary School, 4901 S. 14th St., Tacoma School District (Pierce County). DeLong Elementary was planned and named in 1949. However, construction did not start until four years later in 1953, and it was not occupied by students until 1954. The name selected was that of George Washington DeLong, a graduate of the U.S. Naval Academy, who led an exploration of the Arctic in 1880-1881 in quest of a passage from the Bering Sea to the North Pole. The explorers starved to death in Siberia, but charts developed as a result of the DeLong expedition helped other Arctic explorers.

Denny-Blaine School, Custer and Ninth, Sunnyside School District (Yakima County). Built by funds raised from a public election in 1903. Forty acres of land for the brick schoolhouse and playground were given by "a Mr. Denny and a Mr. Blaine" of the Washington Irrigation Company. Ground was broken in 1904, and the school opened in 1905 as a high school. When a new high school was opened in 1911, Denny-Blaine became an elementary school. In 1954 the school became a junior high school. Denny-Blaine was closed in 1961 and razed in 1966. The site is now that of government offices.

Denny Middle School, 8402 30th S.W., Seattle School District (King County). In September, 1952, the David T. Denny Junior High (later a middle school) opened its doors to students. David Denny and his older brother Arthur came west from Illinois in 1851, headed for the Willamette Valley in Oregon. When Arthur became ill in Portland, David, along with Charles Terry and John Low, traveled north and found Alki Point. The first wedding among the new settlers was David Denny's when he married Louisa Boren, his stepsister, who also has a Seattle school named for her. There was an earlier Denny Elementary school in 1884, part of which was removed in 1906 and the balance in 1929 by the regrading of Denny Hill. The earlier Denny School may have been named for the hill, for Arthur, or for John (David's and Arthur's father), or for the Denny family.

DeSales Junior-Senior High School, Roman Catholic, 919 E. Sumach, Walla Walla, Spokane Diocese (Walla Walla County). Opened and named in 1959 for St. Francis DeSales, a 16th Century Geneva bishop who is now a Roman Catholic patron saint of the learned and the press.

Don Dial Memorial Scoreboard, Palouse School District (Whitman County). The scoreboard at the athletic field was dedicated to the memory of Don Dial in 1978. Dial, who grew up in the Palouse-Potlatch area, was a teacher, coach, and administrator in the Palouse schools.

Emily Dickinson Elementary School, 7300 208th Ave. N.E., Redmond, Lake Washington School District (King County). In 1967 the Lake Washington School

District board of directors adopted a policy of naming new elementary schools from a list of names of "deceased persons famous for their work in science, the humanities, letters, or education." Emily Dickinson School, opened in 1978, is one of the schools named under this policy. Miss Dickinson (1830-1886) was one of the great poets in American literature, in some views, the greatest. She composed more than a thousand unique lyrics dealing with religion, love, nature, death, and immortality, only seven of which were published during her lifetime. A definitive edition of her works did not appear in print until 1955.

Dillenbaugh School, Dillenbaugh School District, Chehalis (Lewis County). Dillenbaugh School District No. 135 was established July 30, 1912, from what had been Dillenbaugh School District No. 16. Dillenbaugh School was located about three miles south of Chehalis on the left side of the Old Pacific Highway (now Jackson Highway) near the Sanderson Road and Dillenbaugh Creek. The two-room building, which has now been razed, sat on a hill that has since been flattened. The first Dillenbaugh School was established sometime before May, 1878, the date on a legal description of the district still on record. The first internal school records date from 1882. The only Dillenbaugh family name in the area was that of A.B. Dillenbaugh, born in 1823 in New York State, who migrated west in 1859 at the age of 36 with his wife and five daughters. He was listed in the 1860 census as a farmer, justice of the peace, and a judge. He also served as Dillenbaugh School District clerk for one year. In those days a school district clerk was the chief administrator. Dillenbaugh School District was consolidated with Chehalis School District on April 11, 1933, and the Dillenbaugh School closed its doors forever.

Dimmitt Middle School, 1320 80th Ave. S., Renton School District (King County). Alva W. Dimmitt came to Renton in 1911 as principal of Sartori School. Over the years he served in a variety of offices and retired as supervisor of elementary schools in 1942. The school named for Mr. Dimmitt opened in 1959. Because of declining enrollment in its attendance area, the school was closed in 1987 and leased to Education Service District 121 as its administrative headquarters. In 1990 some Renton School Board members discussed reopening Dimmitt as a regular school again. No action had been taken at press time.

Discovery Preschool, 18002 "B" St., Spanaway, Bethel School District (Pierce County). Opened in 1989, this preschool is part of the Challenger alternative high school program. (See Challenger.) The preschool-aged children help teach valuable parenting skills to high school students participating in the operation of the preschool. The preschool's name comes both from the educational philosophy of individual discovery and from the Discovery space program. The school is part of the "Extended Learning Family," a unit of the school district's Schools for the 21st Century Project.

Discovery Elementary School, 2300 228th Ave. S.E., Issaquah School District (King County). Named in 1990, this school was not opened until 1991. The school was named by a local child who noted the dual meaning of the word "discovery." The first meaning associates with space exploration and connects nicely with the Apollo and Challenger names of two other district elementary schools. The second meaning relates to how a student "always makes lots of discoveries in school, too," the unidentified student wrote.

Discovery Elementary School, 11700 Meridian Ave., Mukilteo School District, Everett (Snohomish County). No opening date provided. This is one of several schools in the Mukilteo School District whose names are associated with the U.S. space program.

Dorrance Academy, Snohomish (Snohomish County). In 1892 a Snohomish Presbyterian minister named Dorrance raised funds to build an academy "just south of the southwest corner of Second Street and Avenue "A." In 1893 Mr. Dorrance resigned his appointment as pastor of the Presbyterian Church in Snohomish to devote all his energies to the Dorrance Academy. Mr. Dorrance left for

California in the late 1890s, and the school languished in his absence. The building was sold in 1901 and became the Rainier View Hotel. In 1975 the structure was being used under the name Rainier View Apartments.

Dower Elementary School, 7817 John Dower Rd. W., Tacoma, Clover Park School District (Pierce County). Built in 1962, Dower school was named for John Dower Road which, in turn, was named for an early lumber industrialist in the area. Mr. Dower owned 50-some acres on the east and west banks of Chambers Creek at the point the creek flows from Lake Steilacoom. The original Dower home remains on the east bank of the creek in what is now a residential area.

Downing Elementary School, 2502 N. Orchard, Tacoma School District (Pierce County). Named for Mont C. Downing by the Tacoma School Board in 1949, two years after Mr. Downing had died while serving as principal of Jason Lee Junior High School. In addition to his role as principal, Mr. Downing also had been an assistant superintendent for 11 years.

Dunlap Elementary School, 8621 46th Ave. S., Seattle School District (King County). Named for the Dunlap family, who settled in Seattle in 1869. There have been three Dunlap Schools. The first, a one-room school, was near what are now Kenyon and Rainier Avenues. The second was on the site of the old Dunlap home, used in the 1960s for a federal housing project. This site was a four-room unit opened about 1904 and operated until the present Dunlap School was opened in 1924. Joseph Dunlap was born in New Hampshire in 1816. He married Catherine G. Henderson in 1843 in Iowa, where they farmed until 1869. The school has a crayon portrait of the Dunlap family on display. Joseph and Catherine are portrayed as well as their children Charles, George, and Leana.

Ruth Dykeman Children's Center, 1033 S.W. 152nd, Burien, Highline School District (King County). Ruth School for Girls came into existence through the combined efforts of several interested civic leaders, including Judge King Dykeman. In 1921 the Ruth School for Girls, a group home for emotionally disturbed adolescent girls, was founded on the shore of Lake Burien. It was named in honor of Judge Dykeman's daughter. In 1982 the function of the "school" was broadened to include out-patient care and a separate program for boys. The name was changed to the Ruth Dykeman Center to reflect this new charter. The school program, a regular elementary, middle, and high school curriculum for Ruth Dykeman Center clients and community students, is operated by Highline School District staff members. In 1989 the institution's name was changed from Ruth Dykeman Center to Ruth Dykeman Children's Center to more accurately reflect its mission.

E

Eatonville Logging Camp School in Pierce County in 1928 or '29. The school was a converted box car. (Photo from Helen Leonard, Lower Columbia Retired Teachers Association)

Eatonville Lumber Company Camp School, seven miles up the Mashell logging railway from Eatonville (Pierce County). The school, opened in 1929, was held in a railroad boxcar sitting on a sidetrack in the logging camp. The boxcar was fitted with windows, a door, a stove, bookcase, chairs, blackboard, pump organ, and desks of various sizes. The school continued until 1933 or 1934 when the logging camp was closed for lack of a market. Helen Leonard, 1990 member of the Lower Columbia unit of the Washington State Retired Teachers Association and one of the researchers on Cowlitz County schools for this book, was the first teacher in the Eatonville Lumber Company Camp School.

Ebenezer Christian School, Traditional Christian, 9390 Guide Meridian Rd., Lynden (Whatcom County). No information available.

Eckstein Middle School, 3003 N.E. 75th St., Seattle School District (King County). Opened in 1950 as a junior high and changed in 1971 to a sixth, seventh, and eighth grade middle school. Named for former school board member Nathan Eckstein, Bavarian-born business and community leader and patron of the Seattle Symphony. After coming to this country as a child, Eckstein obtained a job in 1897 at the age of 14 working in a grocery store. Later he became president of Schwabacher's, a large grocery chain. In 1926 Eckstein was named Seattle's most useful citizen.

Miles Edgerton Elementary School, 121 E. Whitesell, Orting School District (Pierce County). Miles Edgerton was a teacher and principal in Orting from 1890 to 1899. He also, during his life, served as mayor and as judge. The school bearing his name was built about 1930. The name was changed to Orting Elementary when a new school was built in 1978. Orting Middle School now occupies the old Edgerton School site.

Edison Elementary School, 201 S. Dawes, Kennewick School District (Benton County). Edison was opened in 1960 and named for the American inventor by a vote of the students.

Edison Technical School, Broadway and East Pine, Seattle School District (King County). The first Edison School was of brick, built in 1921 at 1712 Harvard. Substantial additions were constructed in 1942 and 1949. This vocational education school, presumably named for the self-educated Thomas A. Edison, inventor of the incandescent lamp, phonograph recorder, and motion picture machine, was widely used by adults to learn trades or to improve work skills. Edison took over the old Broadway High School site at Broadway and E. Pine after the high school was closed in 1946. That site is now a part of the Seattle Central Community College. Edison had several satellite sites, including the old Holgate Elementary School.

Edison Elementary School, 607 "H" St., Centralia School District (Lewis County). The North End School was completed on this site in 1890. The school was known as Edison by 1910. It was replaced by another

Edison School in 1918. The name honors Thomas Alva Edison, American inventor.

Edison Elementary School, S. 515 Lee St., Spokane School District (Spokane County). Opened in 1893 and closed in 1972. Originally called the Union Park School, this was one of the largest schools in Spokane in 1900. By 1896 the school was being called Edison for Thomas Alva Edison, American inventor. It was closed in 1972 after a school levy failed to get voter approval.

Edison Elementary School, E. Alder, Walla Walla School District (Walla Walla County). Opened in 1936, the school was named Edison at the instigation of school activist George Drennan. Board records do not say that the school was named for Thomas Alva Edison, American inventor (1847-1931). However, his portrait hangs in the school's entryway.

North School in Centralia fielded a football team in the early 1900s. A later school on this site was named Edison. (Lewis County Historical Association Photo from Elizabeth Wedin, Lewis County Retired Teachers Association)

Eels Academy (Stevens County). Established in 1896 as an educational branch of the Congregational Church of Colville. Its purpose was to fill the educational needs of high school students since there was no other high school in the area at that time. The Academy opened in the fall of 1896 with 26 students in attendance. It was named in honor of Cushing Eels, a pioneering Protestant missionary in the area. The Reverend and Mrs. Eels along with Elkhana and Mary Walker established a mission at Ford in 1838. Eels Academy became Colville High School in 1906.

Albert Einstein Middle School, 325 N.W. 195th, Seattle, Shoreline School District (King County). Opened in 1968, Einstein Middle School was named as the result of an essay contest among incoming seventh grade students. Students were instructed to write about persons who had received the Nobel Peace Prize. The winning paper, written by Doug Swanberg, was read by the student on dedication-ceremony day for the new school. Albert Einstein (1879-1955) was born in Germany to Jewish parents. Driven from Nazi Germany in the 1930s, he became an American citizen. A physicist, he is principally remembered for his Special Theory of Relativity.

Eisenhower Middle School, 2500 100th Ave. S.E., Everett School District (Snohomish County). Named on April 7, 1969, after receiving suggestions from the community, for the 34th president of the United States, Dwight David Eisenhower.

Dwight D. Eisenhower Elementary School, 9201 N.W. Ninth Ave., Vancouver School District (Clark County). Opened in 1970 and named by the Vancouver School Board for Dwight David Eisenhower, 34th president of the United States. Mr. Eisenhower had served in 1940 as chief of staff with the Ninth Army Corps at Fort Lewis, Washington.

Eisenhower High School, 702 S. 40th Ave., Yakima School District (Yakima County). Built in 1956 and named for then current President Dwight Eisenhower, who also served as supreme commander of the Allied Forces' Normandy invasion of 1944. The school was opened in the fall of 1957 and, at first, housed a junior high.

Ellisforde SDA School, Seventh-Day Adventist, 32082 Highway 97 N., Tonasket (Okanogan County). No information available.

H.B. Ellison Junior High School, 800 block of Idaho Street, Wenatchee School District (Chelan County). H.B. Ellison was the first principal of a junior high built in 1929. Mr. Ellison died suddenly in 1937 while walking to school in the snow. Soon afterward the school at which he had been principal was renamed for him. In September of 1962 the students and staff moved to a new building, Orchard Junior High School. The Ellison building became an annex of the high school. A new high school was occupied in 1972, and the Ellison building stood empty until it was demolished a few years later.

El-Shaddai Junior-Senior High School, 19830 S.E. 328th Pl., Auburn (King County). No information available.

Elson School District No. 34, Section 36, Township 20 N, Range 4 W; Sect. 1 & 12, Township 19N, R4W; S31-32, T20N, R3W, S5-8, T19N, R3W (Mason County). John Mitchell Elson was born in 1818 in what is now West Virginia. He had studied medicine five years before joining John C. Fremont's expedition to California. He then spent 10 years working in California gold mines. He married Mary Beesecker in 1855, and they had five children. The family moved to Mason County in the Washington Territory where Elson became a farmer and contract mail carrier. The Elson School District was formed in 1896 and named for the Elsons as the first settlers in that part of Mason County. The school later became known as the Brumbaugh School, named for the county superintendent who lived in this district and whose children attended the school. The district was consolidated with the Shelton School District in 1916.

Emerson Elementary School, 801 N. 18th Ave., Pasco School District (Franklin County). Opened in 1954 and named by the Pasco School Board after suggestions from the community. Pasco has several schools named for authors. Emerson was an American essayist, poet, and thinker. His poems as well as his essays are reflective and serious. One of his best known poems is the *Concord Hymn,* sung at the completion of the battle monument at Concord in 1837.

Emerson Primary and Kindergarten School, 201 W. Emerson, Hoquiam School District (Grays Harbor County). Built during the summer of 1921 and named for George H. Emerson, pioneer lumberman and civic leader. Emerson was originally an elementary school but in 1990 had only primary and kindergarten classes.

Emerson Elementary School, 9709 60th Ave. S., Seattle School District (King County). Built in 1903 as Rainier Beach School, Emerson came into the Seattle School District in 1907 as part of a south end annexation. The Seattle School Board changed the school's name to Emerson in 1909. It is not recorded for whom it was named, but a second school—Hawthorne—also was in the same annexation group. Ralph Waldo Emerson and Nathaniel Hawthorne were contemporary writers in the early and middle 19th Century. It is assumed the two schools were named for these writers.

Emerson School of Tacoma had a high school on the second floor. (Photo from Pat Flyn, Community Relations, Tacoma School District)

Emerson Elementary School, South Fourth and St. Helens, Tacoma School District (Pierce County). Named for Ralph Waldo Emerson, essayist and poet, on June 21, 1889. Previously the name had been North School but was renamed when a new six-room building was erected. The school was closed in 1913. In World War 1 it was used to house soldiers. It has since been torn down.

Emerson Elementary School, 8702 Seventh Ave., Everett School District (Snohomish County). Opened in 1957, the school is named for Ralph Waldo Emerson (1803-1882), one of America's most influential authors and thinkers. A Unitarian minister, in 1832 after a three-year stay, he left his only pastorate, Boston's Old North Church, because of doctrinal disputes. A noted lecturer, Emerson called for American intellectual independence from Europe in his Phi Beta Kappa address at Harvard (1837). In the planning stage the building was known as Farmer Road School, that being the old name for Seventh Avenue, on which the school was situated.

Emerson Elementary School, 1103 Pine St., Snohomish School District (Snohomish County). Named in 1892 for Ralph Waldo Emerson, American essayist. The original Emerson building was closed as a school in 1933 and used as a preschool and for vocational training. A new Emerson School was opened in 1954 and was remodeled in 1985.

Enatai Elementary School, 10615 S.E. 23rd, Bellevue School District (King County). Enatai or Enati is a Chinook jargon word meaning "across." This school was named in 1953.

Erikson Home School/Sky View High School, Unaffiliated, 3412 S. Jean St., Kennewick (Benton County). No information available.

Erving Preparatory Academy, Unaffiliated, 20000 68th Ave. W., Lynnwood (Snohomish County). No information available.

Evaline Elementary School, 111 Schoolhouse Rd., Winlock, Evaline School District (Lewis County). Chartered in 1883 as Brown's School, named for an early settler, the school was renamed Evaline for the local post office in 1906. Sedate Porter established a store and post office in his home and submitted three proposed names to the government: Brown, Porter, and Evaline (his wife's name). Evaline was selected. The school was still in operation in 1990.

Jeanette Evans Elementary School, Warden School District (Grant County). Jeanette Swain Evans came to the Warden School District in the early days of World War 2 to become superintendent, principal, and teacher—all at the same time. The Evans school was named for her a few months after her death in 1966.

Explorer Elementary School, 18002 "B" St., Spanaway, Bethel School District (Pierce County). Named while under construction in 1988, this school opened in September of 1989. As are the Challenger High School and Discovery Preschool, also at this address, this school is a part of the district's Extended Learning Family, a unit of the Schools for the 21st Century Project. Its name, as do the names of the other two schools at this site, expresses both an educational philosophy and admiration for the U.S. space program and the Explorer spacecraft.

Explorer Junior High School, 9600 Holly Dr., Mukilteo School District (Snohomish County). Date opened not given by district. Several Mukilteo schools, including this one, have names associated with the U.S. space program.

Students at Aberdeen's Finch School in May 1929, waited to board buses taking them to a circus. Their host was E.C. Finch, local newspaper publisher for whom the school was named. (William Jones Historic Collection Photo from Rosalie Spellman, Grays Harbor County Retired Teachers Association)

F

Fairbanks School District No. 77 (Whitman County). There were some 180 school districts in Whitman County by 1918. Each district was formed to support one rural school. Fairbanks was named for Charles W. Fairbanks, vice president of the United States in the second Theodore Roosevelt administration from 1905 to 1909 and a former senator from a midwestern state. Fairbanks, Alaska, is also named for this same man. It is doubtful that Mr. Fairbanks ever visited either Washington State or Alaska. Why he was selected to be honored by placing his name on a school is unrecorded.

Farwell Elementary School, N. 13005 Crestline, Spokane, Mead School District (Spokane County). Mead School District did not provide an opening date. The school probably is named for an adjacent road. There also is a park in the area named Farwell. District personnel were unable to determine the origin of the Farwell name.

Fawcett Elementary School, 126 E. 60th, Tacoma School District (Pierce County). Named for Angelo Vance Fawcett, five times mayor of Tacoma. He was a veteran of the Civil War, came to Tacoma in the early 1890s, and established a seed and farm equipment business. He was a state senator and a Pierce County commissioner. He also was the prime instigator of a city light, power, and water system. The school board named the school in 1949, but the building was not completed until 1950. Remodeled in 1986.

Fayette School, Adna School District (Lewis County). The first Fayette School was built in about 1878 on land across the Chehalis River from a farm owned by Joel Henry Fay, Sr. The Fay farm was at the edge of a mill town named Burke not far from present-day Adna. That first school was a one-room building. Its small size led to its being called Fayette, the diminuitive of Fay. It was replaced by a four-room, white, frame building in the 1880s, but the name was not changed. The Fay family had migrated west in the 1860s, first from Shrewsbury, Massachusetts, to Illinois and thence to the Chehalis River near Adna. Alice Fay, the elder daughter, was a teacher in the school in the 1890s. In 1892, when a school was started in the Adna District, the Fayette School was rebuilt at the mouth of Deep Creek, Grades 1-12. John William McCutcheon was a teacher there, probably in 1893. Inez Cravatt, one of the pupils, nicknamed the school "The Mud Creek Academy." Eleanor Fay Ponder Jones, granddaughter of Joel Henry Fay Sr., taught at the school in the 1920-1921 school year. The school was consolidated into Adna School District in 1924. The building was moved to a nearby farm and was still in use in 1990 as a farm out-building. Also in 1990, Bob Fay, great grandson of Joel Henry Fay, Sr., still lived on 40 acres of the original Fay property, worked for the Adna School District, and was completing his 30th year as a teacher.

Federal Way High School, 30611 16th Ave. S., Federal Way School District (King County). Named by the school board after two federal highways serving the area in 1929: Military Road and Highway 99 (now called Pacific Highway). In 1990 the community called Federal Way became an incorporated city.

Feenan School District No. 136 (Whitman County). A single rural school named for Frank Feenan, unidentified but probably a school board member or owner of the land on which the school sat or both. The district was consolidated with others in the 1930s.

Felida Elementary School, 2700 N.W. 119th, Vancouver School District (Clark County). No information available.

Fernwood Elementary School, 3934 Jewell Rd., Bothell, Northshore School District (King County). Built in 1988 and named after the 1898 Fernwood Schoolhouse that once served that area. The Fernwood community and the old school no longer exist.

Joel E. Ferris High School, E. 3020 37th Ave., Spokane School District (Spokane County). Opened and named in 1963 after a prominent Spokane citizen. Joel Ferris first visited Spokane as a young man in the 1890s. After graduation from college in 1908, he decided to return to Spokane and make it his home. A businessman and active civic leader, he became president of the Eastern Washington Historical Society and wrote many articles on regional history.

Dr. Vitt P. Ferrucci Junior High School, 3213 Wildwood Park Dr., Puyallup School District (Pierce County). Built in 1982, this school was named for Dr. Vitt P. Ferrucci, a member of the Puyallup School Board for 32 years. He also served as a regent at Washington State University.

Fiker Stadium, Prosser School District (Benton County). Date of construction not provided by school district. Named for Art Fiker, long-time Prosser teacher.

E.C. Finch Elementary School, 1010 Huntley Rd., Aberdeen School District (Grays Harbor County). Named in 1926 for Edward C. Finch, who built Aberdeen's first "skyscraper," the five-story Finch Building. Mr. Finch was a land developer, one-time state senator, philanthropist, newspaper publisher, and all-around civic leader. The Finch School was closed in 1938 and destroyed by fire in 1956. The school site is now a city park named for another local pioneer, Frank Garley.

Finch Elementary School, N. 3717 Milton St., Spokane School District (Spokane County). Named for John Ayland Finch, a wealthy immigrant from England who is remembered as one of Spokane's great philanthropists. The school was named for Mr. Finch in 1924.

Finley Elementary School, Route 2, Box 2670, Kennewick, Finley School District (Benton County). On March 18, 1902, Mr. George E. Finley, a Nebraska farmer, his wife, and stepson (with his wife, a son, and adopted daughter) arrived by wagon over the desert to an area six miles southeast of Kennewick. They settled on land the Seattle, Portland, & Spokane Railroad was devel-

oping in 40-acre tracts for irrigation from the new canal. George Finley felt his grandson and three other children in the area should be attending a school. Under his direction a two-room temporary building was constructed and, in 1904, Finley School District No. 53 became a reality. The people of the community named the school in honor of the man instrumental in building it even though he preferred it be called Central School District. In 1906 a four-room school with a second floor replaced the original one. The community became known as Finley, taking its name from the school.

Fisher Elementary School, 501 N. 15th St., Lynden School District (Whatcom County). Fisher Elementary was built in 1962. It was named for a former teacher and superintendent of Lynden School District, William A. Fisher. He was teacher and coach from 1911 to 1915, superintendent of Sumas School District from 1915 to 1917, and superintendent in Lynden from 1917 to 1954. After his retirement he served a term in the state legislature. He died December 12, 1960.

Fletcher School District No. 49 (Whitman County). From 1872 to 1918, some 180 country schools were established in Whitman County. Most were merged into larger districts in the 1930s. Albert Fletcher was the first clerk of the District No. 49 school board, and thus the school, unofficially at first, became known by his name.

Florence School, Stanwood School District (Snohomish County). This elementary school was built in 1884 on an island at the mouth of the Stillaguamish River. The site had to be elevated because of the tides. Pupils arrived by canoe and rowboat. The number of days the school was open and the length of each school day were usually determined by the tide and the wind. The school was named by the first local postmaster, F.E. Norton, for his former sweetheart. The building, which no longer exists, was constructed by the fathers of the pupils. Most of these fathers were loggers in the area.

Fobes School, Snohomish School District (Snohomish County). The first unit of this school was built in 1884 and expanded in 1885. However, no funds were available to hire a teacher. In 1887 The Reverend J.F. Fobes, Presbyterian minister from Syracuse, New York, began teaching classes at the school, charging a tuition of $6 for 12 weeks instruction. The school year was three to four months long. In 1888 a second story was added to the building providing third and fourth classrooms. Public funds were raised to hire a teacher. Another account more acceptable to the Snohomish Historical Society sets the opening dates of the school at 1904. The structure was still in use as a school in 1963. This second account of the Fobes School history claims the school was named either for a small community between Snohomish and Everett (no longer in existence) or for a man named Warren Fobes who donated the land for the school. Some researchers believe both stories to be true but are about two different schools in the Snohomish area.

Forbes School, Highway 108 and Hurley-Waldrip Road, Forbes School District (Mason County). John Forbes was a school director and donated the land for a schoolhouse in 1897. Both the district and the school were named for him. He was born in Dundee, Scotland, coming to this country with his family when he was a boy. Eventually he came west by oxen-drawn wagon in 1853 to The Dalles, Oregon. By 1883 he, his wife Cornelia Taylor Forbes, and their four children lived on a large farm in Little Skookum Valley near Kamilche where Forbes lived the rest of his life. He was a surveyor, logger, farmer, and the first sheriff of Mason County. The Forbes School existed until consolidation into the Kamilche School District in 1951.

Morris Ford Junior High School, 1602 E. 104th St., Tacoma, Franklin Pierce School District (Pierce County). Morris Ford was superintendent of the Parkland School District and then the first superintendent of the successor consolidated Franklin Pierce School District. This junior high was named for him in 1958.

Henry Ford School in Renton was being used in 1991 for administrative offices. (Photo from Ethel Telban, Renton Retired Teachers Association)

Ford Elementary School, 435 Main Ave. S., Renton School District (King County). Completed in 1922, this school was named for Henry Ford. The automobile was, at that time, revolutionizing travel for the average citizen because of Mr. Ford's mass production techniques. The Renton School District was very short of construction funds. Some of the classrooms at the Ford School remained unfinished for months for lack of money to complete the work. A story is told that the school board named the school for Henry Ford and then petitioned the Ford Motor Company for a grant. The company, still headed up by Henry Ford I, responded with a small photograph of Mr. Ford and no money. In 1970 the school became part of the district administrative center.

Ford School District No. 33 (Whitman County). Another of the early rural schools in Whitman County. This school was named for G.W. Ford, the farmer who owned the land on which the school was sited. By 1900 some sources say that 10 percent of all schools in Washington State were in the relatively sparsely populated Whitman County. They have since been consolidated into larger districts.

Fort Colville Elementary School, 1212 E. Ivy, Colville School District (Stevens County). Fort Colville was established as a fur-trading post by the Hudson's Bay Company in 1825. It was named for Andrew Colville, a London governor of the company. In 1859 Major Pinkney

Lugenbeel was sent by General William Harney to establish a military encampment on Mill Creek, three miles northeast of Fort Colville. His command consisted of Companies A and E, a force of about 250 troopers. The military presence was ostensibly a response to the Indian attacks on miners and gold prospectors in the area. A second and probably more important reason was the Boundary Commission formed to survey the border between the United States and British-claimed territory at the 49th parallel. In 1983 the Colville School Board named an elementary school for Fort Colville to preserve the rich historical heritage of the area.

Fort Henness School, on Ford's Prairie (near today's Greenlawn Cemetery), Centralia (Lewis County). This was a private school operated by Benjamin Henness, captain of the volunteers during the Indian Wars of 1855-1856. Those are the years the school was in operation.

Fort Simcoe Indian School, White Swan (Yakima County). Established in 1861 at Fort Simcoe as a boarding school for Indian youth. Closed in 1922 when the Yakima Indian Agency was moved to Toppenish. The agency then paid tuition for Indian students to attend local public schools.

Fort Vancouver High School, 5700 E. 18th St., Vancouver School District (Clark County). Built in 1970 and named for the Hudson's Bay Company fur-trading fort established on the Columbia River in 1824-1825. The site of the fort has been preserved as a historic landmark. Fort Vancouver High School replaced the old Vancouver High School when that school's building was condemned.

Henry Foss High School, 2112 S. Tyler, Tacoma School District (Pierce County). Named for Henry Foss, son of the founders of Foss Launch and Tug Company. He served as a state senator and Tacoma port commissioner. In 1969 the school site was chosen, the name proposed by the school board, and the school opened in 1973. This was the first time a school in Tacoma had been named for a native Tacoman. Foss' parents were Norwegian immigrants. His mother was the model for the fictional character Tugboat Annie, whose adventures appeared regularly in the *Saturday Evening Post* in the 1930s and '40s.

Foster Senior High School, 4242 S. 144th St., Seattle, South Central School District (King County). South Central's first school board director back in 1891, the year the first school was built, was Joseph Foster. Son of a Methodist minister, Joseph and his brother, Stephen, left their home in the East and started west in 1852. They staked claims in 1853 at the fork of the Black and White Rivers where they join to form the Duwamish River. The first Foster School was built on Foster homesteaded land. Joseph Foster was elected 11 times to the Washington territorial legislature.

Dorothy Fox Elementary School, 2623 N.W. Sierra St., Camas School District (Clark County). The school on this site, built in the early 1950s, was named the Prune Hill School for the area in which it was situated. A new school was built here in the early 1980s and renamed in 1982 for a highly respected kindergarten teacher who had 38 years of service. Miss Fox had cancer. However, she was able to attend the dedication of the school and died soon thereafter.

Franklin Elementary School, 2505 S. Washington St., Port Angeles School District (Clallam County). Opened in 1954 and named for Benjamin Franklin, American scientist, politician, diplomat, printer, and first postmaster of the United States.

Benjamin Franklin Elementary School, 5206 Franklin St., Vancouver School District (Clark County). The present Franklin School was built in 1955 to accommodate a growing population in north Vancouver. The school was so named by the Vancouver School Board to replace the name once used on the "old Franklin School" in another part of town, a school that had been torn down years before. It was the school board's policy in the earlier days to name the schools after presidents or other famous men in American history, in this case the famous printer, writer, scientist, statesman, and postmaster general. Both Franklin schools were built on Franklin Street. Federal offices now occupy the site of the first Franklin School.

Franklin Elementary School, 400 W. Market, Aberdeen School District (Grays Harbor County). Built in 1899 and named for Benjamin Franklin, American revolutionary-era diplomat. The school served elementary children until 1930 when it became the home of Grays Harbor Junior College for five years. The building was razed in 1935. The site is now a part of the Aberdeen park system.

Benjamin Franklin Elementary School, 12434 N.E. 60th, Kirkland, Lake Washington School District (King County). The naming of this school in 1968 complied with school board policy that elementary schools are to be named from a list of persons famous for science, humanities, letters, or education.

Franklin High School, 3013 S. Mount Baker Blvd., Seattle School District (King County). In the fall of 1912 a high school, formerly a part of Washington High School (which was later to be called Broadway High School), was relocated to the Mount Baker area of the city. Residents petitioned to have the new high school named Mount Baker Park. Students at the school favored the board-proposed name of Franklin, for Benjamin Franklin. The early high school names were selected from a list compiled by New York University and called the Hall of Fame of Great Americans.

Franklin Elementary School, 3202 S. 12th, Tacoma School District (Pierce County). Named for Benjamin Franklin in 1889, 10 days before Washington became a state. The building was replaced in 1910, the old building being sold for $250. In 1914 Franklin and Lowell became the first Tacoma schools regularly to offer students hot lunches.

Franklin Elementary School, E. 2627 17th Ave., Spokane School District (Spokane County). Named in 1889 for Benjamin Franklin, American statesman and

inventor. The original school was sold to the Milwaukee, St. Paul, and Pacific Railroad in 1909, the year the present school was finished and opened. In 1953 four classrooms, a library, and multipurpose room were added to the school.

Franklin Elementary School, S.E. 240 Dexter, Pullman School District (Whitman County). Opened sometime before 1916 and named for Benjamin Franklin.

Franklin Middle School, 410 S. 19th Ave., Yakima School District (Yakima County). Franklin School was built on the site of a former orchard and occupied in 1927 even though it was not completed until 1928. At first the school housed seventh and eighth graders, but was later expanded to the ninth grade. In 1990 it was a middle school for sixth, seventh, and eighth grades. The school was named for Benjamin Franklin of early American history.

Franklin Pierce High School (See Pierce.)

Freeborn School, Camano Island (Island County). At about the turn of the 19th into the 20th Century, Peder A. Pedersen donated an acre and a half of land from the northwest corner of his homestead for a school. The Ole Husby children walked to this school via a trail through the woods, using fallen trees to cross swamps. The Sovig and Gabrielson children, as well as Mabel and Ingvar Skogseth, also attended this cedar-log school, hacked out of the wilderness. It is not recorded how the school got the name Freeborn but being that most of its students were the children of immigrants, perhaps the school was a monument to their own children's unlimited future.

Freeman High School and Freeman Elementary School, Rockford, Freeman School District (Spokane County). Freeman School District was formed in 1955 through the consolidation of the Rockford, Lindberg, and Sunnyside No. 117 School Districts and their schools: Mica Peak, Richmond, and Duncan Canyon Schools. Freeman School District was named for a railroad flag stop which, in turn, had been named sometime before 1879 for a railroad attendant at that stop. The first Freeman School was built in 1910 at the intersection of Jackson Road and "the highway." That school was torn down in 1984 with the opening of a new school complex.

Freeport School, on Cowlitz River near Longview (Cowlitz County). This is one of the early schools serving settlers along the Cowlitz River. In 1867 a flood destroyed the school at Monticello, the first regular school north of the Columbia River. A new school was built at Freeport, a trading center a mile and a half farther up the river. The settlement no longer exists. As in other parts of the territory, the early schools were built by the men of the community out of the materials at hand. Such other early schools in the Cowlitz country included a school in the Bozarth home in Woodland in 1855, Kalama in 1871, Martin's Bluff in early 1870s, Huntington (in "the old priest's house") in early 1870s, Silver Lake, Shanghai, Pekin, Pumphrey, Carrolton, Coweeman, Lancaster, Cedar Creek, Chelachie, and Summit by 1873, Mount Coffin (Fowler's) in 1874, LaDu in 1875, Oak Point in 1878, Mount Solo in 1875, Lexington, Rock Point, and Olequa in 1875, Castle Rock in Edwin Huntington's home in 1877.

Robert Frost Elementary School, 1915 N. 22nd Ave., Pasco School District (Franklin County). The school was named in 1964 for the New England poet (1874-1964), who won four Pulitzer Prizes.

Robert Frost Elementary School, 11801 N.E. 140th, Kirkland, Lake Washington School District (King County). Opened in 1969 and named for the New England poet.

Robert Fulton Elementary School, 14th Northwest and 42nd Street, Seattle School District (King County). Named for a developer of steam-powered riverboats, the school was built in 1907. It was torn down and the property sold in 1932.

Built in 1920 as East High School in Seattle, this school's name was changed in 1922 to Garfield at the suggestion of its principal. (Photo from Seattle Public Schools Archives)

G

Gabrielsen Elementary School, LaCenter School District (Clark County). The school was dedicated to Mary Snyder Gabrielsen in 1965, the year she died from cancer. She is buried in the Highland Lutheran Cemetery in LaCenter. Mary Gabrielsen was born in the LaCenter area on January 25, 1903. Except for her college years, she spent her entire life here as child, student, and teacher. She began teaching at 18 just out of normal school and devoted the next 44 years to the teaching profession.

Gaiser Middle School, 3000 N.E. 99th St., Vancouver School District (Clark County). Opened in 1974, Gaiser is named for Dr. Paul Gaiser, who joined the staff of the Vancouver School District in 1934, becoming superintendent in 1941. That same year he also became president of Clark College in Vancouver and served in both positions for the next 11 years. In 1952 he became full-time Clark Community College president until 1958. The student lounge on the Clark College campus also was named for Dr. Gaiser in 1958.

Gale School District No. 178 (Whitman County). One of many rural schools established 75 to 120 years ago in Whitman County. This school was built on land donated by James T. Gale.

Garfield High School, 400 23rd Ave., Seattle School District (King County). This school's name was changed in 1922 from East High School to Garfield High School, a name selected by Principal George N. Porter with concurrence of the school board. The school was built in 1920. Porter selected the name to honor James A. Garfield, president for six months between March and September, 1881, three months of which were spent on his deathbed, the victim of an assassin's bullet.

Garfield School, located on Tacoma tide flats, Tacoma School District (Pierce County). Opened in 1891 in quarters supplied by St. Paul and Tacoma Lumber Company. Named for James Garfield, 20th president of the United States. Closed in 1913.

Garfield Elementary School, 23rd and Pine, Everett School District (Snohomish County). The first Garfield School in Everett was named on March 29, 1902. The present school dates from 1969. Both schools honor the name of James Garfield, 20th U.S. president, who died in 1881 by assassination after six months in office. A mourning nation named more schools for him than for many other former presidents whose terms permitted them to exert more influence on American history.

Garfield Elementary School, W. 222 Knox Ave., Spokane School District (Spokane County). Opened in 1899 and named for James Garfield, 20th president of the United States. In 1980 the old school was demolished and a new school constructed on the site. The new building was dedicated on February 12, 1981.

Garfield Elementary School, 325 N. Plymouth, Olympia School District (Thurston County). Originally named Westside, the school was renamed Garfield in 1902 "honoring the late president" James A. Garfield. In 1930 the building was replaced, and in 1989 another new Garfield Elementary School was built.

Garfield Elementary School, 505 Madison Ave., Toppenish School District (Yakima County). Built in the early 1920s, the Garfield and Lincoln Schools of Toppenish were of concrete block construction, square and two stories high. Despite its masonry construction, Garfield burned and was rebuilt in 1939. Since school district records were lost in a fire that burned the Toppenish Junior High School, dates used here are those remembered by old-timers in the town. Garfield was named for the 20th president of the United States.

Garfield Elementary School, 612 N. Sixth Ave., Yakima School District (Yakima County). In 1907 the first school built on this site was called Longfellow School. A story is told that the name was not after the poet but because the principal was short and the rest of the people were "long fellows." Whatever the merits of the anecdote, when this school was replaced, it was renamed Garfield following the tradition of using presidents' names. President Garfield's assassin, Charles Guiteau, claimed he shot the president because all the newspapers he read vilified Garfield as a traitor to his own party, and some suggested his removal from office. Many newspapers, which had indeed carried such stories, immediately filled their columns with praises for the stricken and dying president in an effort to blunt any further criticism of their earlier treatment of him. Their campaign to praise President Garfield worked so well that schools were still being named for Mr. Garfield, who served as active president for only three months in 1881, well into the 1920s.

Garrison Junior High School, 906 Chase, Walla Walla School District (Walla Walla County). Opened in 1955, the school took its name from Fort Walla Walla and its "garrison" of soldiers from the 1850s into the 20th Century. A painting of a trooper on the door of the old cavalry stable, thought to be the work of a soldier at the fort in about 1900, is kept in a showcase at the school. The school's colors of blue and gold were the colors of trooper uniforms during the early days of the West.

Royal Garrison School, Unaffiliated, Pullman, Grades 1-12 (Whitman County). No information available.

Garry Junior High School, E. 725 Joseph Ave., Spokane School District (Spokane County). Named for Chief Spokane Garry, chief of the Spokane Indian tribe at the time (mid-1850s) of the Indian Wars in Washington Territory. The name Spokane was applied to several small bands of Salish Indians who lived on or near the Spokane River. Chief Garry was an educated man who spoke French and English as well as several Indian languages.

He was also a Christian missionary to his people, often translating sermons given by English-speaking preachers. Chief Garry was present at a special peace council called by Territorial Governor Isaac Stevens in 1855. He agreed to take the governor's proposal back to the tribes he represented and put it up to a vote. He said his people had voted once before on a similar proposition in which the federal government would buy their land. On that occasion the Spokanes had voted it down. So he could not accept the proposal without another vote. He left the council meetings and never returned. Nevertheless, the federal government imposed its will on the Indians and their land.

Garvey School, Independent, Seattle (King County). No information available.

GATES Secondary School, 813 S. 132nd St., Tacoma, Franklin Pierce School District (Pierce County). GATES is an acronym for Greater Alternatives to Education for Students. In 1990 the school served as a junior and senior high for students who might otherwise drop out of school if they had to stay in the regular secondary school program.

Gates School District No. 41 (Whitman County). One of more than 180 rural schools that existed in Whitman County between 1872 and 1918. Many lasted until the 1930s before they were consolidated with other small districts. George Gates donated the land for this school. Later in its history it was also known as the Parvin School for a family prominent in the area.

Gatzert Elementary School, 2101 S. Jackson, Seattle School District (King County). Opened at 615 12th Ave. S. in 1922, the school was named for Bailey Gatzert, leading citizen of the 1870s, former mayor of Seattle, early banker, and businessman, who hosted President Rutherford B. Hayes, the first president to cross the Rocky Mountains. The school name was suggested by then school board member Nathan Eckstein. Gatzert was related to Mrs. Eckstein. The new building at 2101 Jackson opened in September, 1988.

Gault Middle School, 1115 E. Division Lane, Tacoma School District (Pierce County). Opened in 1926 and named Gault Intermediate School by the school board for Franklin B. Gault, superintendent of Tacoma schools from 1888 to 1892.

Gause Intermediate School, 1100 34th St., Washougal School District (Clark County). Completed in 1953, this school was named for a then recently deceased former school board member who had worked hard to get the much-needed school built. Omer Gause was a civic leader. In addition to his school board service, he had been a member of the hospital and county library boards. In 1918 Omer Gause moved from his farm near Washougal and settled in the town itself. He began a job with the U.S. Department of Agriculture in the Soil Conservation Service. He worked there for 37 years. He died after a heart attack at age 60 in 1952.

Geiger Elementary School, 621 S. Jackson, Tacoma School District (Pierce County). William Geiger was district superintendent for 20 years (1912-1931). He was principal of Stadium High School from 1911 to 1912. He was first to urge the opening of a polytechnical school. On June 3, 1948, he turned the first shovel full of dirt to begin construction on the school that was to bear his name. The school was not opened until 1949.

Built in the 1920s, Garfield School of Toppenish was burned and rebuilt in 1939. (Photo from Ron Ott, Yakima, via Virginia Campbell, Yakima Retired Teachers Association)

Genaro School District No. 175 (Whitman County). Country school established about 1910 on land donated by Napoleon and Emma Genaro. The school district was consolidated with other schools in the 1930s.

Gess Elementary School, Box 47, Chewelah School District (Stevens County). No information available.

Gilbert Elementary School, six miles west of Coulee City, southwest corner, Section 23.T25N, R27E, Coulee City-Hartline School District (Douglas County). Named after Riley and Emma Gilbert, who took a homestead and timber culture claim in 1878 six miles west of Coulee City in Douglas County. The school, on land donated by the Gilberts, opened in 1903, operated until 1940. It was then closed and consolidated with the St. Andrew School District. That district consolidated with the Coulee City School District in 1953. The original Gilbert School was abandoned and went to ruin. The building was burned and cleared from the land in the 1960s.

Gilbert Elementary School, 410 N. 44th Ave., Yakima School District (Yakima County). H.M. Gilbert was a successful fruit grower of Yakima. He was active politically and was civic-minded. The land on which this school stands was part of his property. Gilbert Elementary was built in 1951 and expanded in 1955.

Frank Givens Community Elementary School, 1026 Sydney Ave., Port Orchard, South Kitsap School District (Kitsap County). Frank Givens served for 20 years on the Port Orchard School Board. His other community activities included the Kiwanis Club, the Chamber of Commerce, and the Masonic Lodge. He served as Port Orchard mayor and was postmaster until the time of his death in 1937. The present Givens School was remodeled in the 1970s to be an open-concept school. Plans in 1989 were to close the Givens School and build another school in a different location.

Gladish Middle School, Pullman School District (Whitman County). Named in 1972 for Oscar E. Gladish, former principal of Pullman High School, former teacher of history and government, and former mayor (after his retirement from the school district) of Pullman. Mr. Gladish died in 1980. In 1990 the school was being used for district administrative offices and a private kindergarten and preschool.

Glover Junior High School, W. 2404 Longfellow Ave., Spokane School District (Spokane County). The school was named in 1958 for James Glover, early pioneer of the area often identified as the "father of Spokane." In 1873 the 36-year-old Glover, son of covered wagon pioneers to Oregon, came to the Spokane Falls in Washington Territory. He bought the rights of two squatters—J.J. Downing and S.R. Scranton. He then enlisted the financial aid of two businessmen from Salem, Oregon—J.N. Matheny and C.F. Yeaton—to build a sawmill at Spokane Falls. Three years later he bought out his partners and became sole owner of 160 acres in what became the center of the city of Spokane. In addition to the sawmill, he ran a general store, opened the Spokane *Chronicle* newspaper, was president of a bank, mayor of the city, justice of the peace, named many of Spokane's streets, operated mines in Kellogg, Idaho, and went broke in the Panic of 1893. He died in difficult economic circumstances in 1921.

Golding School District No. 165 (Whitman County). Late 19th or early 20th Century rural school in Whitman County named for W. Golding, first clerk of the school board.

Goldworthy School District 93 (Whitman County). Another of the early rural schools in Whitman County, now consolidated with other districts. T. Goldworthy was the clerk of the school board. Schools weren't always formally named. They just took the name of a prominent person or nearby landmark by common usage.

Samuel Gompers School, 8815 Seward Park Ave. S., Seattle School District (King County). The address given above is that of Rainier Beach High School which opened in 1960. That school originally was named Samuel Gompers for the English-born founder of the American Federation of Labor. The school board rescinded the action at the request of the Seattle-King County Labor Council, which asked that a vocational school be given that name rather than a conventional high school. Gompers name was then given to a vocational training unit at Edison Technical School, no longer in existence.

Gonzaga Preparatory School, Roman Catholic, E. 1224 Euclid Ave., Spokane Diocese (Spokane County). Opened as a high school in 1887, staffed by Jesuits. Named for St. Aloysius Gonzaga of Italy, who died in 1591 at age 24 after working among the sick.

Nellie Goodhue School, 13720 Roosevelt Way N., Seattle School District (King County). This special education school was opened in the Shoreline School District and acquired by the Seattle School District by annexation in 1954. It was named for a Shoreline teacher. Goodhue was a center of education for the mentally disabled. Nellie Goodhue was a leader of special education for the disabled students in the Shoreline School District. The school was closed in June 1961.

Goodman Middle School, 9010 Prentice Ave., Gig Harbor, Peninsula School District (Pierce County). Miss Lucy Goodman very likely had the longest teaching career (from 1888 to 1964) in the territory and state of Washington, a total of 76 years. She retired from the public schools after 41 years. She then started the first kindergarten on the Gig Harbor peninsula where she taught 33 more years, after which she continued her association with the school until her death in 1964. Lucy wasn't the only member of her family to be involved in education. Her father, Joseph Goodman, settled in the Gig Harbor area in 1883 and set up a school in the evening in his home. By 1886 the school had 10 Indian and white children taught by 17-year-old Anna Goodman, Lucy's older sister. The Goodman Middle School, formerly Gig Harbor High School, was named for the Goodman family in 1947.

Virginia Grainger Elementary School, Okanogan School District (Okanogan County). In the early 1900s Virginia Hancock Grainger and her husband homesteaded in what is now the town of Okanogan. She later gave 10 acres to the Okanogan School District. On part of that land now stands a school named for her. The current building has been there since 1937. Mrs. Grainger was born on Whidbey Island, Washington Territory, in 1858. Trained as a teacher, she was both a student and a teacher at the Washington Territorial University in Seattle. At 19, she was elected the first woman school superintendent in Jefferson County. In 1884 she married James Grainger and moved to the Okanogan area. In 1890 she became the Okanogan County superintendent of schools, presiding over an area from the Canadian border to the Wenatchee River. Her second husband, Charles Herrmann, owned a store in Conconully.

The first Virginia Grainger School near Okanogan was built in the early 20th Century. (Photo from Okanogan County Historical Society)

Grand Coulee Dam Junior High School, Coulee Dam, Grand Coulee Dam School District (Grant County). Named for the giant hydroelectric, flood-control, navigation, and irrigation dam completed in 1939. The dam changed the region from desert into an agriculture center and helped bring in industries in search of cheap power.

Grant Elementary School, 1430 S.E. First, East Wenatchee, Eastmont School District (Douglas County). Built and named in 1953 for Ulysses S. Grant, Union general and 18th president of the United States. The school was built before Robert E. Lee Elementary School, in the same district, was even conceived. Nevertheless the name of the Grant School had a strong influence on the naming of the Lee School in a spirit of national unity. In East Wenatchee, Grant is located south of Lee.

Grant Elementary School, Third and "F" N.W., Ephrata School District (Grant County). No information available.

Grant Elementary School, 1018 N. Prospect, Tacoma School District (Pierce County). Built and opened in 1900 and named for Ulysses S. Grant, former U.S. president. The name was proposed by an unnamed school board member. In 1955 a new Grant School was built on the same site.

Grant Elementary School, E. 1300 Ninth Ave., Spokane School District (Spokane County). Opened in 1900 and named for Ulysses S. Grant, Union General in the Civil War and 18th president of the United States. The school was replaced with a new building in 1980.

Grant Street Elementary School, 16th and Grant Streets, Port Townsend School District (Jefferson County). Built and named in 1956 for the street on which it is located. The street is named for former President Ulysses S. Grant.

Grantham Elementary School, 1253 Poplar, Clarkston School District (Asotin County). In April, 1975, the year Winfred Grantham, the principal of Poplar Grade School, was scheduled to retire, the Poplar teachers secretly circulated in the community a petition asking that the school name be changed to Grantham. This met with favor among citizens and with members of the school board. At his retirement party, Mr. Grantham was surprised with the news.

Robert Gray Elementary School, 4622 Ohio St., Longview School District (Cowlitz County). Robert Gray Elementary was built in 1955 and named for the early explorer whose charts and maps helped define the Columbia River, leading eventually to the settlement of the Longview area.

Captain Gray Elementary School, 1102 N. 10th, Pasco School District (Franklin County). Named for Captain William P. Gray (1845-1929), an early pioneer and landowner and one of Pasco's leading citizens. He was an early steamboat captain on the Snake and Columbia Rivers. He became one of Pasco's promoters. In 1887 he organized the first Sunday School in Pasco because he thought the children should not spend so much time in front of the saloon. Captain Gray Elementary School was built and named in 1948.

Robert Gray Elementary School, 900 Cleveland, Aberdeen School District (Grays Harbor County). This school was named for the famous explorer, the first white man to sail a river he named for his ship, the Columbia. On earlier maps that river was called the "Great River of the West" and the "Oregan," in writings by Captain Jonathan Carver of Connecticut. William Cullen Bryant, in his masterpiece, *Thanatopsis,* had called it "Oregon," a spelling that stuck, not on the river but rather on the northwestern land mass. Gray's name was affixed to Grays Harbor on the coast of what became Washington Territory and then Washington State. The present Robert Gray School opened in Aberdeen in 1950.

Gray Middle School, 3109 S. 60th, Tacoma School District (Pierce County). Named for Captain Robert Gray, American naval officer and explorer. In May 1792, he sailed his ship into a river he named the Columbia. This school, first called South Tacoma, opened as Gray Intermediate School in 1926. Its name was chosen in a Tacoma *Daily Ledger* naming contest.

Great Northern Elementary School, N. 3115 Spotted Rd., Spokane, Great Northern School District (Spokane County). Great Northern School District is one of the older districts in Spokane County. It was consolidated with the White Bluff School back in the 1920s. It is believed that funds were provided for the building by the Great Northern Railroad (now Burlington Northern), for which the school and district are named. The district has only one building, opened in 1900, and serves kindergarten through sixth grade.

Greene Memorial Field, Third and Nelson, Sedro-Woolley School District (Skagit County). The high school athletic field was named in 1938 soon after the death from pneumonia of Gaylard Wilson Greene, superintendent of schools in Sedro-Woolley for four and a half years. That same year a high school athlete and member of a prominent local family died of a broken neck suffered in a football game. There was considerable local sentiment to name the field after the athlete. But the publisher of the *Courier Times,* Frank Evans, prevailed on the school board to honor the former superintendent.

Gribble School, S.E. Corner, Section 12, T25 N., Range 27E, Coulee-Hartline School District (Douglas County). The school was listed as in operation in the 1915 Standard Atlas of Douglas County, published by George A. Agle & Company, Chicago. The school was closed in 1929 and consolidated with St. Andrew's School. In the early 1940s, the school building was moved three miles east and two miles north to become an addition to the St. Andrew's Grange Hall. The building still stands but was not in use in 1989. The school was named, probably informally, for W. Gribble who had a farm and home across the road from the original site of the schoolhouse.

Griffen Elementary School, 6530 33rd Ave. N.W., Olympia, Griffen School District (Thurston County). Arthur Eugene Griffen was an Olympia-area pioneer. He was born in 1862 and died in 1947. He was an attorney and judge in the Olympia area. In 1926 he donated the land on which the school now sits.

Grinnell School District No. 179 (Whitman County). One of the last of the country school districts to be formed in Whitman County early in this century. The origin of the name has been lost, but likely it is the name of a school board member, a school board clerk (who functioned as a school superintendent does today), or a farmer who gave land on which to build the school.

Grisdale Elementary School, 1363 Grisdale, Montesano, Lake Quinault Schools (Grays Harbor County). The Grisdale School was named for a logging camp boss named George Grisdale. He was identified by one source as a "bull of the woods." Grisdale was at the peak of his career in the 1930s and '40s. The school was located at Camp Grisdale, a Simpson Logging Company camp named for the same man. The camp and the school came into being in 1948. Grisdale is no longer listed as an operating school.

Gross School District No. 112 (Whitman County). Early 20th Century country school built on land given by Jacob and Nancy Gross.

Guardian Angel-St. Boniface Consolidated School, Roman Catholic, Colton, Spokane Diocese, Grades 1-8 (Whitman County). St. Boniface School was founded in Uniontown (Whitman County) in 1884 by Benedictine Sisters. After the order left Uniontown in 1893, the Sisters of the Holy Names Jesus and Mary came to St. Boniface School where they taught until 1979. In 1968 the school moved from Uniontown to merge with Guardian Angel School of Colton. St. Boniface School was named for a Catholic Bishop who was sent to bring discipline and correct teachings to the Germanic churches in 719 to 722 at the request of Pope Gregory II. He later sought to establish the Roman Church's authority over the Frankish Kingdom and, even though he had the protection of a Frankish ruler, Charles Martel, Boniface and 53 companions were massacred during a mission to the Frisians.

Guyette School, on Lateral B one and three-quarters mile south of the Fort Road, Wapato School District (Yakima County). John Deese Guyette built this school on his land in about 1909. That property is now known as the Rosie Jacobs place. Rosie was Guyette's daughter. Guyette was of French and Indian parentage, his wife of English and Indian blood. The building was moved or rebuilt in 1916 at the corner of Lateral B and the Fort Road. The school offered instruction to all grade levels. It was closed in 1936 and its pupils transferred to Bradshaw School. The Guyette School building no longer exists.

Guardian Angel-St. Boniface School is a merger of two predecessor schools in Colton. (Photo from the school)

Helen Haller Elementary School of Sequim. (Photo from Sam Kenzy, Clallam County Retired Teachers Association)

Haddon Elementary School, 1525 N. Lafayette, Bremerton School District (Kitsap County). Named after Lulu Davis Haddon (1881-1964). Mrs. Haddon served 14 years on the Bremerton School Board. She served two terms as state representative and chairman of the education committee of that body. She served two terms as state senator and chairman of the common schools committee. She was an early advocate of community colleges and initiated the college movement in Bremerton. She was a founder of the PTA in Bremerton. The school named for her opened in 1942 at a dedication ceremony attended by Mrs. Haddon. The Haddon school was closed and was torn down in 1985.

Dr. Arthur K. Harris Stadium, N.E. 22nd Avenue and Ione Street, Camas School District (Clark County). This stadium and football field complex was opened in the fall of 1958. It was named for Dr. Arthur K. Harris, a local physician who volunteered his medical services on the field to Camas High School football players over a period of many years. He rarely missed a home game. He also offered free physical examinations to Camas athletes until his retirement.

Nathan Hale High School, 10750 30th Ave. N.E., Seattle School District (King County). Built on the site of a golf course, Hale opened in 1963. Named for a Revolutionary War patriot (1755-1776) captured and hanged as a spy without trial by the British. The June 23, 1986, issue of *Newsweek* magazine quoted then Central Intelligence Agency Director William Casey as saying that Nathan Hale "fouled up the only mission he was given." Casey objected to a statue of Hale at CIA headquarters, preferring one of William "Wild Bill" Donovan, founder of wartime predecessor of the CIA, the Office of Strategic

Services. Some Hale High School students in Seattle were incensed at the unkind words directed toward their school's namesake and offered to have the offending statue sited on the Hale campus. Their proposal never received a direct response from Washington, D.C.

Helen Haller Elementary School, 503 N. Sequim Ave., Sequim School District (Clallam County). Sequim's first elementary school, a one-room building on Dungeness Way built in 1885, was succeeded by a two-story building in 1911. Another new building followed in 1949 on Alder Street. Helen Haller had been a teacher and principal in Sequim School District for 46 years (1921 to 1967). The elementary school was named in her honor at her retirement. In 1990 a newer Haller school stood behind the Alder Street building. Helen Haller was married in Sequim to Glen Harbough but continued to be known by her professional name.

Sadie Halstead Elementary School, 331 S. Calispel Ave., Newport School District (Pend Oreille County). More than 700 citizens attended the 1953 dedication of this then-new school and its naming for Sadie Halstead. Miss Halstead not only was present, she was and remained for seven more years a member of the school's teaching staff. Sadie Halstead was born in Jacksonport, Wisconsin, in 1889, the year Washington became a state. She began her teaching career in 1908. In 1924 her brother's wife died, leaving him with a 15-month-old baby boy to raise. That brother lived in the state of Washington. Sadie packed her bags and came west to help her brother both in raising the boy and in running a logging camp on Russian Creek west of the Pend Oreille River. Later she became principal of the school in Metaline Falls and then held other positions in education including being a member of the school board, Pend Oreille County Board of Education, and the board of the Washington Education Association. In 1939 Miss Halstead left the northern part of the county and settled in Newport where she was elected county superintendent of schools. After one term she returned to the classroom as a teacher once again. She retired in 1960 but continued to work as a substitute teacher for several years. In 1970 she was named Senior Citizen of the Year by the Washington State Council on Aging. She moved to Prosser late in life to be near her adopted son, Dwight, and his family. She died there in 1981.

Hamblen Elementary School, S. 4005 Napa St., Spokane School District (Spokane County). Opened in 1954 and named for Laurence R. Hamblen, Spokane attorney and member of the Spokane Park Board from 1912 to 1956, whose family donated the land for the school.

Hamilton Elementary School, 1822 W. Seventh St., Port Angeles School District (Clallam County). Opened in 1956, this school was named for Alexander Hamilton, first secretary of the treasury.

Hamilton Middle School, 1610 N. 41st St., Seattle School District (King County). Opened January 31, 1927, as the first intermediate (junior high) in Seattle. It became a middle school in September, 1971. It was named for Alexander Hamilton in accordance with a policy of naming schools after prominent Americans.

Hamilton Elementary School, E. 545 Wellesley, Spokane School District (Spokane County). Built in 1903 and known as the Kenwood School until 1908 when it was annexed into the Spokane School District (from Stevens County). It was renamed Hamilton after the first secretary of the U.S. treasury, who was born in the West Indies. In the early days, Indians often camped on the west side of the school grounds and came to the school to draw water from its well. The school was closed in 1972, its oldest section razed. The 1949 addition still existed in 1989 and was being used by a church group.

Hamilton School District No. 111 (Whitman County). This early country school serving farm families in Whitman County was built on land owned by S. and H.P. Hamilton.

Hamilton School District No. 166 (Whitman County). The origin of this school is similar to the Hamilton School above except that the person for whom the school was named is not now known. It may well be for some other member of the same Hamilton family for whom District 111 was named.

Robert J. Handy Reception Center, Camp Waskowitz, North Bend, Highline School District (King County). A visitors' reception building was erected at Camp Waskowitz in 1975. It was named for a former Seattle teacher and founder of the Washington School Employees Credit Union, Robert J. Handy, who was a frequent benefactor to this outdoor education center.

Hanson Field, Walla Walla School District (Walla Walla County). An athletic field named in 1962 by popular acclaim for Franklin "Pete" Hanson, former superintendent of schools.

Harlan School District No. 163 (Whitman County). The origin of the name of this early-day Whitman County School is lost. It is probable that Harlan was either the landowner of the school site or a member of the school board in this turn-of-the-century school.

Harney Elementary School, 3212 E. Evergreen Blvd., Vancouver School District (Clark County). Named after Lt. Gen. William S. Harney, who served in the 1850s as an Indian pacifier in the West from Utah to the Washington Territory. He and his troops also served as protectors of the disputed boundary between the United States and British Columbia. In 1859 he was dispatched to an Army post near Fort Vancouver. He later owned land in the Vancouver area. There have been three Harney Schools at the same site. The first was built in 1890, the second in 1922, and the third in 1944. There also have been several additions to the building, the most recent in 1965.

Hathaway Primary School, 630 24th St., Washougal School District (Clark County). Alpha Hathaway and his twin brother, Omega, were born to pioneer parents in what is now Clark County in 1864. His early years were spent on a farm, but later he became a successful dealer in real estate. Alpha Hathaway donated land in Washougal for a park that today bears his name. He also donated the land for a Methodist Church and parsonage and for a school. That school was built in 1936, and it too bears Mr. Hathaway's name. In 1990 it was operated as a kindergarten through Grade 2 primary school.

Gordon Hauck Center, 11133 N.E. 65th, Kirkland, Lake Washington School District (King County). Opened in 1965. No information about the school's namesake was provided.

Hauptly-Webb School, Webb Hill Road and Highway 106. Lower Skokomish School District (Mason County). In 1889 school was held in the home of Jacob Hauptly, Swiss-born farmer who had come to the Washington Territory in 1862. He married for the first time when he was 50 and his bride 18. He outlived that wife and married again at 74 to a woman of 27. He died in 1928 at 98 years of age, outliving his second wife by 12 years. In 1891 school was held at a new schoolhouse on the road between the Hauptlys and the home of Mr. and Mrs. Thomas Webb. Mr. Webb was an Irish-born farmer, who supplied food to the logging camps. Both Mr. Hauptly and Mr. Webb were school directors. Since the school had been built on the boundary line between their properties, it was called the Hauptly-Webb School. The school no longer exists.

Havermale Junior High School, W. 1300 Knox Ave., Spokane School District (Spokane County). Opened in 1927, this school was named for The Reverend Samuel Havermale, famous Spokane pioneer minister. The building was closed in 1981. In 1990 the old school housed the Jantsch High School.

Lydia Hawk Elementary School, 7600 Fifth St. S.E., Olympia, North Thurston School District (Thurston County). Opened in 1959, Hawk School was named for Lydia Jane Hawk, daughter of pioneers John and Sara Hawk. The school site is part of the original 1855 homestead of the Hawk family. The land was inherited by George Mayes, son of Lydia Jane Hawk Mayes. When he

sold the land to Alvin and Evelyn Thompson and Gaylor Montgomery, he stipulated that a school to be built on that land be named for his mother. The Thompsons and Montgomery donated the 20-acre school site to North Thurston School District.

Hawkins Middle School, Highway 3, Belfair, North Mason School District (Mason County). In 1983 when the new North Mason High School was completed, the old high school was remodeled and renamed Hawkins Middle School. The name honored a favorite teacher—Bill Lane Hawkins—who had taught junior and senior high students in Belfair for 23 years when he died suddenly in 1978 at 53.

Hawthorne Elementary School, 3520 W. John Day, Kennewick School District (Benton County). Built in 1956, the school was named for American fiction writer Nathaniel Hawthorne.

Hawthorne Elementary School, 4100 39th Ave. S., Seattle School District (King County). Hawthorne School was built in the Columbia City area of southeast Seattle in 1909. It is believed to have been named for Nathaniel Hawthorne, American fiction writer. However, a neighborhood in Columbia City was called Hawthorne Hill and might have lent its name to the school. The school is now closed.

Hawthorne Elementary School, 28th and East "F" Street, Tacoma School District (Pierce County). On June 21, 1889, East School was renamed Hawthorne. A new Hawthorne School was built in 1913. It was closed in 1963. From 1966 to 1973 Hawthorne housed early childhood education programs. Until 1980 the school housed the Puyallup Tribe's Chief Leschi School. The building was closed and razed in 1981 to make room for the Tacoma Dome stadium. The name Hawthorne is believed to have been for Nathaniel Hawthorne (1804-1864), American novelist.

Hawthorne Elementary School, 1110 Poplar, Everett School District (Snohomish County). Named on February 13, 1951, for Nathaniel Hawthorne (1804-1864),

American fiction writer born in Salem, Massachusetts, who helped establish the short story as an art form. He is the author of *Twice-Told Tales, The House of the Seven Gables,* and *The Scarlet Letter.* His name was selected for the school at the recommendation of the local PTA, which had suggested the school be named for either a former president or a poet. The PTA committee apparently was under the impression Hawthorne was a poet. The predecessor to Hawthorne School was a collection of temporary buildings known as the Baker Heights School. In 1982 third grade students at Hawthorne petitioned for approval of naming a mountain peak in the Poet's Peak section of the Cascade Mountain Range. A peak north of Lake Wenatchee was named Hawthorne Peak, further extending Hawthorne's undeserved reputation as a poet. That summer the school's principal, Norman Keck, and five of the school staff members scaled the newly named 5,898-foot peak.

Hawthorne Elementary School, W. 714 Fourth Ave., Spokane School District (Spokane County). Opened in 1898 and closed in 1932, this school was named for the author Nathaniel Hawthorne. The school was reopened in 1940 for use by the federal Works Progress Administration (WPA). It later was used as a vocational training school. For awhile, Hawthorne was an annex of Lewis and Clark High School but was again closed and demolished in the 1960s to make way for Interstate Highway 90.

John Hay Elementary School, 411 Boylston, Seattle School District (King County). The school opened in 1905 for Grades 1-7. Following the suggestion of Reuben Jones, secretary of the school board, the school was named for the noted statesman, John Hay, who had recently died. Hay had served as a private secretary to President Abraham Lincoln but was better known as secretary of state under Presidents William McKinley and Theodore Roosevelt. After the school had been named, Jones further suggested that the school write a letter to the widow of John Hay and tell her of the naming of the school for her husband. In return she sent the

school a portrait of Hay which was placed in the front hall. The picture was still in the school's possession in 1990.

Hazelwood Elementary School, 11815 S.E. 304th St., Auburn School District (King County). Opened in 1990 and named for an early independent school district which was incorporated into the Auburn School District years ago.

Hazen High School, 1101 Hoquiam Ave. N.E., Renton School District (King County). Oliver M. Hazen was superintendent of Renton Schools from 1936 to 1966, the longest tenure of any Renton superintendent. The school was dedicated in his honor at its opening in 1968. The school board selected the name.

Amanda Hebeler Elementary School, campus of Central Washington College of Education, Ellensburg School District (Kittitas County). From the 1930s into the 1950s Amanda Hebeler was principal of the College Elementary School, a teacher training school on the campus of what was then primarily a teachers' college in Ellensburg. The college is now known as Central Washington University. Miss Hebeler is well-remembered by many teachers throughout the state. The Hebeler School, on the other hand, has been one of the most difficult on which to get definitive information. It appears that either the campus training school or a new building constructed to replace the College Elementary School was named for Miss Hebeler on a date unknown. The information on the Hebeler School is sketchy and contradictory. Even the spelling of her name is uncertain. The Ellensburg School District administration office referred an inquiry about the school to the university. The university administration did not answer the inquiry. A submission about the school from the local retired teachers' unit was apparently lost in the mail and was not resubmitted. The school was not listed in the 1989 issue of the Washington Education Directory.

Heistuman School District No. 134 (Whitman County). One of many country schools built in Whitman

County between 1872 and 1918. The land on which this school was built was owned by J.T. Heistuman.

Wayne M. Henkle Middle School, 480 N.W. Loop Rd., White Salmon Valley School District (Klickitat County). The name of this school was changed on June 10, 1986, from White Salmon Middle School to Henkle Middle School to honor the town's long-time "country doctor," Wayne M. Henkle. Dr. Henkle had come to White Salmon after serving in the Army Medical Corps in Europe during World War 2. Born in Afton, Iowa, and trained at the University of Iowa, Dr. Henkle served the White Salmon-Bingen community for 40 years, assisted for all of those years by the same nurse, Wilma Driver. Dr. Henkle died at the age of 69, five months after the school was named for him.

Sam Henry School, near Winlock (Lewis County). This school was established in 1902, probably being named for the person donating the land. There is no known record now of Sam Henry. In 1910 the school was consolidated with Winlock Schools and renamed King

School. Again, no reason is given for the name. In 1913 the school was closed but reopened in 1914 and operated until 1927.

Bess Herian Elementary School, P.O. Box 270, Cusick Consolidated Schools, District No. 59 (Pend Oreille County). In the small, northeastern Washington town of Cusick an elementary school was named in 1950 for Bess Herian, a beloved teacher. The school opened for classes the following January. Bess Herian was born south of Spokane on August 6, 1898, to homesteaders James and Elizabeth Mullen. After being trained at Cheney Normal School, Bess Mullen arrived in Cusick as a beginning teacher in 1919. She left teaching after her marriage to R.J. Herian in the early 1920s but returned to the classroom during the teacher shortage of World War 2. Mrs. Herian died of cancer in 1950.

Hickson School, six miles northwest of Sedro-Woolley, by Fairhaven and Southern Road (Skagit County). Skagit Valley pioneers George and Myrtle Hickson decided they needed a school for their children and

The second Hickson School of Sedro Woolley was built in 1915 and used as a school until 1942. (Photo from Eloise Stendal, Skagit-Island-San Juan Counties Retired Teachers Association)

those of other families in the area in about 1909. Over the years Hickson was a logger, stump-puller, and dairyman. The first Hickson School was built in 1910, followed by a larger building in 1915. The second Hickson School was in continuous operation until 1942. George Hickson died in 1948. The school has been demolished, but the site is occupied by a community hall and gun club.

Hickman School District No. 66 (Whitman County). Country school built before the turn of the century and named for the man who donated the land for the school: Henry Hickman.

Highline High School, 225 S. 152nd St., Burien, Highline School District (King County). As late as November, 1924, the new high school in Burien, which had opened for business the previous September, had no name except for the state designation: Union High School, District R, which meant it was formed by a union of several elementary school districts, and it was a rural school. A year earlier, in November, 1923, School Board Clerk George Hannan had received a letter from some of the planned school's prospective students. They liked the name Abraham Lincoln for the new school but realized that name was already overused. So they proposed Warren Harding High School instead for the following reasons: "President Harding came to the Northwest to look into Alaska's possibilities which are so vitally connected with ours and practically gave his life for our interests. Furthermore, he was the only president that entered Alaska. He was a good man   one whose footsteps could well be followed. Therefore, we respectfully send our choice of names." The letter was signed by Marie Weber, a member of the soon-to-be "upper grades." A year later the school board chose the name High Line (two words) after a brick road that served the area. An award of $10 was given to a Mount View Elementary School student for suggesting that name. That student, to whom everyone in the Highline School District should be grateful, is not mentioned by name in the records.

Highline Hotel School, Second Street and Sunnyside Avenue, Granger (Yakima County). This was never the official name of the school but a colloquialism describing the origin of the school building. A "luxurious, modern hotel of 75 rooms built at a cost of $55,000" and named The Highline was established in Granger in 1898. It did not turn out to be a profitable investment. By 1920 the three-story brick building had been standing empty for some years. That year the Upper Columbia Conference of the Seventh Day Adventists bought the old hotel and turned it into a boarding high school named the Yakima Valley Academy. Additional buildings were incorporated into the campus and included the elementary grades. The academy operated until 1945 when it was closed and moved to Spangler and renamed the Upper Columbia Academy. Stadium High School in Tacoma also had its beginnings as a hotel.

Lea Hill Elementary School, 30908 124th Ave. S.E., Auburn School District (King County). Named in 1965 for an Auburn-area pioneer homesteader.

Hillyard High School, Regal Street, Spokane School District (Spokane County). Named after the rail yards and shops of the Great Northern Railroad and its president, J.J. Hill. The first Hillyard School was started in 1907. A new building was constructed in 1912 and a substantial addition completed in 1922, the year Hillyard was annexed by the Spokane School District and city. In 1932 a new high school was built to serve the Hillyard area. The new school was named John Rogers for a former state governor. The old Hillyard High School was sold and turned into an apartment house.

Hilton Elementary School, Fourth and Dean, Zillah Public Schools (Yakima County). Named for Geoffrey Hilton, an accountant and businessman. He helped people of the area with their income tax returns. The school is called Zillah Grade School by most people, but its official name is Hilton, named when it was built in 1950. A 1962 fire destroyed parts of the school, which were rebuilt the same year.

Holy Rosary School of Moxee opened in 1915 and closed in 1968. (Photo from Sisters of Providence Archives, Seattle)

Hofstetter Elementary School, 640 N. Hofstetter, Colville School District (Stevens County). Hofstetter School opened in September, 1952. The land had been acquired in 1950 by the school board from the state game farm. The school was named by Mrs. D. M. Hurt for the street on which it is situated and for the man credited with founding the city of Colville. John U. Hofstetter was an infantry soldier under the command of Major Pinkney Lugenbeel. He was one of those soldiers sent by Lt. Gen. William Harney (see Harney School) in 1859 to establish a military encampment near Fort Colville. Fort Colville had been founded as a fur-trading post by the Hudson's Bay Company in 1825, named for Andrew Colville, London governor of the fur-trading company. After his tour of duty, John Hofstetter stayed on at what was then called Pinkney City. He helped to plat the community, which became known as Colville, in 1883. He also built the town's first brewery.

Holgate Elementary School, on the edge of George-town, Seattle School District (King County). No information available. Believed to have been named for

an area pioneer or for Holgate Street. In its later years Holgate served as a branch of Edison Technical School.

Oliver Wendell Holmes School, Chicken Coop Road, Blyn, Sequim School District (Clallam County). Opened in 1893, a year before the death of its namesake Oliver Wendell Holmes Sr., physician, poet, novelist, and medical writer. The school was closed in 1921 and its service area consolidated into the Sequim School District.

Holmes Elementary School, W. 2600 Sharp, Spokane School District (Spokane County). Named for Oliver Wendell Holmes Sr. (1809-1894), a noted physician and famous author and poet (*Deacon's Masterpiece, Old Ironsides*). The school was opened in 1901.

Holy Rosary School, Roman Catholic, Moxee (Yakima County). The school was founded on September 25, 1915, by the Holy Rosary Parish. The Sisters of Providence were asked to staff the school with teachers. A falling enrollment, and a reduced number of Sisters of Providence available as teachers led to the closure of the school in June of 1968. The school was named for the rosary, a form of mental and vocal prayer centered on mysteries or events in the lives of Jesus and Mary.

Hoover Elementary School, 400 W. Viola, Yakima School District (Yakima County). Built in 1947 and named for Herbert Hoover, 31st U.S. president. The school has a large facility for disabled children including a swimming pool.

Hopewell School District No. 49, Ethel (Lewis County). A one-room school offering instruction from Grades 1-8. The school was built in 1882 or 1883. In 1944 the school was consolidated with Onalaska, and the building was used for a cattle feeding barn. Origin of the name of the school was not recorded.

Mabel McKinlay Hopkins Junior High School, 359 N. Division, Aberdeen School District (Grays Harbor County). Hopkins Junior High, named for Mabel Hopkins, opened in 1958. She was an elementary teacher and secretary of the school board from 1900 to 1907. This school was closed in 1982, and in 1990 the building was being used for a continuation high school and a Head Start program for preschoolers.

Hopp School, 638 Salmon Creek Rd., Toledo (Lewis County). An early school that later became known as the Salmon Creek School, it was consolidated with the Toledo School District in 1921. Date the school first opened is not known. The school was located on a corner of Henry Hopp's farm and was named for the Hopp family.

Hopwood School, Section 23, Township 10 N., Range 44 E.W.M. (Asotin County). District No. 9's schoolhouse was ready for occupancy in 1887. The first school was built, unwisely as it turned out, near Asotin Creek about 10 miles west of the town of Asotin. Ten years later, in 1897, there was a cloudburst in the Blue Mountains to the west. It was on the afternoon of May 20 that Mr. Jim Barkley, the teacher, heard the faraway sound of rushing water. He got the youngsters out of the building and up the side of a nearby hill in time to see the school torn from its foundation and carried away on the crest of the

raging Asotin Creek. The building was soon smashed. A new Hopwood School was built some years later about a mile up that hill the students were standing on that rainy May day in 1897. Both Hopwood Schools were named for William Hopwood who gave land for the school. In 1928, Hopwood School was consolidated with the Asotin School District. The schoolhouse was vacated June 4, 1929. It was eventually torn down and its lumber used to build a house for a rancher named Arch Watkins.

Horn School District No. 125 (Whitman County). This rural school was built at the turn of the century on land owned by A.K. Horn.

Horton School District No. 138 (Whitman County). Another of the early Whitman County schools, this one built in 1899 on land owned by Andrew Horton. The land was later sold to a Mr. Zaring, and the school was thereafter known by the Zaring name.

Hough Elementary School, 1900 Daniels St., Vancouver School District (Clark County). Patrick (Paddy) Hough (pronounced Howk) was one of Vancouver's pioneer teachers. He was born St. Patrick's Day in Ireland in 1846. A school teacher in Ireland, Hough moved to Paris as a newswriter in 1870 to cover the Franco-Prussian War and to serve as a battlefield stretcher-bearer. After losing his arm in a battle, he migrated to Canada where he worked as a teacher for 13 more years and thence to Vancouver, Washington, where he headed a parochial school. He was named public school principal in 1881 and served until 1906. Afterward he was named deputy superintendent of Clark County Schools and ran unsuccessfully for the superintendent's post. He died in 1925 at 79. After his wife's death, his estate became a trust fund for the use of the Battle Ground School District Future Farmers of America and Future Homemakers of America in northern Clark County. A new Vancouver school was named for Mr. Hough in 1941. The school was built to replace both the old Franklin and Columbian schools.

Housel Middle School, 2001 Highland Dr., Prosser School District (Benton County). Prosser Middle School was renamed Housel Middle School in 1973 in honor of Charles C. Housel, who had been a teacher and principal at the school from 1944 to 1973. Mr. Housel came from Melda, Idaho, in 1944 to work at Hanford. He took the position of principal of Prosser Junior High that fall as well as teacher of Washington State history.

Howard School District No. 109 (Whitman County). This school district was formed in about 1885 to oversee one school. It was named for Nelson Howard, who is not identified.

Fred Howe Gymnasium, 1612 N.E. Garfield St., Camas School District (Clark County). The gymnasium was opened in the fall of 1953 and was named for Fred Howe, a long-time teacher and principal in the Camas schools, at the suggestion of students at Camas High School. A dedication and open house were held on November 23, 1953.

Hoyt Elementary School, 2708 N. Union, Tacoma School District (Pierce County). The school was named in 1959 for Nell Hoyt, Tacoma resident who founded a pre-school Parent-Teacher Association in 1914, an idea which spread throughout the nation. Her husband, Elwell, was a Tacoma druggist who served on the Tacoma School Board from 1912 to 1918.

Hubbard School District No. 51 (Whitman County). Another of the early rural schools in Whitman County. This one was named for Charles Hubbard who gave the land for the school.

Hubbard School District No. 75 (Whitman County). Another early-day Hubbard School in Whitman County, this one named for the Joe Hubbard family. They might well have been related to the Hubbards of District No. 51, but the schools were established some years apart.

Hudson's Bay High School, 1206 E. Reserve St., Vancouver School District (Clark County). Named for the Hudson's Bay Company, a British trading firm founded in 1607. Fort Vancouver, near the present-day site of the city of Vancouver, was a Hudson's Bay Company enterprise established in 1825 principally for fur trade. The high school was built and named in 1955.

A.G. Hudtloff Junior High School, 7702 Phillips Rd. S.W., Tacoma, Clover Park School District (Pierce County). At a ceremony on January 29, 1958, this junior high was named for Arthur G. Hudtloff, first superintendent of the Clover Park School District. In 1928 five local elementary school districts—American Lake South, Custer, Lake City, Lakeview, and Park Lodge—elected to form a union high school district. Mr. Hudtloff, himself a teacher, was selected by the board of directors of the Union High School District No. 204 as superintendent. Over the next 27 years, until his retirement in 1955, Mr. Hudtloff guided the school district through rapid growth, merger with the original five elementary districts and expansion of facilities in the Lakewood area.

Hulen School District No. 10 (Whitman County). From 1872 until 1918, farm families in Whitman County were so isolated from towns and community services that they had to bring civilization to themselves. They formed school districts for their children under county charter and elected school boards to oversee the common school program and control the spending of money. Hulen School was named for the first member of the school board, Beeker H. Hulen.

Hughes Elementary School, 7740 34th Ave. S.W., Seattle School District (King County). Opened in 1926, the school was named for E.C. Hughes, a former member of the school board and a prominent attorney. He was on the school board during the first decade of the 20th Century, a time of rapid school population growth.

Humptulips School, Quinault Lake Schools (Grays Harbor County). Named for a subtribe of the Quinault Indian Nation. By 1986 this school was no longer in use for classes.

Warren D. Hunt Elementary School, 12801 144th St. E., Puyallup School District (Pierce County). Named for a former school board member, businessman, and Puyallup civic leader. The school was opened in September, 1990.

Hunt Middle School, 6501 S. 10th St., Tacoma School District (Pierce County). Named in 1958 for Henry F. Hunt, a Tacoma educator for 34 years. He was principal of Stadium High School for 16 years and district assistant superintendent for nine years.

Huntington Junior High School, 500 Redpath, Kelso School District (Cowlitz County). Built in 1956 and named for Harry Darby Huntington, an early 1850s settler, at Monticello on the west bank of the Cowlitz River. Huntington helped build the first school in what became the state of Washington. Huntington also was a member of the first Washington Territorial legislature. The name of the school was selected by a contest.

George Huntley Building, Aberdeen School District (Grays Harbor County). A part of Weatherwax High School, the Huntley Building, constructed in 1955, houses activity-centered courses such as woodshop, music, auto shop, and printing. The building was named to honor a shop teacher who taught high school in Aberdeen during the first three decades of the 20th Century.

Hutton Elementary School, E. 908 24th Ave., Spokane School District (Spokane County). Named in 1921 for Levi W. Hutton. Hutton arrived in Spokane in 1881 and began his career on the Northern Pacific Railroad. He later transferred to Wallace, Idaho, where he was an engineer for 17 years, having worked his way up from a job in the roundhouse. He and his wife were childless. In Wallace Hutton invested in what became the famous Hercules silver mine, giving Hutton the fortune he needed to fulfill a dream. He built the Hutton Settlement, which provided long-range residential care for orphans, needy, or dependent children. Hutton himself had been an orphan from age six.

I

Illahee Junior High School, 36001 First Ave. S., Federal Way School District (King County). Illahee is a Chinook jargon word meaning "earth" or "dirt." The school was named in 1971.

Image Elementary School, 4400 N.E. 122nd, Vancouver, Evergreen School District (Clark County). Opened in 1976 and named Image by popular choice of community. "Image" was a buzzword in the 1970s, connoting the impression a person leaves in others by his or her own actions, statements, and appearance.

Imbler School District No. 81 (Whitman County). J.W. Imbler was an early day Whitman County postmaster who gave his own name to the rural post office and thus to the nearby school. The school district has since been assimilated into a larger district.

Indian Trail Elementary School, W. 4102 Woodside, Spokane School District (Spokane County). Named in 1964 for the school's location on an ancient Indian trail. The site was once a part of a well-worn path from the southern portion of what is now Washington State and traveling north to Mount Spokane.

Ingersoll Stadium, 1302 North St., Olympia School District (Thurston County). In 1967 representatives of the Olympia Lions Club, of which Oliver Ingersoll was a member, recommended that the William Winlock Miller High School football field and grandstand be named for Ingersoll. On September 27, 1968, the dedication ceremony took place just before the opening game of the season. Oliver Ingersoll was first elected to the Olympia School Board in December 1945, and served as board president five times.

Ingraham High School, 1819 N. 135th, Seattle School District (King County). The school was named after Major Edward Sturgis Ingraham, Seattle's first superin-

tendent of schools and an avid mountaineer. It was opened on September 9, 1960. Ingraham was appointed superintendent of schools in 1883. He retained his military title of major even after re-entering civilian life.

Irene School District No. 89 (Whitman County). Irene was the first name of a girlfriend of the man who carried a petition from farm to farm at the turn of the century to get signatures supporting creation of a new school district. His name has been lost to history. The resulting school also was known as Bowers School for James Bowers who gave the land for the new school. The school district was absorbed years ago through consolidation.

Washington Irving Elementary School, Seattle School District (King County). Built in 1915 in Ballard, closed and torn down in 1940. Named for an American writer, Washington Irving (1783-1859), author of *Rip Van Winkle, The Legend of Sleepy Hollow,* and *Astoria.* He was U.S. minister to Spain from 1842 to 1846.

Irving Elementary School, W. 1716 Seventh Ave., Spokane School District (Spokane County). Opened in 1890, closed in 1972. The school was named for the American 19th Century writer, Washington Irving. The building was razed in 1973 except for the multipurpose unit. In the 1979-1980 school year the site housed the district's first teacher center. In 1981 the building was sold as surplus property to the Spokane Elks Lodge.

Irving School, South 25th and Walnut Streets, Tacoma School District (Pierce County). Built and named in 1890 for Washington Irving (1783-1859), American writer. Among his works is *Astoria,* the story of the founding of the city at the mouth of the Columbia River. In 1930 the school in Tacoma named for Irving was closed and demolished in 1934.

Isom Intermediate School, 8461 Benson Rd., Lynden School District (Whatcom County). Isom houses Grades 3 through 5 and was built in 1989. It is named for Elbert R. Isom, superintendent of Lynden schools from 1954 until 1967. He was the second superintendent of the Lynden School District. In 1990 Mr. Isom was 83 years of age.

The Andrew Johnson School of Winlock was not named for a former president of the U.S. (Photo from Lewis County Historical Museum via Elizabeth Wedin, Lewis County Retired Teachers Association)

J

Jackson School, near Dayton (Columbia County). Named for the Richard A. Jackson family on whose land the school was built. The Jacksons had 12 children. Mr. Jackson had large flocks of sheep which summered in the Blue Mountains and wintered along the Tucannon River on the Jackson ranch. The school, also named District No. 51, was founded in 1893 and operated until 1924 or 1925 when it was consolidated with White Bird District No. 19.

Jackson Elementary School, 3700 Federal Ave., Everett School District (Snohomish County). The first Jackson School in Everett was named on March 29, 1902, for Andrew Jackson, seventh president of the United States. That school was succeeded in 1949 by the present Jackson Elementary School. The old Jackson School was on Rucker Hill, 36th and Norton, a site that now serves as a grass playground.

Armin Jahr Elementary School, 900 Dibb St., Bremerton School District (Kitsap County). Opened in 1968 and named for a former superintendent of schools (1950 to 1968) who died one month before his planned retirement. This building is believed to be the first open concept ("school without walls") school in Washington State.

Janikula Building, Southern Heights Elementary School, 11249 14th Ave. S., Seattle, Highline School District (King County). A plaque bearing the Kiwanis International seal has been placed on the building. It reads "In memory of Don H. Janikula whose leadership made the construction of this building possible." It was built in 1961 as a private kindergarten at a time before Highline School District offered public kindergarten classes. The building later was used for special education, music, and exercise classes for physical therapy. It

became a kindergarten again in 1990. Mr. Janikula was treasurer of a local Kiwanis Club for several years. His children attended Southern Heights Elementary School and the private kindergarten on that site.

Joseph Jantsch Continuation High School, W. 1300 Knox Ave., Spokane School District (Spokane County). Built in 1930 and named Havermale Junior High School for a Spokane area pioneer preacher. In 1959 the building use was changed to an alternative high school and called Continuation High School. In 1976 it was renamed for an educator in the Spokane schools who promoted the concept of alternative education for students who don't produce their best work in the traditional school setting. Alternative education in Spokane began in 1930 with a one-teacher (Joseph Jantsch), one-room operation in Lewis and Clark High School.

P.C. Jantz Elementary School, Odessa School District (Lincoln County). In April of 1951 the Odessa School Board named a new school building for the elementary principal who had been in their district for 27 years at that time and would remain as the town's only elementary principal for another three years, serving those years in a school named for him.

Jefferies School District No. 152 (Whitman County). Rural school of late 19th or early 20th Century, now consolidated with other rural schools. The school was named for S.M. and S.N. Jefferies, probably local farmers who owned the land on which the school was built.

Jefferson County Schools were in existence soon after Jefferson County was formed out of part of Thurston County in 1852. The first woman county superintendent of schools was 19-year-old Virginia Hancock, who ran for office while still a student at the Territorial University in Seattle in 1880. She defeated her high school teacher, a man named Ryan. Miss Hancock later married a farmer named Grainger and moved to Okanogan County where she again ran successfully for county school superintendent. A school in that county is named for her. Jefferson

County historical records show that there was a West Uncas School there between 1900 and 1918 when it merged with Discovery Bay School. Uncas was the name of a character in a story by James Fenimore Cooper. In 1890 the Tarboo School existed in a community named Coyle on Hood Canal. Tarboo is an Indian word meaning "windy." Tukey School, named for John Tukey who settled the area in 1852, was founded in 1920 at a site used by the Chevy Chase Golf Course in 1991. Other historic names of schools in Jefferson County include the Hoh School of 1920, named for the Indian tribe or the river; Quilcene School named for the Quilcene Indians; Cooper School, probably named for a pioneer family; Spruce School of 1923 near the Bogashiel River. Other Jefferson County schools on which more historical data has been gathered are listed separately under their own names. (See index.)

Jefferson Elementary School, 1525 Hunt, Richland School District (Benton County). The old Jefferson School building was first occupied in September 1944. By 1980 the building needed so many costly repairs the school board decided to build a new school on the same site. The new Jefferson school was occupied on February 22, 1982. The old building was demolished that same year. The name Jefferson had been selected because

Thomas Jefferson Senior High School of Federal Way. (Photo from Margit Larson, South King County Retired Teachers Association)

Thomas Jefferson was president of the United States during the Lewis and Clark Expedition which opened the Pacific Northwest to settlement.

Jefferson Elementary School, 218 E. 12th St., Port Angeles School District (Clallam County). Jefferson School, named for President Thomas Jefferson, was built on the site of the old Fourth Ward School in 1922. The school was still in operation as of 1989.

Thomas Jefferson High School, 4248 S. 288th St., Auburn, Federal Way School District (King County). Opened in 1969 and named after the third president of the United States.

Jefferson School, 4720 42nd Ave. S.W., Seattle School District (King County). Built in 1911; torn down in 1985.

Jefferson Elementary School, Centralia School District (Lewis County). Built in 1924 and demolished in 1978. Its name was transferred to Centralia's Lincoln School which became Jefferson-Lincoln. It was not the first time Jefferson had been part of a merger with another school. The old Roosevelt Elementary School, built in Centralia in 1923, was combined with Jefferson from 1930 to 1937.

Jefferson-Lincoln Elementary School, Woodland and Summa, Centralia School District (Lewis County). A new Lincoln School was built in 1957. An addition was built in 1978, the year the old Jefferson School was closed. The expanded Lincoln School became the Jefferson-Lincoln Elementary School.

Jefferson Elementary School, 4302 N. 13th, Tacoma School District (Pierce County). In 1906 some portable buildings were placed on the present school site and named Jefferson by the school board. In 1908 the present school was built and has been modernized and modified several times since. It was named for the third president of the United States.

Jefferson Elementary School, 18th and Blackburn, Mount Vernon School District (Skagit County). Opened in 1956 and named for the third president of the United States, a tradition in the Mount Vernon School District. Building additions were completed in 1960, 1972, and 1983.

Jefferson Elementary School, 2500 Cadet Way, Everett School District (Snohomish County). Named for Thomas Jefferson, third president of the United States (1801-1809), this is the second school in Everett to bear his name. The first was opened in 1894 at 3100 Hoyt Avenue. That site is now the main branch of the United States Post Office in Everett. The current Jefferson was built in 1964. In the planning stages the new Jefferson was referred to as Eastmont for the residential area in which it is located.

Jefferson Elementary School, S. 3612 Grand Blvd., Spokane School District (Spokane County). Opened in 1908 and named for the third president of the United States.

Jefferson Middle School, 2200 Conger Ave. W., Olympia School District (Thurston County). Opened in 1956 and named for the third president of the United States.

Jefferson Elementary School, N.W. 1150 Bryant, Pullman School District (Whitman County). Built in the 1950s, the school was named for the third president of the United States.

Jefferson Elementary School, 1600 S. 10th St., Yakima School District (Yakima County). Built in 1918 and closed in 1988. A new Martin Luther King School now serves students who would have attended Jefferson or Ruth Childs School (also closed and demolished). Jefferson was named for the third president of the United States.

Jemtegaard Middle School, 35300 E. Evergreen Blvd., Washougal School District (Clark County). Completed in August and dedicated September 12, 1982, the school was named for Gudrun Jemtegaard, who migrated to the Washougal area from Norway with her parents when she was seven years old. She was graduated from Washougal High School in 1923, earned teaching credentials at Ellensburg Normal School, returned to Washougal where she taught elementary school for 42 years. In 1989 Miss Jemtegaard was living in a nursing home in nearby Vancouver. The Washougal School Board chose to name a school for her because of the kindness, love, and learning she gave to every child she had in class.

Jenkins Middle School, Box 47, Chewelah School District (Stevens County). No information available.

Jenne-Wright School, 9210 Silverdale Way N.W., Silverdale, Central Kitsap School District (Kitsap County). Named in 1985 for Carl Jenne, superintendent of Central Kitsap School District from 1939 to 1965, and for J. Aubrey Wright, principal of Silverdale Grade School from 1923 to 1962. Mr. Jenne spoke at the school's dedication, speaking highly of Mr. Wright who was by then deceased.

Leonard M. Jennings Elementary School, N. 1207 Morton St., Colfax School District (Whitman County). Formerly named Colfax Elementary School, the name was changed in the fall of 1970 to Jennings Elementary in honor of a long-time teacher and principal. He began teaching in Colfax in 1938 at the Hamilton School. He was then principal of the Martha Washington School from 1940 to 1954 when the new Colfax Elementary School replaced both the Hamilton and Martha Washington schools. Jennings retired in 1970, the year his school was renamed for him.

Jensen Shelter, Camp Waskowitz, North Bend, Highline School District (King County). An outdoor classroom shelter near the river at the Highline School District's outdoor education camp in the foothills of the Cascades in eastern King County. The shelter was named in 1977 for Carl Jensen, former district superintendent who retired in 1971. Jensen was a pioneer in outdoor education in Washington State.

Jereta School District No. 148 (Whitman County). Another rural school, one of 180 such schools in Whitman County between 1872 and 1918 now nearly forgotten. The origin of the name has also been forgotten.

Andrew Johnson School, Winlock School District (Lewis County). The Andrew Johnson School (also known as Winlock School for the town) was named for a pioneer settler in the area who was a member of the school board. Johnson came to Lewis County in 1885 and became an "important figure in the industrial life of the community," according to local historical sources. The school was built in 1921 and used for many years. As was customary in that time, the elementary school was on the first floor, the high school on the second floor.

Johnson Christian School, traditional Christian, Colville (Stevens County). No information available.

Johnson School, eight miles west of Harrah on Fort Road, Wapato School District (Yakima County). Built in 1918 and named for the family who donated the land. The school was closed in 1936 and has since been remodeled into a residence.

Rufus Jones School, Independent, 444 21st St., Bellingham, Grades P-12 (Whatcom County). No information available.

Jones School District No. 146 (Whitman County). Early 20th Century rural school named for Viola Jones, first clerk of the school board. The school has since consolidated with other rural schools in the county.

Chief Joseph Junior High School, Stevens and Baldwin Streets, Richland School District (Benton County). Built in 1951, this school was named for the son of Old Joseph, veteran of the Washington Territory Indian Wars of the 1850s and chief of the Nez Perce Indians. Old Joseph's successor—Chief Joseph—became the most famous Indian general in U.S. history. He lived from 1840 to 1904. Resisting a fraudulently obtained treaty in which the Indians supposedly had ceded their homelands to the U.S. government, the Nez Perce tribe, under Chief Joseph, was pursued a thousand miles by U.S. troops. In 1877 Joseph led his whole tribe of warriors, women, children, and elders, across a wintry West, evading capture until he was intercepted only 30 miles from the presumed safety of Canada. Chief Joseph School in Richland was closed in 1983 because of enrollment decline. For awhile the building was used as an alternative high school and the auditorium opened for public performances. Operating costs forced its total closure in 1987. In 1990 the city was considering reopening Chief Joseph School as a community activities center.

Kessler School in Longview as it appeared in 1947. This building was torn down and replaced by a brick structure in 1973. (Photo from Helen Leonard, Lower Columbia Retired Teachers Association)

Kalles Junior High School, 515 Third St. S.E., Puyallup School District (Pierce County). Built in 1955 and named Puyallup Junior High School. In 1962, when the second junior high was built in Puyallup, the name of the first school was changed to East Junior High. In 1970, when another junior high was built, the name was changed to Eileen B. Kalles Junior High School. Eileen Kalles served eight years on the Puyallup School Board and a number of terms on the state board of education.

Kamiache School District No. 58 (Whitman County). A variation on the name of Chief Kamiakin who was a Palouse Indian even though he became chief of the Yakimas. This was one of the one-school districts established in Whitman County between 1872 and 1918. Neither the district nor the school now exists. Most such schools were consolidated with larger school districts in the 1930s.

Kamiakin High School, 600 N. Arthur, Kennewick School District (Benton County). Named for Chief Kamiakin of the Yakima tribe. At the Walla Walla Council called by Washington Territorial Governor Isaac

Stevens in 1855, Chief Kamiakin opposed the government's proposal to purchase Indian land. He repudiated the treaty. He is believed to have organized raids against white settlers and miners traveling inland from the Coast to Colville. One of those who lost his life was A. J. Bolan, Indian agent, on his way to join Governor Stevens in the Spokane country. Although involved in many Indian wars against federal troops, Chief Kamiakin was never taken and may well have died of old age at his cabin on the Palouse River in about 1880. The school was built in 1971 and the name chosen by student vote.

Kamiakin Junior High School, 14111 132nd Ave. N.E., Kirkland, Lake Washington School District (King County). Opened in 1974. No information forthcoming on this school. Presumably it was named for the same Indian chief for which the other Kamiakin schools in the state were named.

Chief Kamiakin Junior High School, Ninth and Edison, Sunnyside School District (Yakima County). This school (but not this building) traces its beginnings back to 1911. The current school was named as the result of a student essay contest in 1954. (See discussion of Chief Kamiakin under Kamiakin High School in Kennewick, Benton County, above.)

Karshner Elementary School, 12328 Eighth Ave. N.W., Puyallup School District (Pierce County). Built in 1953 and named for Dr. Warner M. Karshner, a pioneer physician, civic leader, and noted world traveler from Puyallup.

Keene-Riverview Elementary School, 832 Park Ave., Prosser School District (Benton County). Renamed from Riverview to Keene-Riverview in 1976 in honor of Edna Keene, a valued teacher who had taught and then been principal in that school for her whole career, 44 years. She retired in 1969. In 1989 Keene-Riverview was a primary school serving kindergarten, first, and second grades.

Perry G. Keithley Middle School, 12324 S. "L" St., Tacoma, Franklin Pierce School District (Pierce County). The school was built in 1961. It is named for Perry G. Keithley Sr., superintendent of the Midland School District, prior to consolidation and the Midland School principal after it became part of the Franklin Pierce School District.

Keller School, five miles north and one mile east of Wheeler, six miles east of Moses Lake (Grant County). Named for the Keller brothers, early homesteaders.

Helen Keller Elementary School, 13820 108th Ave. N.E., Kirkland, Lake Washington School District (King County). Opened in 1970 and named for Helen Keller (1880-1968), noted writer and lecturer of the early 20th Century. At 19 months old, an illness left her deaf and blind. Her ability to overcome these physical limitations inspired both the hearing and the deaf, the seeing and the blind.

Kelley School, N.E. Quarter, Section 11, Township 7 N., Range 45, E.W.M. (Asotin County). Kelley School, also called County School District No. 17, was organized in August, 1881. The schoolhouse was located high in the eastern end of the Blue Mountains, near the breaks of the Grande Ronde River canyon. The schoolhouse was named for pioneer settler Hiram Kelley, who had served in the Civil War with the 42nd Wisconsin Regiment. Kelley was one of the first settlers in this remote Asotin County area, finding his roots about five miles east of what is now the town of Anatone. Kelley and his wife donated the land for the school and helped construct the rough-lumber building. District No. 17 was merged into Anatone School District in 1917. Students were hauled to town by wagon or sleigh, depending on the season. The Kelley School building was demolished in 1940.

Kellogg Middle School, 16045 25th Ave. N.E., Seattle, Shoreline School District (King County). When a new junior high school was to be opened in September 1953, sixth grade classes from surrounding feeder schools held an essay contest to select a Nobel Peace Prize recipient for whom to name the school. Matthew King, then a student at Lake Forest Park Elementary School, won the contest with an essay on Frank Billings Kellogg, American diplomat who co-authored (with a French diplomat) the Briand-Kellogg Peace Pact of 1928 to outlaw war.

Mrs. Kelly's Kitchen School, Sunnydale, Highline School District (King County). Mike Kelly, an early settler in the Burien area of south King County, named his place Sunnydale soon after he and his family arrived in 1878. Within months, Mrs. Kelly was holding school in her kitchen for her own children and a few of the nearest neighbors' children. By 1882 a log cabin school had been built on the Kelly property. It had an enrollment of 28 and was called the Sunnydale School. There is still a Sunnydale Elementary School operating on that site. The oldest unit of that building was built in 1904.

John F. Kennedy Memorial High School, Roman Catholic, 140 S. 140 St., Seattle Archdiocese (King County). Opened in 1966 and named for the U.S. president who had been assassinated only three years before. John F. Kennedy was the first Roman Catholic president of the United States.

Kenova School District No. 131 (Whitman County). An early 20th Century school, now consolidated with other districts, named for a nearby siding of the Chicago, Milwaukee, and St. Paul Railroad. The siding was named by H.R. Williams, a railroad vice president who named many Milwaukee sidings as the rails stretched west.

Kenroy Elementary School, 601 Jonathan Ave., East Wenatchee, Eastmont School District (Douglas County). Kenneth Randall owned and operated a hardware store in East Wenatchee. He and Roy McMahon bought land for an investment and later sold the property to the Eastmont School District for a new elementary school, built in 1958. Teachers and students of the school were asked to suggest a name. One suggestion was that the name be a combination of the first names of the two men who had sold the school site to the district.

Kent's Prairie School, Arlington School District (Snohomish County). In 1884 settlers in north Snohomish County petitioned the county superintendent of schools to form a school district in their area. These settlers thought a school district would influence new immigrants to settle in the north county area. The resulting school district boundaries contained 600 square miles. The Prairie School was the first school in north Snohomish County. It had split cedar walls and roof and a fir puncheon floor. It cost $150, making it the best and most expensive structure in the north county. The land for the school was leased from J.L. Kent of Kent's Prairie. Lumber for the school was produced at a sawmill at Utsaladdy, loaded into a canoe, poled up the river to Gifford's Landing, loaded on horses, and packed to Kent's Prairie. The new school opened for three students under the tutelage of John McEwen in 1886. By 1890 the railroad had come to Arlington, and the Prairie School already was too small.

Kessler Elementary School, 1902 E. Kessler Blvd., Longview School District (Cowlitz County). Opened in 1923, Kessler school was the first school built in the new city of Longview. Until it opened, elementary students went to school in a bunkhouse on Baltimore and Oregon Way. The high school students went to school in the St. Helen's Inn. The Long Bell Company built the school at a cost of $202,000. It was rented to the Longview School District until 1930 at $10,000 a year. The west unit was built in 1926. The school served both elementary and high school students until 1928 when high school students moved to the new R.A. Long High School. In 1930 the school district bought the Kessler school for $210,000. Kessler was torn down in 1973 except for the auditorium, and a new school was built around the auditorium. The new school opened in 1975. The school was named for George Kessler, one of the planners of the city of Longview. He lived in St. Louis, Missouri, and laid out parks and boulevards for Kansas City and many other cities. He was landscape planner for the St. Louis Exposition of 1904. The street in front of the school and the school were named for Mr. Kessler by the Long Bell Company despite suggestions from the school board that the new school be named Lewis and Clark.

Kilo Junior High School, 4400 S. 308th, Auburn, Federal Way School District (King County). No information available.

Kimball Elementary School, 3200 23rd Ave. S., Seattle School District (King County). The present Kimball School, which opened in February, 1971, had its beginnings as an all-portable annex of Beacon Hill School named Kimball in 1964. At that time the overcrowded district did not have the funds for a new school, and students and staff had to wait for the new building that also would be named for George Kimball. Captain Kimball was born in St. Paul, Minnesota, and joined the Seattle Police Department in 1924. In 1928 Captain Kimball organized the first junior safety patrol in Seattle.

Martin Luther King Jr. Elementary School, 4801 Idaho St., Vancouver School District (Clark County). Built in 1970 and named for the famous Baptist minister, black activist, and civil rights leader of the 1960s.

King Early Childhood Education Center, 3201 E. Republican, Seattle School District (King County).

Harrison Elementary School, first opened in September 1913, named for the street on which it was located, was renamed for Martin Luther King in the 1970s. King, a Nobel Peace Prize recipient, was a martyred civil rights activist and Baptist preacher of the 1960s.

Martin Luther King Jr. Elementary School, 2000 S. 18th St., Yakima School District (Yakima County). Named in 1988. Built on the site of the Ruth Childs School. Changing the name of the school to King engendered some public complaints which the board attempted to disarm by naming the school library for Ruth Childs and by hanging the Childs School plaque in the Childs Library.

Helen Kinzel Auditorium-Gymnasium, Entiat School District (Chelan County). The Entiat Board of Education named the auditorium-gymnasium for Helen Kinzel in 1952 when the building was erected. Ms. Kinzel served Entiat schools as a teacher from 1920 to 1934, as high school principal from 1934 to 1944 and again from 1950 to 1957. Ms. Kinzel was widely recognized and appreciated within her profession and in her community. The North Central Washington District of the Federated Women's Clubs set up an educational scholarship in her name.

Peter Kirk Elementary School, 1312 Sixth St., Kirkland, Lake Washington School District (King County). Opened in 1974 and named for Peter Kirk, Scottish immigrant founder of Kirkland.

Roland Kirkby Field, 301 Garl, Burlington-Edison School District (Skagit County). Roland Kirkby was a 1947 graduate of Burlington-Edison High School. He excelled in football, basketball, and track. His pole vault record stood for more than two decades. He went on to play football for the University of Washington. His jersey number 44 is one of three retired at the University of Washington. He later served in the Army in Korea. The football field at Burlington-Edison High School was named for Kirkby at the homecoming game in 1950 and rededicated at the homecoming game in 1978 after Kirkby's untimely death from cancer.

Kirkwood-Mount Adams Intermediate School, 403 S. Juniper St., Toppenish School District (Yakima County). Kirkwood was built in 1957 as a neighborhood elementary school. Kirkwood-Mount Adams is a combined name of two buildings. The school houses third grade students. It is named for Allan Kirkwood, who farmed on the outskirts of the city and served as a member of the Toppenish School District board of directors from 1935 to 1946.

Kiwanis Vocational School, 2901 Sawall Ave., Centralia (Lewis County). No information available.

Klickitat County Schools (Klickitat County). In the late 19th Century, Klickitat County had many country schools named for the land-giver or the clerk of the school board or the name of the nearest farm, the same way schools were named all over the West during settlement days. These school names are recorded in the Klickitat County Historical Society, but as yet no one has connected these early school names with their namesakes. Nonetheless, some of those school names should be recorded here: Dutch Flat, Warwick, Van Hoy, Lowery, Halstead, SixProng, McKinley, Cleveland, Claussen, Chamberlin, Blockhouse, Lucas, Camp Seven, Laurel, Snowden, Fulda, and Panakanic.

Knab School, Cedar Creek Area east of Toledo near Eden Road on Layton Prairie (Lewis County). In the early 1860s a one-room log school was erected at Eden on Layton Prairie. It was open three or four months a year. In 1888 a board and batten building was constructed on the site and later relocated across from Eden Road. The most recent Knab School building was erected in 1899 and in 1990 still stood, although no longer a school. The area was consolidated into the Toledo School District in 1939. The Knab School and post office were named for John Knab, born in Buffalo, New York, July 15, 1856. Knab came to Washington Territory in the early 1880s.

Mary M. Knight School District No. 311, Matlock (Mason County). The mailing address is Route 1, Box 134, Elma. Mary M. Knight, a teacher from the time she was 16 in Michigan, moved with her husband and daughters to Mason County, Washington State, in 1890. She became County Superintendent of Schools in 1905 and worked to consolidate small schools in the western part of the county in order to provide more services to students. When consolidation was finally achieved and a new school built in 1924, it was named in her honor. She wrote a letter to the school board saying, in part, "I thank you all most cordially and hope with all my heart that the Mary M. Knight School may always be, as now, the place where 'dreams come true' educationally and socially."

Knight School District No. 83 (Whitman County). One of Whitman County's one-school districts founded between 1872 and 1918 and later consolidated with other districts. Knight was named for a Riley Knight, reason not known. The school was also called Missouri Flat.

Knowledge Hill School, on top of hill on road between Hanaford Valley and Skookumchuck Valley, near Bucoda (Thurston County). An early rural school, dates unknown.

Esther R. Knox Administrative Service Center (See Washington Middle School, Olympia.)

Kopachuck Middle School, 10414 56th St. N.W., Gig Harbor, Peninsula School District (Pierce County). The school name is really two Chinook Indian words, kopa and chuck. Kopa means "near" and chuck means "water." Another definition of Kopachuck is "five waters." The school was constructed near several beaches in 1982. There's also a state park nearby named Kopachuck.

Kopachuck Elementary School, Gig Harbor, Peninsula School District (Pierce County). A new elementary school has been erected near the Kopachuck Middle School. It housed pupils from Artondale School while that school was being remodeled. Kopachuck opened to its own student body in the fall of 1989.

Martin C. Kosche Classroom Building and Campus (See Zion Lutheran School of Snohomish County.)

Norm Kramer Athletic Field, Colton School District (Whitman County). Norm Kramer, a Colton native and lifelong resident, the retired Colton postmaster and owner of the Colton Fountain, has been leading community efforts to maintain and improve school properties in Colton for many years. In the summer of 1989 he led a drive for funds to renovate the baseball field, helping to raise more than $2,000 from the community to get the job done. The school district athletic field was named for him in appreciation of Mr. Kramer's untiring efforts.

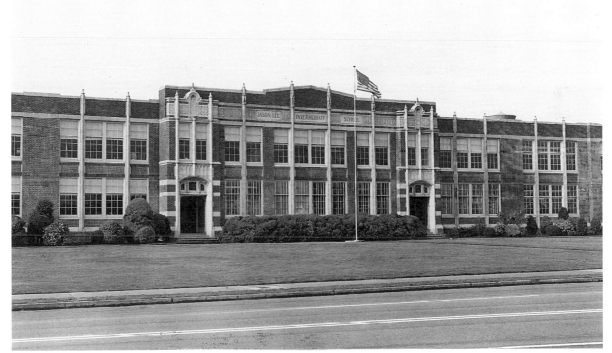

Jason Lee School of Tacoma, named for a pioneer missionary. (Photo from Pat Flynn, Community Relations, Tacoma School District)

L

LaDow School District No. 21 (Whitman County). Another of the early Whitman County rural school districts established between 1872 and 1918. This one-school district was named for Tom LaDow (as was nearby LaDow Butte), the first mail carrier in the area. This school consolidated with Garfield School before 1910. The school also was called Byrne School after a long-time school board member.

LaEscuelita Bilingual School, Unaffiliated, 2500-A N.E. 49th, Seattle (King County). No information available.

Lafayette Elementary School, 2645 California S.W., Seattle School District (King County). Opened in 1919, the school was named for Marie Joseph Paul Yves Roche Gilbert du Motier, Marquis de Lafayette (1757-1834), French general and statesman, who became a major general in the U.S. Continental Army during the American Revolution. He designed the modern French flag in 1789. An earlier school built on the same site in 1893 was called West Seattle Grammar and High School. That school became a part of the Seattle School District when West Seattle joined Seattle in 1907. The elementary section of that school was renamed Lafayette in 1919. The old Lafayette building was so badly damaged by the 1949 earthquake it had to be abandoned. It was replaced by a new brick building in 1950.

Lake Roosevelt High School (See Roosevelt.)

Lakota Junior High School, 1415 S.W. 314th St., Federal Way School District (King County). One source identifies "Lakota" as a Native American word meaning "meeting place of friendly people." No particular tribe or dialect is cited. No other information given.

Lancaster-Willada School District No. 22 (earlier called **Downing**) (Whitman County). An early (probably before 1900) rural school district named for James Lancaster, the first postmaster of the area. The local post office also was named Lancaster. The depot agent objected to the name and called his railroad siding "WillAda" after himself and his wife Ada. He built a second school with the same district number and called it Willada.

Larrabee Elementary School, 1409 18th St., Bellingham School District (Whatcom County). The original Larrabee Grammar School was built in 1890 at 21st and Larrabee Streets. It was replaced by a new school in 1920 at the 18th Street address given above. In addition to being named for a street, this school is indirectly named for C.X. Larrabee, an early-day land developer particularly in the Fairhaven section of Bellingham. The Larrabee Company still has many land holdings in the area.

Laurence School, Ashue and Branch Road, Wapato School District (Yakima County). This school was built on the property of the Laurence family in 1909 and is sometimes referred to as the Ashue School. From 1923 to 1936 the school was known as the Liberty School. By 1938 most such schools had been consolidated into larger districts to which students were bussed. The Laurence Schoolhouse no longer exists.

Laurin Intermediate School, 1360 N.E. 97th Ave., Vancouver, Battle Ground School District (Clark County). No information available.

LaVenture Middle School, 1200 LaVenture Rd., Mount Vernon School District (Skagit County). The original property owner (J. LaVenture) was a farmer. No other biographical information on this man has been unearthed as of this writing. In the original planning it was the intent of the school board to name the school Garfield Middle School. However, there was some public objection to the name as being in too common use in other school districts and for other reasons more obscure. So the new Mount Vernon School was built, dedicated, and named in 1971 for the street on which it was located.

Lawton Elementary School, 4017 26th Ave. W., Seattle School District (King County). No information available.

Lee Academy, Unaffiliated, 4626 191st Ave. S.E., Issaquah, Grades P-6 (King County). Oral response not followed up by written response. Named for the mother of the school's administrator in office in 1990.

Jason Lee Elementary School, 1702 Van Giesen, Richland School District (Benton County). Classes first occupied this building in 1952. It was named for a Methodist-Episcopal minister who lived from 1803 to 1845. He came to the Oregon Territory in 1834 and founded a mission on the Willamette River. He also traveled with explorer Nathaniel Wyeth to Fort Vancouver, north of the Columbia. During his travels he showed special concern for education of children and helped set up early schools at several sites.

Jason Lee Middle School, 8500 N.W. Ninth Ave., Vancouver School District (Clark County). Named after Jason Lee, a prominent Methodist-Episcopal missionary and pioneer in the Oregon Territory. He arrived at Fort Vancouver in 1834, stayed for a short time, and then moved south to present-day Salem. The name for the school was chosen in 1964 by student body vote. Lee was born in Stanstead, Quebec, and attended Wesleyan Academy in Wilbraham, Massachusetts.

Jason Lee Middle School, 602 N. Sprague, Tacoma School District (Pierce County). First called West Intermediate School, it opened as Jason Lee Intermediate School in 1924. Jason Lee was a Methodist-Episcopal missionary to the Oregon Country from 1834 until his death in 1845. He cooperated in drawing a petition for territorial government. He was a founder of the Oregon Institute (now Willamette University).

Robert E. Lee School of Eastmont is a representative of schoolhouses built in the 1950s and '60s—flat, horizontal, one-level structures built for efficiency and economy. (Photo from Eastmont School District, Douglas County)

Robert E. Lee Elementary School, 1455 N. Baker Ave., East Wenatchee, Eastmont School District (Douglas County). Completed in the 1956-57 school year, two years after Ulysses S. Grant Elementary was built in the same district, Lee school's name was a conscious effort to honor representatives of both sides in the War Between the States. Ironically, Lee School is in the northern part of the district, Grant School in the southern part.

Lemon Building, Camp Waskowitz, North Bend, Highline School District (King County). A building at the outdoor education camp owned by the Highline School District was named in 1980 for Harry Lemon, long-time teacher and camp naturalist. Once each year Lemon regaled his young students by saying, "All of you have seen a fuzzy peach. Now you've seen a Harry Lemon."

Leroue School, seven miles south of Ashue, Wapato School District (Yakima County). Another country school named for a family, probably the owners of the land on which the school was built in the early part of the 20th Century. Little else is known of the school.

Leschi Elementary School, 135 32nd Ave., Seattle School District (King County). This school was built in 1909 and named for Chief Leschi. Leschi was a Nisqually Indian farmer who had been elevated to chief by Territorial Governor Isaac Stevens in a vain attempt to build Indian support for Stevens' treaty transferring Indian lands to the federal government. Instead, Chief Leschi became an ally of Chief Kamiakin, Palouse Indian who had become chief of the Yakimas and who successfully mounted "hit and run" military actions against white settlers, miners, and federal troops. Eventually Chief Leschi was tried and hanged for ambushing a U.S. military officer, a charge of which most modern historians believe he was innocent. Pioneer Ezra Meeker wrote a book on Chief Leschi which largely finds him a tragic rather than guilty figure.

Chief Leschi School, Unaffiliated, 2002 E. 28th, Tacoma (Pierce County). An elementary, middle, and high school operated by the Puyallup Tribal Schools and named for a famous Indian leader of Washington territorial days. Originally Chief Leschi School was housed at the old Hawthorne School. It was moved to its present site, the former Cushman Hospital, in 1981. The school was named by the Puyallup Tribal Council.

Lewis Junior High School, 4100 Plomondon St., Vancouver School District (Clark County). (See Bagley Downs.) Bagley Downs Elementary School was built in 1943 and named for the Bagley family who had owned the property and had operated a race track there. In 1946 the building became known as Lewis and Clark Elementary. The name Clark was dropped to avoid confusion with Clark Community College, and the school became a junior high. The building was being used in 1989 for book storage and classes offered by the Vancouver Parks and Recreation Department. It was once again known by the name Bagley Downs.

Lewis and Clark Elementary School, 800 Downing St., Richland School District (Benton County). Named after Meriwether Lewis and William Clark, who led an expedition across the Rocky Mountains to the Pacific Ocean and back (1804-1806). Originally the plan was to name the grade school Lewis and the high school Clark. However, the high school was used only one year after the big influx of students during construction of the atomic energy plant. When a new high school had to be

built, it was decided to give both the Lewis and the Clark names to the grade school. The first Lewis and Clark Elementary School was named in 1943, used until 1971 at which time a new building of the same name was opened.

Lewis and Clark Elementary School, 1130 Princeton, Wenatchee School District (Chelan County). William Clark and Meriwether Lewis led an expedition to explore the Pacific Northwest from 1804 to 1806. They followed the Missouri River and its tributaries, crossed the Rocky Mountains to the navigable waters of the Snake and Columbia Rivers, thence to the Pacific Ocean. The North End School District No. 7, organized in 1889, renamed its only school Lewis and Clark School shortly after its consolidation with South End School District to form Wenatchee School District No. 46 in 1905. The original Lewis and Clark School frame structure was replaced by a brick building destroyed by fire in 1922. The third building, with additions, served until June 1988, when a completely new structure was erected on the site adjacent to the existing school. The vacated school was demolished in September 1988.

Lewis and Clark High School, W. 521 Fourth Ave., Spokane School District (Spokane County). First opened in 1883 as Spokane High School, this school was renamed South Central High School in 1908. South Central burned and was rebuilt in 1911 and renamed for Meriwether Lewis and William Clark, the famous American explorers of the Pacific Northwest.

Lewis and Clark Middle School, 1114 W. Pierce, Yakima School District (Yakima County). Built in 1966 as a junior high, it became a middle school in 1988. The school was named for Captain Meriwether Lewis and William Clark, the American explorers of the Pacific Northwest.

Libby Middle School, E. 2900 First Ave., Spokane School District (Spokane County). Opened in 1928 as a junior high and named after Isaac Chase Libby, former Latin teacher in Spokane High School (later called Lewis and Clark High School) in the 1880s and '90s.

Liberty Bell High School, Twisp, Methow Valley School District (Okanogan County). No information available.

Liberty School, Granger School District (Yakima County). The first school in the lower Yakima Valley was held in a small building on the Mason farm at Punkin Center. The school opened on November 18, 1892. A short time later it was moved to the corner of Hudson Road and what was later called Highway 12. Jasper Stone, who owned a half section west of the Liberty Road, donated a parcel of his land for a school in the early 1900s. The building at Hudson Road was moved to the new site. It was called Liberty District School No. 31. It is believed that Liberty Road may have been named for the school rather than vice versa. By 1907 the one-room school had grown to three rooms and offered classes for the first eight grades and two years of high school. The wooden school burned on an undetermined date and was replaced by a brick building which still stood in 1990 but was not an active school.

Lieser Elementary School, 301 S. Lieser Rd., Vancouver School District (Clark County). Named for Louis Lieser who took up a donation land claim of 640 acres in 1851. The school stands on part of this land claim and was built in 1943. A great grandson of Louis Lieser, Dr. Miles Lieser, D.D.S., still lived on a section of the Lieser property in 1989.

Robert Lince Elementary School, W. Naches Ave., Selah School District (Yakima County). In 1986 a campus that had been named Selah High School since 1926 was remodeled to accommodate elementary-age children and given a new name. The faculty and students suggested several names. The final selection—Robert Lince—was chosen by popular vote. Robert "Bob" Lince documented the history of Selah and the surrounding area for some 30 years. In 1984 he published a book entitled *The Selah Story.* Mr. Lince was born and reared in the valley. He owned and operated a grocery store for many years. He and his wife had eight children, all daughters. He died on the fourth of July, 1986.

Lincoln Middle School, 1945 Fourth Ave., Clarkston School District (Asotin County). The new Lincoln Elementary opened in the fall of 1928. The name was chosen by a contest among students in the eight grades. Later the elementary grades moved out and the school became Lincoln Junior High. In 1971 Lincoln Junior High was closed when a new middle school was opened in Clarkston Heights. In 1989 the old Lincoln building was sold to Vernon Dinke whose plans at that time were to turn it into an apartment building.

Lincoln Elementary School, 4901 W. 21st Ave., Kennewick School District (Benton County). Named for the 16th president of the United States on the completion of the building in 1983. The school board had sought to involve the students, parents, and the community in the naming of the new school. Several names were submitted for board consideration: Horizon, Union, Union West, Horse Heaven, and Mountain Ridge. Board Member Jensen added his favorite to the list: Lincoln. The board then voted and adopted Lincoln three to one on the grounds that every district should have a Lincoln School.

Lincoln Elementary School, 1224 Methow St., Wenatchee School District (Chelan County). The first Lincoln School, a four-room brick building, was erected in 1909. The building was used until the new school was built in 1957, diagonally across Methow Street. The old building and site was sold in 1958 and the building was torn down.

Lincoln Elementary School, Eighth and "C" Streets, Port Angeles School District (Clallam County). This Lincoln School was named in 1894 for the 16th president. The building then was a single-room log cabin. The site had been obtained from the U.S. Patent Office. Another school, called the Fourth Ward School, was constructed nearby and, in 1916, was replaced by a new Lincoln School. Additions were made in 1922, 1939, 1940, and 1951. The school was closed in 1978 and the building used for community functions.

Lincoln Elementary School, 4200 Daniels St., Vancouver School District (Clark County). This school was given its name in 1921 when a collection of portable buildings was placed at the present school site. The first permanent structure was built in 1924. The school was named for the 16th president of the United States.

Lincoln Elementary School, 700 Wood Ave., Hoquiam School District (Grays Harbor County). The original school was situated at Lincoln and Raemer Avenues and was named for the 16th president of the United States. The newer Lincoln School on Wood Avenue was completed in 1967.

Lincoln School, 1610 Blaine St., Port Townsend School District (Jefferson County). Named for the former U.S. president, Port Townsend's Lincoln School was completed in 1892. It was originally a three-story building with a tower and bell. The third story was deemed unsafe and removed when a wind of hurricane force blew off the roof in 1934. The building subsequently fell short of the fire code requirements and was closed in 1980. In 1989 the Port Townsend School District was still waiting for realistic proposals for the practical community use of the old school. The goal was to convert its 36,000 square feet to a community purpose.

Lincoln High School, 4400 Interlake Ave. N., Seattle School District (King County). Opened in the fall of 1907. Named for former U.S. President Abraham Lincoln. The school was closed for lack of enrollment in 1981.

Lincoln Elementary School, 200 S. Sampson, Ellensburg School District (Kittitas County). Named for Abraham Lincoln, 16th president of the United States, in 1949.

Lincoln Elementary School, 400 W. Summa, Centralia School District (Lewis County). In 1889, the South School was built on the northwest corner of Pearl and Rock Streets on land donated by George Washington, black man and early Washington territory settler and founder of Centralia. In January, 1922, an eight-room building replaced the South School and was named Lin-

coln. In 1958 Lincoln was closed, becoming part of Centralia College in 1967. A new school, built in 1958 at the Summa Street address, was eventually named Jefferson-Lincoln to honor two former presidents and commemorate two former schools.

This photo of Port Townsend's Lincoln School likely was taken some years before World War 1. Tower and third floor were removed after a 1934 wind storm. (Photo from Jefferson County Historical Museum)

Lincoln Elementary School, Fifth and Cota Streets, Shelton School District (Mason County). The opening exercises at this school were held on February 12, 1909, at which time the school was named Lincoln High School. In 1924 a new high school was built, and Lincoln no longer housed high school classes. In 1932 a junior high was built, and Lincoln then held only Grades 1 through 6. It operated as a school until June, 1958, and was torn down that same summer.

Lincoln Elementary School, South 17th and "K" Streets, Tacoma School District (Pierce County). Named June 21, 1889. Previously it had been known as West School. The school was closed in 1938 when the building was condemned.

Lincoln High School, 701 S. 37th, Tacoma School District (Pierce County). Named for President Abraham

Lincoln in 1911. An elementary school earlier had been named for Lincoln in 1889. In 1914 the high school became known as Lincoln Park High School. By 1917 the word "park" was dropped from the school name.

Lincoln Elementary School, 1005 S. 11th, Mount Vernon School District (Skagit County). The original three-story building was erected in 1891 and named for the 16th president of the United States. The present building was constructed in 1938 as a Public Works Administration project. The school was remodeled in 1983. The original school was the high school from 1891 to 1907, after which it became a grade school.

Lincoln Elementary School, 2400 Colby Ave., Everett School District (Snohomish County). Everett, as did Tacoma, had two schools named for Abraham Lincoln. The first and original Everett Lincoln School was a wooden building on the east side of Colby Avenue (site of the current Everett Civic Auditorium, a part of Everett High School). This school was razed in 1938. The second Lincoln School was a brick building at 25th and Oakes. It replaced the 1902 wooden Everett High School (later renamed Central School). The Lincoln building became the main building for Everett Junior College when that level was a part of the Everett School District and before the Everett Community College moved to its present site at 801 Wetmore in 1958. The second Lincoln building was demolished in 1981, and the site now serves as a physical education and athletic field.

Lincoln Elementary School, W. 25 Fifth Ave., Spokane School District (Spokane County). Opened in 1888 and closed in 1967. This school evolved from the earlier Cowley School. The school was on Cowley Street. In 1926 the old school was badly damaged by fire and later turned into headquarters for the district's grounds department, repair shops, and warehousing. A new Lincoln School was built at the W. 25 Fifth Avenue address in 1930. The last few years Lincoln was open its principal was Paul O. Abraham, who answered the school telephone with "Mr. Abraham, Lincoln."

Lincoln Elementary School, 213 E. 21st, Olympia School District (Thurston County). The first Lincoln School in Olympia, named for the 16th U.S. president, was occupied in 1890. A new Lincoln School was built in its place in 1924 and is still in use, the oldest school in the Olympia district. In 1989 the school was awarded a plaque commemorating its historical significance.

Lincoln School, Bellingham School District (Whatcom County). The school was in operation from 1891 to 1952, at which time the school district traded the Lincoln site for 135 acres at the end of Lake Whatcom, the Gordon L. Carter Environmental Education Site, where the district now operates an environmental education program. The site of the old Lincoln School is occupied by the Shuksan Convalescent Center on James Street.

Lincoln Middle School, S.E. 315 Crestview, Pullman School District (Whitman County). Built and named for President Lincoln in 1962.

Lincoln School, west and south of White Swan on Pine Cone Road, Mount Adams School District (Yakima County). The dates of this school are hazy, but probably it was built in the early years of this century. Unlike the other Lincoln Schools, this one was named for Abe Lincoln, an Indian pawn shop owner in Toppenish. He was an active citizen of the community and probably donated the land for the school. The building eventually was moved into White Swan where, in 1990, it was in use as a private home.

Lincoln School, Lincoln Avenue and Sixth Street, Sunnyside School District (Yakima County). Built in 1927 for Grades 1-6, Lincoln was remodeled in 1941 and again in 1955. In the 1970s the school was closed and reopened to house kindergarten and primary classes, the superintendent's office, and the migrant office (dealing with the special needs of pupils from migrant farmworker families). It was named for President Abraham Lincoln.

Lincoln Elementary School, 309 N. Alder, Toppenish School District (Yakima County). The first Toppenish Lincoln School was built in the early 1920s, but it was substantially rebuilt in 1941. As are most Lincoln Schools, it was named for President Abraham Lincoln, Kentucky-born farm boy who probably never accumulated more than one year of formal schooling in his whole lifetime.

Lincoln Elementary School, North Third, northeast corner of "D" Street, Yakima School District (Yakima County). Built as a high school in 1890, it became a grade school when Yakima High School was built in 1907. The school has since been torn down and merged with Barge School on "I" Street. A building at 219 E. "I" Street has been given the name of the two schools it replaced: Barge-Lincoln. (Also see Jefferson-Lincoln, Barge-Lincoln, and Paine.)

Lindbergh High School in Renton was designed by Fred Bassetti, nationally recognized school architect. (Photo from Ethel Telban, Renton Retired Teachers Association)

Charles A. Lindbergh High School, 16426 128th S.E., Renton School District (King County). Completed in 1971 but unused for one year due to lack of funds. The school was named at a dedicatory ceremony held May 23, 1973, for aviation pioneer Charles Lindbergh, who, in 1927, became the first man to fly the Atlantic Ocean solo. Attending the dedication was Miss Wendy Lindbergh, then-16-year-old granddaughter of "Lucky Lindy."

Lindley School District No. 155 (Whitman County). Another of the late 19th and early 20th Century country schools in Whitman County that later consolidated into larger districts. This one was named for J.L. Lindley, who donated the land the school was built on.

Lister Elementary School, 2106 E. 44th, Tacoma School District (Pierce County). Named in 1949 by the school board and built in 1950, this school name honors two brothers. Alfred Lister was a Tacoma city comptroller and school board member. He became board secretary and school district business manager for 22 years. He also served at one time as president of Tacoma Savings and Loan and later as a trustee of the University of Puget Sound. His brother, Ernest Lister, served on the Tacoma city council and was elected to two terms (1912 and 1916) as governor of the state. He died in office in 1919. A previous building on this site, constructed in 1943, had been named Salishan School for a nearby housing project.

Little School, Othello (Adams County). Built in 1906 and named for the Little family who donated the land for the school. This rural school operated for about one year.

Little Red Schoolhouse, Lake Stevens area (Snohomish County). Built in the 1890s by families in rural Snohomish County near Lake Stevens, this school served mostly the children of Scandinavian immigrants. The nearest student to the school walked two and a half miles each way along difficult trails.

Little Kentucky School, Toledo area (Lewis County). This school is marked on a map in the Lewis County Historical Museum. It is believed that this school served immigrant families from Kentucky. It is likely that it later became part of the Lone Yew School District.

Litzenburger School District No. 95 (Whitman County). The single school in this district, no longer in existence, was named for Henry Litzenburger, member of the school board.

Ruth Livingston Elementary School, 2515 Road 84, Pasco School District (Franklin County). Built in 1978 and named for Ruth Corbett Van Slyke Livingston, who served on the Pasco School Board from 1926 to 1951 and held many other positions of leadership in her community and in the state. She was a 1908 graduate of the University of Wisconsin and a former high school Latin teacher. She was a charter member of the Washington State Board of Education and served one term as Franklin County auditor. She and her husband ran Livingston Dairy until his death in 1941. The name of the school was recommended to the school board by the Pasco-Kennewick Chapter of the American Association of University Women, the Franklin County Historical Society, and by C.L. Booth, former superintendent of Pasco School District.

Lochburn Junior High School, 5431 Steilacoom Blvd. S.W., Tacoma, Clover Park School District (Pierce County). No information available.

Loeffelbein School, half mile west and four miles north of Ruff (Grant County). Named for a family in the area in territorial days.

Logan Elementary School, 1330 Rose St., Centralia School District (Lewis County). The first Logan School was built in 1909. A portrait of Mr. Logan hung in the front hallway. The building was destroyed by earthquake in 1949 and replaced by a new building. The portrait, however, and the identity of Mr. Logan, have been lost. From 1968 to 1972 the school served as a kindergarten center. It was closed in 1972 and reopened in 1973. In 1978 it became a special services site serving Centralia and Chehalis School Districts' preschool through elementary pupils having "identified handicaps." At the end of the 1989-90 school year, Logan was closed once again and became a school storage warehouse.

Logan Grade School, S. 21st and "I" Streets, Tacoma School District (Pierce County). In 1891 the University School opened in a building vacated by the College of Puget Sound. The name of the school was changed to

Logan in 1896 when the Grand Army of the Republic, an organization of Union veterans of the Civil War, offered to give the school a flag. John A. Logan was a Civil War Union general and a founder of the Grand Army of the Republic. The school was closed in 1924, the building demolished in 1925, and McCarver Intermediate School erected on the site.

Logan Elementary School, E. 915 Montgomery Ave., Spokane School District (Spokane County). The school was named in 1889 for John Alexander Logan, a Union Army General and political leader. He helped organize the Grand Army of the Republic, a Union Army veterans organization. He also was a co-founder of Memorial Day in 1868. Logan served as a U.S. representative and senator from Illinois. His association with Spokane is not readily apparent. Perhaps the school board was offered an American flag as was the Tacoma School Board in the naming of its John A. Logan School.

Lone Star School District No. 167 (Whitman County). This one-school district in early Whitman County must have been named by a homesick, displaced Texan.

R.A. Long High School, 2903 Nichols Blvd., Longview School District (Cowlitz County). Robert A. Long and Victor Bell formed a partnership in Kansas City, Missouri, in 1870. The two men produced hay for awhile and then, in 1891, formed the Long Bell Lumber Co., one of the largest in the South. The company opened operations in the area between the Columbia and Cowlitz rivers in Washington State in the 1920s. A new city was built—Longview—and schools financed by the Long Bell Company were placed under the administration of a small rural school district. By 1926 a high school was needed. Mr. Long built the school at a cost of $750,000 and gave it to the city. He spoke at the dedication ceremonies July 23, 1928. Mr. Long died in 1934 at the age of 84.

Longfellow Elementary School, 301 N. 10th Ave., Pasco School District (Franklin County). The first school at this site was called West Side School and served all grade levels through high school from 1909 until 1921. Thereafter, the school became Longfellow Elementary School, which burned down in the summer of 1949. A new building was completed and occupied in 1951. The school was replaced in 1988 by another new building. The school was named for Henry Wadsworth Longfellow (1807-1882), American poet who wrote *Evangeline, The Song of Hiawatha, The Courtship of Miles Standish, Paul Revere's Ride,* and *The Village Blacksmith.* Five Pasco schools are named for writers.

Longfellow Elementary School, South 25th Street and Pacific Avenue, Tacoma School District (Pierce County). On June 21, 1889, South School was renamed Longfellow for the American poet, Henry Wadsworth Longfellow. The school was condemned as unsafe and closed in 1936.

Longfellow Elementary School, 3715 Oakes Ave., Everett School District (Snohomish County). Longfellow School was constructed in 1911 on a site that had housed the wooden 37th Street School. Longfellow was named for the poet, Henry Wadsworth Longfellow (1807-1882). The school was closed in 1971 and reopened in 1980 as an administrative building. In 1990 the Longfellow Building housed the school district's business offices and other administrative and instructional offices. The late Senator Henry M. Jackson lived about a block from Longfellow as a youngster and attended school there.

Longfellow Elementary School, 800 Providence Ave., Spokane School District (Spokane County). Opened and named in 1893 for Henry Wadsworth Longfellow, American poet.

Longmire School, 12 miles north of Selah on the North Wenas Road (Yakima County). In 1911 a new school, which was also to be used for church services, was opened in the Wenas Valley. The members of the community gathered for a dedication ceremony at which the school was named for David Longmire, a member of the school board and community leader. In the 1930s the Longmire School was consolidated into the Selah School District. The Longmire School later was purchased by

Grange No. 874 and, in 1990, was still used by the Grange and as a community center.

Loop Field, 12th and Franklin, Shelton School District (Mason County). When a new junior high school was built next to the school district athletic field in 1932, the field was named after the superintendent of schools— H. Enzo Loop—who had earlier served as coach and had always been an advocate of school athletics. "Prof." (pronounced prawf) Loop, as he was known by adults and students alike, came to Shelton in 1909 as principal and physics teacher at Lincoln School, which served all grade levels through high school. He was named superintendent of schools in 1912 and served until 1944. After that, until 1947, he taught at Mary M. Knight High School in western Mason County. He died in 1974 just before his 93rd birthday.

Lotzgesell School, Dungeness Valley, Clallam County School District No. 1, Sequim (Clallam County). In 1896 the J. Thornton Lane School was closed and relocated on the Lotzgesell farm and renamed the Lotzgesell School. In 1912 the Lotzgesell School was closed and consolidated into the Macleay School, which became a part of the Sequim School District in 1920.

Frank Love Elementary School, 303 224th S.W., Bothell, Northshore School District (King County). Built in 1990, this school was named in honor of Dr. Frank Love who served as Northshore superintendent of schools from 1981 until his retirement in 1988, shortly before his death from cancer.

Lowell Elementary School, 1058 E. Mercer St., Seattle School District (King County). The original unit of the frame building at Lowell School was started in 1889 and opened for the school year 1890-91. At that time and for a number of years afterward, it was known as Columbia School. In September, 1910, soon after Columbia City had been annexed by Seattle, the school's name was changed to Lowell after James Russell Lowell, American writer and scholar. Lowell's picture and autograph hang in the school hallway.

Lowell Elementary School, 810 N. 13th, Tacoma School District (Pierce County). Lowell School was named in 1890 when two Tacoma area school districts combined. It had earlier been known as First Ward School in 1869 and was then located on North 28th and Starr Streets. That school burned in 1875. A new school was built near the old site in 1885, and, in 1892, another new school was built at this site. It was destroyed by an earthquake in 1949 and rebuilt in 1950. The school was named for James Russell Lowell, American poet, diplomat, Harvard professor, and one-time editor of the *Atlantic Monthly.*

Lowell School of Tacoma, named for the New England poet, diplomat, professor, and editor. (Photo from Pat Flynn, Community Relations, Tacoma School District)

Lowell Elementary School, 23rd and Inland Empire Highway, Spokane School District (Spokane County). Opened in 1899, closed in 1933, re-opened in 1940, closed in 1941, re-opened in 1943, closed in 1954. Named for American poet, educator, and philosopher James Russell Lowell. In 1919 a brick structure replaced the original building. The re-opening in 1940 was to house National Youth Administration classes, a Roosevelt New Deal program to help the nation recover from the Great Depression. Northwest Air College rented the

building in the 1955-56 school year. In 1968 the building was sold for $3,000.

Lowell Elementary School, 935 14th St., Bellingham School District (Whatcom County). Lowell School was preceded on this site by the 14th Street School built in 1890. The Lowell School was built next door in 1914, and the site of the old school is now a Lowell School playfield. It is believed that the school was named for James Russell Lowell (1819-1891), poet, essayist, professor of modern languages, and U.S. minister to London.

Wing Luke Elementary School, 3701 S. Kenyon, Seattle School District (King County). Ground-breaking for the new building to be known as Wing Luke Elementary School took place on March 26, 1970. The school was named for the man who, in 1962, became not only the first Asian to be elected to the Seattle City Council but is believed to be the first Asian elected to public office anywhere in the mainland United States. Born in Kwangtung Province in China, Wing Luke was brought to Seattle at the age of six. He attended Seattle public schools, graduating from Roosevelt High School and the University of Washington Law School. While a member of the city council, he was killed in an airplane crash in May 1965.

Lum Schoolhouse, where Lum Road joins Ford's Prairie-Waunch Prairie Road (Lewis County). James K. Lum took up a donation claim in 1853 northeast of Ford's claim on Ford's Prairie. Lum was born in Braintown, Pennsylvania, in 1823. He was a watchmaker, taxidermist, musician, surveyor, world traveler, inventor, painter, and poet. In about 1875 he surveyed the first plat of Centralia, then called Centerville. A lifelong bachelor, he died in 1881. An early-day rural school, situated on Lum Road, took his name. The school no longer exists.

Lummi Tribal School, Unaffiliated, 1790 Bayon Rd., Bellingham (Whatcom County). No information available.

Lutacaga Elementary School, 795 S. Seventh, Othello School District (Adams County). Named for a

Wanapum Indian word meaning "Finish what you have started." The school was opened in 1952 and was still in operation in 1990.

Lynch School District No. 118 (Whitman County). This old rural school was named for the family that donated the property. The school no longer exists.

Lyon Elementary School, 101 E. 46th, Tacoma School District (Pierce County). Mary Lyon championed education for women. She founded Mount Holyoke College, Massachusetts, in 1837 and was its president until her death in 1849. In 1909 a Mary Lyon School opened in Tacoma at South 46th and "A" Street. In 1924 a new Mary Lyon School was built at the East 46th site noted above.

Iva Alice Mann stands under the name of the junior high school named for her in 1951. (Mann family photo via Doris Anderson, Pierce County Retired Teachers Association)

Mabana School, Camano Island (Island County). Named about 1910 by Nils "Pegleg" Anderson for his daughter Mabel. He used the first syllables from her first and last names and added an "a" to make the coined word euphonious. The school was closed in 1937 and in 1990 was a private residence. Anderson operated a logging camp on the south end of Camano Island. One of the early teachers in Mabana School was Pearl Anderson. It had not been determined at the time of this writing whether she was of the same family as Nils Anderson. Pearl Anderson later became Pearl Wanamaker, one of the most influential state superintendents of public instruction this state has ever had.

Mac Field, 12033 N.E. 80th, Kirkland, Lake Washington School District (King County). Mac Field is the athletic field on the Lake Washington High School campus. It was built in the 1950s under the supervision of William J. McLaughlin, who was then the athletic director for the district. It was first named William Bowie Field in honor of the school board member who was a firm supporter of the construction of the new field. In 1973 Mr. McLaughlin retired after 25 years in the Lake Washington District as teacher, coach, school administrator, and district administrator. In 1984 the Lake Washington High School alumni petitioned the school board to rename the field for "Mr. Mac." The family of Mr. Bowie was consulted and approved the name change.

Angus MacDonald High School, Colville (Stevens County). Angus MacDonald opened as the new high school in Colville in 1911. It was a two-story brick building housing 12 classrooms, an auditorium, library, and superintendent's office. The school was named for a factor or general manager of the Hudson's Bay Company's Fort Colville at Kettle Falls in early territorial days.

Macleay School, Macleay Road, Sequim (Clallam County). Don M. Macleay purchased 8,000 acres from General Mills of the U.S. Army between 1870 and 1880. The Macleay School was established in 1912 when the Rena (also known as Long Prairie) and Heath Elementary Schools were combined into the new Macleay School built on land given by Don Macleay. In 1920 the Macleay School became part of the Sequim School District. The building was being used in 1989 as a community center.

Madison Middle School, 3429 45th Ave. S.W., Seattle School District (King County). Opened as a junior high on September 23, 1929, this school was named for former U.S. President James Madison, who also had served as secretary of state under President Jefferson.

Madison Elementary School, 907 E. Fir, Mount Vernon School District (Skagit County). Built, dedicated, and opened in 1954. Following tradition, the school board selected the new school's name from a list of former U.S. presidents. The year this school was built, one of many rapid school construction projects across the state, Mount Vernon's Madison School cost the least—at $10 per square foot. A west wing was added in 1960. A building modernization and east wing addition were completed in 1983.

Madison Elementary School, 616 Peck's Dr., Everett School District (Snohomish County). Madison was completed in 1947, Everett's first school built after World War 2. It was named by the school board for James Madison, fourth president of the United States, a name selected from recommendations made by members of the community.

Madison Elementary School, W. 319 Nebraska Ave., Spokane School District (Spokane County). A small frame building called Madison School opened in 1910. A new school replacing the original Madison was built adjacent to Franklin City Park in 1949. Both schools were named for James Madison, fourth president of the United States.

Madison Elementary School, 812 Central St., Olympia School District (Thurston County). Opened in 1956, this school was named for former President James Madison by consensus of students, a citizens' advisory board, and townspeople.

Manchester School District No. 48 (Whitman County). Named for Benjamin T. Manchester who owned a large tract of land in the area and probably donated some of it for this school. This is one of many country schools built in Whitman County between 1872 and 1918. It no longer exists.

Horace Mann Elementary School, 17001 N.E. 104th, Redmond, Lake Washington School District (King County). While serving as secretary of the Massachusetts State Board of Education, Horace Mann (1796-1859) pioneered a movement for professional education standards in the schools. He later was a U.S. representative from Massachusetts and president of Antioch College where he demonstrated the practicality of coeducation of male and female students. The elementary school in Redmond named for Horace Mann opened in 1964.

Horace Mann Elementary School, 21st and E. James Streets, Block 6 of Barclay Addition, Seattle School District (King County). Built in 1902, Mann Elementary originally was called Walla Walla after the neighborhood in which it was located. Walla Walla is the name of an Indian tribe in the southeastern part of the state. In 1921 the school's name was changed to Horace Mann, named for the champion of free common schools in the United States. Horace Mann School has been closed for many years.

Mann Elementary School, 5211 S. "K," Tacoma School District (Pierce County). Named for Horace Mann (1796-1859), the famous Massachusetts educator who established the first normal school for teachers. This Tacoma elementary school was built in 1901 at South 54th and "J" Streets. In 1953 a new Mann School was built at the present site.

Iva Alice Mann Junior High School, 11509 Holden Rd. S.W., Tacoma, Clover Park School District (Pierce County). The school was built in 1959 and named for a woman held by many area citizens to be the founder of the Clover Park School District. In 1923 Mrs. Mann was clerk of the Park Lodge school board. She witnessed the rivalries among Park Lodge and four other small school districts serving the area south of Tacoma. She worked to consolidate the districts in order to improve educational services to children. In 1940, when School District No. 400 was formed, she served as administrative assistant and business manager. She also was instrumental in starting the district's vocational training school later called Clover Park Vocational Technical Institute. Mrs. Mann also is credited with naming the new school district for the clover-covered area on which the high school was built. Mrs. Mann was co-founder and past-president of the Washington State School Directors Association.

Horace Mann School, Sharp Avenue and Howard Street, Spokane School District (Spokane County). Opened in 1913 and closed in 1943. Named for the pioneer American educator of the 19th Century. Originally an apartment building, the structure was remodeled into a nine-room school. It replaced Field School as a facility for children with special learning problems. While the building was closed as a school in 1943, the district's health department occupied the building until 1948. In 1956 the building was sold at public auction.

Manning School District No. 46 (Whitman County). No reason was given for the name of this late 19th Century school, but likely the land was donated by the Manning family. Building also was known as the Green Hollow School.

Maple Elementary School, 4925 Corson Ave. S., Seattle School District (King County). Jacob Maple and his son, Samuel, staked claims in the Duwamish River Valley September 14, 1851, two months before the arrival of the Denny-Terry-Boren party at Alki. Another son, John Wesley Maple, arrived in 1862. Settlers built a school in about 1863 on land given by Samuel Maple. That site now holds the King County Airport Boeing Field administration building. John Wesley Maple was the first teacher at that school. Of his experience he recalled, "I was often sorry that I had undertaken it as it was about the hardest work that I ever had undertaken to do in my life." In 1909 a Maple School was built up the hill near the site of today's Cleveland High School. In 1926, when construction began on Cleveland, Maple School was moved to 17th and Lucille Streets. In 1972 a new Maple School was built on Corson Avenue. The school is listed as being named for Samuel Maple, who originally gave school land but not the present site.

Maranatha SDA School, Seventh-Day Adventist, Route 2, Box 295, Usk, Grades 1-8 (Pend Oreille County). No longer listed in the Washington Education Directory. No information available.

Mariner High School, 200 120th S.W., Mukilteo School District, Everett (Snohomish County). Another of several schools in the Mukilteo School District whose names are associated with the U.S. space program. The year the school opened was not provided by the district.

Marion Elementary School, 134 N. Marion, Bremerton School District (Kitsap County). No information available.

Market Street School, 23rd and Jackson, Seattle School District (King County). Built in 1890 at a time when 23rd Avenue was called Market Street, this school was preceded by the Jackson Street School built on leased land across Market and to the north. The Market Street School eventually became known as Rainier School, which continued as an eight-grade elementary school until 1940 when most of its pupils were transferred to the Colman School. After remaining empty until 1943, it was reopened as the Building Trades Unit of the Edison Technical School. The Edison Technical School no longer exists. Most of its functions have been absorbed by the Seattle Central Community College.

Edwin Markham Elementary School, 4031 Elm Rd., Pasco School District (Franklin County). Named for Edwin Markham (1852-1940), American poet born in Oregon City. He is best known for *The Man with the Hoe.* For several years he worked as a school teacher and superintendent of schools in small California communities. It is customary in Pasco to name schools for writers. When this school was built in 1962, community opinions supported naming it for Markham.

Marquette Middle School, Roman Catholic, 212 N. Fourth St., Yakima Diocese, Grades 6-8 (Yakima County). Built in 1909 and 1910 and named for Father Jacques Marquette, French missionary, Jesuit priest, and explorer. With Louis Joliet, in 1673, he explored the Mississippi River. The driving force behind getting the Marquette School built was Father Conrad Brustin, pastor of St. Joseph Church in Yakima. Money subscribed for the construction of the school came largely from a part of the community having a French cultural heritage. Originally the school was called Marquette College and served boys from fifth grade to high school. In 1989 it was a co-educational middle school.

Marrion Elementary School, 10119 N.E. 14th St., Vancouver, Evergreen School District (Clark County). Built in 1968 and named for a local family having large land holdings in the area. Seth Marrion, a farmer, owned orchards in a part of the community once known as Ellsworth. He gave some of this land to the Evergreen School District for a school site. When that school became overcrowded, the land was divided into two parts. That part south of Mill Plain Avenue became known as Ellsworth. The land north of Mill Plain Avenue became the Marrion School area.

George C. Marshall Elementary School, 6400 MacArthur Blvd., Vancouver School District (Clark County). The first Marshall School was built in 1942, a one-story wooden structure on Mill Plain Boulevard between Morrison and Andersen Roads. This building was closed and torn down in 1953. In 1962 a second Marshall Elementary School was built at the present site. General George C. Marshall was chief of staff for much of World War 2 and secretary of state in President Harry Truman's cabinet. But this Vancouver school was named for him largely because he had served as a commander of the Fifth Infantry Brigade at the Vancouver Barracks from 1936 to 1938. There is an irony in locating a school named for George C. Marshall on a street named for General Douglas MacArthur. The two men were opposites in almost every way, and yet both were recognized as great military leaders.

John Marshall Intermediate School, 520 N.E. Ravenna Blvd., Seattle School District (King County). The school, named for a man who served as secretary of state in President John Adams' cabinet and as a precedent-setting chief justice of the U.S. Supreme Court from 1801 to 1835, was built in 1927. In the fall of 1971 Marshall School became an annex to Roosevelt High School, becoming known as Roosevelt "M." In 1989 Marshall was an alternative secondary school offering instruction for students who had not succeeded in the traditional secondary school setting.

Mason Middle School, 2812 N. Madison, Tacoma School District (Pierce County). Built in 1926 and named for Allen C. Mason, a Tacoma pioneer lawyer, former school principal, author of textbooks and teachers' guides, real estate developer, and railroad executive.

Matlock School District No. 87 (Whitman County). The land for this late 19th Century rural school was given by John and Norda Matlock.

Mattson Junior High School, 16400 S.E. 251st, Kent School District (King County). Mattson Junior High was named for the original family who settled on the property now occupied by the school. A Mattson still lived on that property when it was purchased by the Kent School District in 1979.

Mayfield School District No. 62, (Lewis County). Established in 1895 and named for early settler Henry C.

Mayfield. Later the community served by the school took the name Mayfield.

McAlder Elementary School, 15502 96th St. E., Puyallup, Sumner School District (Pierce County). The McAlder School was named after the merger in 1968 of two smaller schools named McMillin and Alderton. The Alderton School had been named for its community which, in turn, had been named for piles of alder logs along the local roadway awaiting shipment to the mill. The McMillin School had been named for John S. McMillin, president of the Roache Harbor Lime Co. operating in the area. In 1989 the old McMillin School was still in use as a Grange Hall.

In 1968 two Sumner area schools—McMillin and Alderton—were merged to form a new school—McAlder. This photo is of Alderton School, one of the two predecessor schools. (Photo from Ernest Louk, Pierce County Retired Teachers Association)

Christa McAuliffe Elementary School, 23823 N.E. 252nd, Redmond, Lake Washington School District (King County). Opened in 1990 and named for the teacher-astronaut killed in the 1986 Challenger spacecraft accident.

Christa McAuliffe Academy, Unaffiliated, 1125 Fruitvale Blvd., Yakima, all grade levels (Yakima County). Named for the teacher-astronaut killed in the Challenger space shuttle explosion on January 28, 1986, the school was started in the summer of 1988. The owners of this private school chose to name the school for Mrs. McAuliffe because she represented the kind of dedication and commitment to educational excellence that they wanted the school to reflect.

McCarty School, 6915 E. Fourth Plain Blvd., Vancouver School District (Clark County). When the McCarty and Vancouver School Districts consolidated in 1918, a school, formerly called McCarty, was renamed Roosevelt. Origin of the name McCarty does not appear to have been recorded. The building no longer exists.

McCarver Elementary School, 2111 S. "J" St., Tacoma School District (Pierce County). McCarver served as an intermediate school when it opened in 1925, then in 1928 as a junior high. In 1938, at the closure of Lincoln Elementary School, McCarver offered some elementary classes as well as junior high classes. Since 1968 it has been an elementary school. It was named for Morton Matthew McCarver, a Kentuckian by birth, who has been recognized as the father of the city of Tacoma. McCarver was a farmer, goldminer, and politician. He was elected to the Oregon legislature in 1844, to the California legislature in the 1860s. He developed the McCarver apple and grew horseradish as a cash crop. He bought the Carr claim in Tacoma in 1868 and in 1869 built the first clapboard house in what was to become Tacoma.

McClure Middle School, 1915 First Ave. W., Seattle School District (King County). Named in 1964 for Worth McClure, who had served in the Seattle School District from 1916 to 1944, the last 14 of those years as superintendent.

McClure Elementary School, 913 W. Second, Grandview School District (Yakima County). In 1978 Grandview High School moved into a new building, and what had been the old high school became an elementary school. The school board named this school for Clarence R. McClure, an educator in the Grandview District from 1944 to 1966. As an educator Mr. McClure was a leader in providing educational services to the children of migrant farm families. He offered such services long before that effort became a need recognized by state and federal agencies. He also was instrumental in starting an evening adult education program for persons seeking naturalized U.S. citizenship.

McClure Elementary School, 1222 S. 22nd Ave., Yakima School District (Yakima County). Built and named in 1951 for William L. McClure, who began his career at 19 as a teacher in the Swauk gold mining area of central Washington, an experience requiring book learning and boxing ability. He then taught at Central School in Yakima to earn funds to study for a career in medicine. In later life he served on the Yakima School Board and led a successful effort to institute a health program for students in the district.

McDermoth Elementary School, 409 N. "K" St., Aberdeen School District (Grays Harbor County). McDermoth School was built in 1930 and named for an Irish-born Methodist-Congregational minister who served in Aberdeen from 1885 to 1888. The Reverend McDermoth returned to Aberdeen in 1899, retiring from the ministry there in 1926.

McDonald Elementary School, 144 N.E. 54th St., Seattle School District (King County). The first unit of the McDonald School was under construction in 1913 when Judge F.A. McDonald, president of the Seattle School Board, died. The building was to have been named the Bryant School, but was instead named for the judge. F.A. McDonald came to Seattle after completing law school in Michigan, working in California, and becoming a land judge in Oregon. He arrived in the Green Lake area of Seattle most probably in the late 1880s. The school bearing his name opened in 1915 and has been closed for many years.

McDonald Elementary School, S. 1512 McDonald Rd., Spokane, Central Valley School District (Spokane County). McDonald was a valley pioneer who was involved in the formation of a water district primarily for irrigation. The small community of Veradale was named for McDonald's daughter, Vera. The McDonald School was built in 1956.

Robert B. McFarland Junior High School, 790 S. 10th, Othello School District (Adams County). Robert McFarland was principal of Othello Junior High School until his death from cancer in 1963. In 1964 a new junior high was built and named for him. During his career Bob McFarland was a prime mover in starting a number of youth activities in Othello. He was a leader in Boy Scouts, in organizing the Little League program, and in getting a swimming pool built. He also organized and taught Red Cross swimming lessons.

James W. McGee Elementary School, 4601 N. Horizon Dr., Pasco School District (Franklin County). On November 15, 1981, a dedicatory ceremony was held to name this school for James W. McGee (1926-1979), an outstanding teacher who taught sixth grade in the district for 21 years in a career of more than 30 years.

McIlvaigh Middle School, 1801 E. 56th, Tacoma School District (Pierce County). In 1963 the Tacoma School Board named this school for Harry S. McIlvaigh, a local labor leader who helped with many campaigns to pass the district's levy and bond election issues. He was secretary of the Central Labor Council for 30 years and was a co-founder of a local labor newspaper, *Union Advocate.*

McGilvra Elementary School, 1617 38th Ave. E., Seattle School District (King County). John J. McGilvra was a U.S. Attorney for the Territory of Washington in the Lincoln administration. Before he entered government service, he and Mr. Lincoln had had adjoining law offices in Springfield, Illinois. The experience as Washington Territory U.S. Attorney caused McGilvra to migrate to Seattle in 1864. Later, as a judge, McGilvra purchased 420 acres of land from the U.S. government and built the first home on the shore of Lake Washington. On December 2, 1891, the Seattle School Board authorized the purchase of Block 7 of John J. McGilvra's Second Home-

stead Addition. The Lake School was built on the property in 1899. In 1913 a new and larger building was under construction. In 1914 the school board changed the school's name from Lake to McGilvra.

McKinley High School, Emerson Avenue between Sixth and Seventh, Hoquiam School District (Grays Harbor County). Opened in 1892. School board minutes and newspaper accounts before 1900 refer to the school as "the schoolhouse" or "the high school." In 1903 a local city directory lists it as "McKinley School." President William McKinley was assassinated in 1901, and the school probably was named in his memory that same year. The school was dismantled in 1925.

McKinley Elementary School, 3702 McKinley Ave., Tacoma School District (Pierce County). The first Tacoma McKinley School opened in 1906 at E. "H" and Columbia. In 1908 a new school was built at the present site. The school is named for William McKinley (1843-1901), 25th president of the United States, who was shot by anarchist Leon Czolgosz near the beginning of his second term.

McKinley Elementary School, North 117 Napa Street, Spokane School District (Spokane County). This eight-room brick building opened for classes in 1903. A nine-room addition was completed that year. In 1917 a prevocational junior high program was added. In 1928 the junior high students were transferred to new junior high schools. In 1962 the McKinley School was closed and eventually sold as a storage warehouse to Spokane Transfer.

McKinley Elementary School, 1412 Grand Blvd., Olympia School District (Thurston County). The first Olympia McKinley School, named for the 25th president of the United States, was built in 1908. A new McKinley School was built in 1949. In 1989 McKinley students moved to the new Centennial Elementary School and McKinley was closed as an elementary school.

McKinley Elementary School, rural school southwest of Toppenish, Toppenish School District (Yakima

County). Built in the early 1920s and named for the 25th president of the United States, this school was closed in 1939. In 1949 it was purchased by a private college and completely remodeled. In 1990 it was part of the Heritage College campus outside Toppenish.

McKinley Elementary School, 621 S. 13th Ave., Yakima School District (Yakima County). Built in 1911 on 12th Avenue between Division and McLaren Streets. Enlarged over the years to become the largest school in the district. A new building was completed in 1976, and the old building was knocked down. McKinley was named for former President William McKinley.

John H. McKnight Middle School, 2600 N.E. 12th, Renton School District (King County). John Henry McKnight was a partner in Williams and McKnight General Merchandise and a member of the Renton School Board from 1923 to 1941. This school was named for him when it opened in 1954.

McLane Elementary School, 200 Delphi Rd., Olympia School District (Thurston County). The rural McLane School District consolidated with Olympia School District in 1966. The district and school were named for William McLane, pioneer landowner in the area. McLane not only turned over title to the school land to the McLane School District but, in 1883, also gave the district title to almost 10 acres for a McLane Cemetery "in trust for the use of the public for burial purposes only—conditioned that said cemetery shall be free to all without reference to color or creed...." The first McLane School was built in 1883, the fourth in 1942, and the current school in 1987.

McLoughlin Middle School, 5802 MacArthur Blvd., Vancouver School District (Clark County). The school was named for Dr. John McLoughlin, Canadian-born physician and chief factor for the Hudson's Bay Company in Oregon from 1824 to 1846. He established a fur-trading headquarters for the company at Fort Vancouver on the Columbia River in 1825. Part of the school was built in 1943. Substantial additions were made and the school was named for Dr. McLoughlin in 1956. It is said that Dr.

McLoughlin lost his job in 1846 because he was too accommodating to American settlers and missionaries. At the time Fort Vancouver was established there was no uncontested valid claim to the Pacific Northwest by either the American or British governments. American settlers came into the area and, welcomed there by Dr. McLoughlin, eventually turned the territory into the American West.

McLoughlin Junior High School, 2803 Rd. 88, Pasco School District (Franklin County). The building at North Third Street in Pasco, once called McLoughlin Junior High, was built in 1922 to serve as Pasco High School. When the present high school was built in 1953, the old high school became Pasco Junior High. The name McLoughlin Junior High was adopted in 1961 at the suggestion of Mr. Wilbert Mills' history class. The school is named for John McLoughlin (1789-1857), to honor the "chief factor" (manager) of the Hudson Bay Company outpost at Fort Vancouver on the Columbia River who had helped many settlers in the Pacific Northwest. In 1983 the students and the school's name were moved to a new building in West Pasco.

McManamon School, Othello (Adams County). The school, also known as Deadman's Bluff School, was built on property donated by the McManamon family at a site called Deadman's Bluff in memory of a cowboy who had ridden his horse off a cliff in the dark. No dates available on when this school opened and closed but it was probably in territorial days.

McMicken Heights Elementary School, 3708 S. 168th, Highline School District, Seattle (King County). This school was built in 1949 on the highest point in the Highline School District, almost 500 feet above sea level. The mound called McMicken Heights, on which the school sits, was named for Maurice McMicken. Young Maurice, born in 1860, came west from Minnesota with his family in 1874. His father was surveyor general of the Washington Territory. The family moved to Olympia. Maurice McMicken, by then a lawyer, moved to Seattle in 1881 where he became a law clerk with the firm of Struve and Haines. In 1890, with several partners, he incorporated the South Seattle Land Company, giving his name to a parcel of land that company was to develop.

McMurray Intermediate School, Route 2, Box 320, Vashon Island School District (King County). No information available.

Margaret Mead Elementary School, 1725 216th Ave. N.E., Redmond, Lake Washington School District (King County). Opened in 1980 and named for the noted American anthropologist Margaret Mead (1901-1978), author of *Coming of Age in Samoa.*

Meany Middle School, 301 21st Ave. E., Seattle School District (King County). The original school at this site was called Longfellow School, an eight-grade elementary built in 1902. There have been many additions and modifications since. By 1941 the school had been renamed for Edmond S. Meany, member of a pioneer family who became a professor of history at the University of Washington specializing in the history of Washington Territory and State.

Meeker Junior High School, 12600 S.E. 192nd, Renton, Kent School District (King County). Ezra Meeker came west to Washington Territory along the Oregon trail in 1852. In 1906, trying to stir interest in preserving the historic route to the West, he made the journey again— again behind a team of oxen. Along the way he painted inscriptions on landmarks. In 1910 he repeated the trip. In 1916 he retraced most of the trail by automobile, and, in 1924, at age 94, he did it again, this time by airplane. Meeker died in Seattle in 1928. His wagon has been in the Washington Historical Society Museum in Tacoma since 1915. In 1963 a batch of Meeker's private papers was found under the wagon floorboard. The Kent school was named for him in 1969 when it opened.

Meeker Elementary School, 409 Fifth St. S.W., Puyallup School District (Pierce County). Named for Ezra Meeker, an early pioneer in the valley and writer about his times. The school was first built in the 1930s and underwent major remodeling in 1977. Ezra Meeker platted and named the city of Puyallup. He also wrote a stirring defense of Chief Leschi, whom he believed to be innocent of the murder for which he was executed.

Meeker Middle School, 1526 51st St. N.E., Tacoma School District (Pierce County). The school was named in 1958 for a locally famous American Indian, Jerry Meeker. Meeker was born in 1863. His parents worked for Ezra Meeker. Eventually their son took Meeker as his last name. He was one of the first Tacoma Indians to attend the Indian school in Forest Grove, Oregon. Meeker became a land developer, held several offices in the reservation government, and represented the tribe in negotiations in Washington, D.C. In later years he became a well-known public figure in the Tacoma community.

Mellis School District No. 5, near Wapato (Yakima County). Established in 1912 by parents who split from the Parker Bottom School over some disagreement now forgotten. The school was named for a Northern Pacific Railroad siding, a flag stop and fruit loading spur named for the William Mellis family, settlers in the area in 1890. The Mellis School later was used as a Grange Hall and was subsequently torn down.

Asa Mercer Middle School, 1600 S. Columbian Way, Seattle School District (King County). Built in 1957 and named for Asa Mercer, first president of the Territorial University. In 1860 Mercer went to Lowell, Massachusetts, to recruit female teachers for the Seattle area. He brought nine of them back with him, one of whom, Lizzie Ordway, became a force in Washington education for many years. Mercer became so popular for helping to fill the local shortage of marriageable females, he was elected to the territorial legislature. On his second trip to the East to recruit females, he openly avowed that they would have multiple chances for matrimony. He married one of his recruits of the second trip.

Mercer School, Fourth Avenue North and Valley Street, Seattle School District (King County). Mercer

School was built in 1890 near the center of a community then known as North Seattle. The building was erected on part of the Thomas Mercer donation claim. Mr. Mercer was an early director of the school district. The Denny regrade project in the early 1900s caused the building to be closed as a school. But it was still used for school business, once as a training school for custodians, until 1948 when it was removed to make way for the school district's Administrative and Services Center.

Meridian Alternative Junior-Senior High School, Unaffiliated, 17011 Meridian Ave. N., Seattle, Grades 7-12 (King County). No information available.

Mill A School District No. 31, Mile Post 1.11 R Jessup Rd., Cook (Skamania County). The district has one school serving kindergarten through eighth grade. The school name is taken from the larger of two sawmills situated on a large flat on either side of the Little White Salmon River. Mill A was on the west side of the river, Mill B on the east side. The flat area on the Mill A side was larger and encouraged settlement of an area that became known as Mill A Flat. The school built to serve the children of this community became known as the Mill A School. It is still in operation.

George B. Miller Junior High School, 100 E. Lindstrom, Aberdeen School District (Grays Harbor County). The current Miller Junior High opened in 1979. The first Miller School opened at Fourth and "I" Streets in 1923. George Miller served as high school principal from 1910 to 1914. He then was superintendent from 1914 to 1930. During his time as superintendent he and a student association organized the financing for construction of the natatorium swimming pool and gymnasium at 820 Willard Street. That building also was named for George Burdette Miller in 1926. He died in 1930.

Miller School District No. 29, Daniels and Grunert Roads (Mason County). Captain Edward Miller donated land for a school built in 1894 and named for him. He had operated a school on his property for a few years before the official school district was formed. Captain

Miller began farming a donation land claim on Big Skookum Inlet in Mason County in 1853 at the age of 20. He married a local girl, Sarah Shepherd, in 1870. He acquired the title of Captain because in the 1880s and '90s he owned a sailing ship. He transported farm produce to logging camps along the waterways. He later built and operated several tugboats. In 1912 the Miller School was consolidated with Chapman's Cove District No. 7 and Cape Horn District No. 33. The eventual destiny of the Miller schoolhouse was not recorded.

William Winlock Miller High School, 1302 North St., Olympia School District (Thurston County). William Winlock Miller was a quartermaster during the Washington Territory Indian Wars. Later he invested in land in Thurston and Lewis Counties. His widow, Mary McFadden Miller, deeded Block 68 to the school district in Olympia at no cost. A condition of the gift was that the school to be built there would be named for her late husband. If the school was not so named, the property would revert to the Miller family. A Miller High School was built in 1907. It burned in 1918. A new William Winlock Miller High School was dedicated in 1919. In the late 1950s that school was no longer central to the population it served and was on property coveted for the state capitol campus. A new high school was needed at another location. Olympia Superintendent Roland Upton and Board Member Esther Knox drove to Seattle in 1958 to confer with Attorney Pendleton Miller, grandson of William Winlock Miller, about the reversionary clause in the property title at the old high school. Mr. Miller agreed that the property could be disposed of if the Miller name were transferred to another school and if there always would be a school in Olympia named for William Winlock Miller. That new school was built in 1961.

Nellie S. Milton Elementary School, Eastsound, Orcas Island School District (San Juan County). Nellie Sweeney became a teacher by passing a state teachers' examination when she was 16 upon her graduation from Friday Harbor High School in 1898. She taught in various

San Juan County schools and became county superintendent of schools in about 1914. She married Ben Milton, who operated a shingle mill in Bellingham and a still in West Sound, Orcas Island. He was sent to prison for moonshining. In 1932 Mrs. Milton returned to Orcas where she had lived as a child and where she had spent part of her teaching career. It is believed she came as teacher and principal of the Eastsound School. By 1937 she also was superintendent of schools on Orcas Island. She left Orcas for a teaching job in Richland in 1948 and from Richland to a private school in California in 1953. She died in McKinleyville, California, in 1972 at the age of 90. A new elementary school was built near Eastsound in 1948 and, in 1950, was named Nellie S. Milton Elementary in recognition of the many educational programs she had introduced to the children of Orcas. She returned to Orcas Island in 1950 for the dedication ceremony.

T.T. Minor Elementary School, 1701 E. Union, Seattle School District (King County). Named for Dr. Thomas Minor, born in 1844 on the Island of Ceylon. His missionary parents returned to the United States in 1852. Minor served on the Union side in the Civil War, emerging as a captain and assistant surgeon. He moved to the Washington Territory and served as mayor of Port Townsend at one time and later mayor of Seattle from 1886 to 1888. He also served on the Seattle School Board and, as a board member, proposed construction of four new schools. One of those new schools opened in the fall of 1890, less than a year after Dr. Minor's death. It was named in his honor. In 1941 a new brick structure replaced the old Minor School at the same site.

Minter Elementary School, 12617 118th Ave. N.W., Gig Harbor, Peninsula School District (Pierce County). An early settler named George Minter came to the northwest shore of Henderson Bay and bought a tract of land in about 1882. A school was built in the area in 1884, another school in 1888, and another school in 1907. Both of the latter two schools were known as Minter School and Elgin School. They went by both names. Origin of the Elgin name is not known, but it may be that of

another early settler. Classes were held in the 1907 school until the early 1940s. The building is now a private residence. A new Minter School was opened at the above address in 1986.

Mint Valley Elementary School, 2745 38th Ave., Longview School District (Cowlitz County). For many years the acreage in the west part of the Columbia Valley, an area diked against the Columbia River in 1923 when Longview was built, was planted in mint. When the crop was harvested for distilling, the fragrance wafted over the area. Development and crop disease in the early 1940s drove out the mint. But a school built in the area carries the name Mint Valley to remind people of that earlier period. The school was built in 1969.

Mizpah Gardens School, Unaffiliated, Route 1, Box 524, Raymond, Grades 1-11 (Pacific County). No information available.

Moby Dick Academy, Unaffiliated, Ocean Park, Grades K-12 (Pacific County). No information available.

Mockonema School District No. 25 (Whitman County). An early rural school that took its name from an Indian word for "little shoe."

Monroe Elementary School, 300 S. Monroe, Port Angeles School District (Clallam County). Built in 1949-1950, the school was named for James Monroe, fifth president of the United States. In 1990, the school was still in operation.

James Monroe Junior High School, 1810 N.W. 65th St., Seattle School District (King County). On February 2, 1931, James Monroe Junior High School opened its doors to 759 pupils. The building was designed by architect F.A. Naramore. The school was named for former U.S. President James Monroe.

Monroe Elementary School, 10901 27th Ave. S.E., Everett School District (Snohomish County). Opened in 1969, the school was named for the fifth president of the United States. The first Monroe School in Everett was built in 1893 in the 2700 block between Pine and Maple Streets. It was torn down after being damaged in a 1965 earthquake. The district's bus barn now occupies that site.

Monroe Elementary School, Eighth and Division, Yakima School District (Yakima County). In 1921 the old Capitol Hill School, built in 1908, was reopened as Monroe School, named for President James Monroe. It was abandoned and torn down in 1928.

Montessori Schools, a group of independent schools using an educational philosophy and instructional techniques developed by Maria Montessori (1870-1952) in Italy. Dr. Montessori, the first female physician to be graduated from an Italian university, was a psychiatrist. She opened a school for retarded children in 1907 that placed each child in a "manipulative environment," one in which the child was self-motivated by learning games. She later used the method successfully with normal preschoolers. She wrote extensively on her learning method. Montessori schools at various grade levels up to the sixth grade were operating in 1989 on Bainbridge Island, in Bothell, Lynnwood, Spokane, Seattle, Port Townsend, Richland, Federal Way, Burien, Sumner, Kirkland, and Gig Harbor.

Monticello Middle School, 28th and Hemlock, Longview School District (Cowlitz County). The first school founded in 1850 by settlers north of the Columbia River was at a site along the Cowlitz River. After 1852 the school district was identified as District 1, Washington Township in Lewis County, Washington Territory. Lewis County later was divided into Lewis and Cowlitz Counties. The school was built on Nathanial Stone's Donation Land Claim and took the name of the settlement it served—Monticello. The town, which had been named for Thomas Jefferson's home near Charlottesville, Virginia, was swept away by floods in 1867, but its name is preserved by Monticello Middle School in Longview, built in 1952 as a junior high and converted to a middle school serving Grades 6, 7, and 8 in 1978.

A new Moran Prairie School was opened in 1990. But there had been at least one earlier Moran Prairie School in the Spokane area. This photo appears to have been taken about 1910. (Photo from Eastern Washington State Historical Society, Spokane)

Moran Prairie Elementary School, East 4101 57th Avenue, Spokane School District (Spokane County). The latest Moran Prairie School opened in the fall of 1990. Named for Joseph F. Moran, pioneer farmer who settled the prairie that bears his name and whose home was a supply station for travelers.

Morgan Center School, 3423 Sixth St., Bremerton School District (Kitsap County). Operated by the Bremerton School District for residents of Francis Haddon Morgan Center, a state institution for children who are either autistic, emotionally disturbed, or mentally retarded with severe behavior problems. The Morgan Center School opened in 1973 and, like the Francis Haddon Morgan Center, was named for a former state senator and advocate of special education. Her mother was Lulu Davis Haddon, for whom another Bremerton school is named.

Morgan Middle School, 400 E. First Ave., Ellensburg School District (Kittitas County). John L. "Pop" Morgan held many jobs in the field of education, including membership on the faculty of Ellensburg Normal School. He earlier had been the last of the territorial superintendents of schools, having been appointed to that post in 1888 by Governor Eugene Semple. Morgan also was the first president of the Washington Education Association. At the time in 1934 that a new junior high school in Ellensburg was named for him, he was principal of Ellensburg High School. Educated at Furman University in South Carolina, Morgan came to Washington Territory right out of school to teach in Waitsburg and Ellensburg. He also was a principal in Waitsburg and superintendent of schools for Walla Walla County—all before statehood.

Mark Morris High School, 1602 Mark Morris Ct., Longview School District (Cowlitz County). Mark Morris was the nephew of R.A. Long, proprietor of Long Bell Lumber Co. He came to work for a Long Bell venture on the Columbia River in Washington State in 1922 with instructions from his uncle to build a town and a lumber mill. The name selected for the new city was Longview; however, the city planners found that there already was a Long View in Washington's Benton County. It was a whistle stop of only three families. The U.S. Post Office, however, recognized its name and delivered mail there. Long View residents agreed to give up their town's name in exchange for a new roofed mail-drop platform alongside the tracks. Mark Morris accepted the offer and authorized a company expenditure of $25 (more than $350 in 1989 U.S. money) to build the platform. Long View changed its name to Barger. When a new high school was built in Longview in 1956, the school board received a petition signed by hundreds of citizens recommending that the school be named for Mark Morris, the man who had bought the town its name. The Kate Felker Library in the high school was named for the wife of Mark Morris. In 1989 the school underwent substantial renovation.

Morrison School, rural Grant County near Moses Lake (Grant County). Named in 1906 for several Morrison families who had homesteaded the area in 1904. The school was on land then known as Morrison Flat, land donated for the school by one of the Morrison families. The school no longer exists. A school preceding the Morrison School was unnamed. It actually was the cabin of a bachelor homesteader who had little furniture and did not use his cabin during the day. So a local homesteader and teacher, Mrs. Emma Richard, convinced the bachelor to let her use his cabin as a schoolhouse during the day. He obliged.

Morrow School District No. 145 (Whitman County). Named for the school board's first clerk, W.C. Morrow. In early school districts the clerk was the chief executive officer.

Chief Moses Junior High School, 1517 S. Pioneer Way, Moses Lake School District (Grant County). Built in 1955, Chief Moses Junior High was named for an Indian chief famous in the Big Bend area of the Columbia River. The chief's name earlier was given to the lake for which the city is named. Chief Moses was one of the negotiators for Indian claims during and after the Indian Wars of the 1850s in Washington Territory. He and his followers were removed to the Colville Indian Reservation to live out the rest of their lives.

Moys School District No. 85 (Whitman County). A late 19th Century country school named for the school's first board clerk, C.R. Moys.

Muckleshoot Tribal School, Unaffiliated, 39015 172nd Ave. S.E., Auburn, Grades K-3 (King County). Opened in September, 1985, and named for the Muckleshoot Indian tribe which oversees the school's operation. "When the federal government established the reservation," wrote James F. Kolessar, principal/superintendent, in 1990, "they referred to it as the 'Muckleshoot Reservation;' consequently, all of the Native Americans living within its boundaries at that time, became known as Muckleshoot Indians." If the word "Muckleshoot" has a particular meaning, Mr. Kolessar did not give it.

John Muir Elementary School, 14012 132nd Ave. N.E., Kirkland, Lake Washington School District (King County). No response to query, but it is assumed that this John Muir is the same as the John Muir described below.

John Muir Elementary School, 3301 S. Horton St., Seattle School District (King County). The first school on this site was built in 1903 by a country school district outside the city limits. It was called Wetmore School, named for a pioneer family in the area. In 1907 the country school merged with the city schools. It was soon expanded and its name changed to York in recognition of the large English immigrant population in the region. In 1921 York Principal Jessie Lockwood was asked to suggest a new name for the school. She was an advocate of conservation of natural resources and an admirer of John Muir (1838-1914), Scottish-born American naturalist. She chose his name for the school.

Mullan Road Elementary School, E. 2616 63rd, Spokane School District (Spokane County). The first wagon road over the Rockies from Washington to Montana, Mullan Road was a military route built under the direction of Lt. (later Capt.) John Mullan, Army surveyor, between 1859 and 1862. It was 624 miles long from Fort Walla Walla in Washington to Fort Benton on the Missouri River in Montana. By the time it was completed, the military need for the road (Indian wars) was over. But its historic importance to Washington's Inland Empire, that part of Washington of which Spokane is the center, led to adoption of that name for a new Spokane elementary school in 1977.

Tom Mullen Grandstand, Third and Nelson, Sedro-Woolley School District (Skagit County). The grandstand at Greene Memorial Field was named for Tom Mullen, a much respected football coach at Sedro-Woolley High School from 1936 to 1945. The grandstand was built in 1965 with volunteer labor and donated lumber and other building materials. The dedicatory plaque reads "Tom Mullen: Football coach, educator, volunteer fireman. Later in fields of labor relations and apprentice training."

Mullenix Ridge Elementary School, 3900 S.E. Mullenix Rd., Port Orchard, South Kitsap School District (Kitsap County). This school opened September 5, 1990. It is named for a highway and a freeway intersection. The Mullenix family members were pioneers in South Kitsap. Mr. Mullenix was clerk of the South Kitsap County School District from 1895 through 1907.

Munger School, Unaffiliated, 4845 S.E. Horstman, Port Orchard, Grade 10 (Kitsap County). No information available.

N

Naches Trail Elementary School, 15305 Waller Rd., Tacoma, Bethel School District (Pierce County). In 1979 this school was opened and named for the first wagon road across the Cascade Mountains into Pierce County. In 1853 a wagon train of 180 persons from Indiana, Illinois, Iowa, Missouri, and Kentucky entered Pierce County after an 18-day trip from Selah on the east side of the Cascades. The Naches Trail is still accessible today to travelers on foot or horseback. Part of the old trail is followed by the Chinook Pass Highway. In 1990 a pyramid marker commemorating the early wagon train trail was alongside the roadway in the town of Greenwater on the Chinook Pass Highway 410.

Natural High School, 3602 Memorial Park Dr., Longview School District (Cowlitz County). This school was established in 1975 as an alternative high school for "at risk" students—students unlikely to stay in the traditional high school setting. The first students at this school named it Natural High, a reference both to the more relaxed atmosphere of the school and to the alternative of a "natural" versus a chemically induced "high" emotional experience.

Naval Avenue Elementary School, 900 Olympic Ave., Bremerton School District (Kitsap County). No information available.

Navy Yard City School, Bremerton School District (Kitsap County). No information available.

Nazarene Christian School, Traditional Christian, 940 Israel Rd. S.W., Tumwater, Grades K-4 (Thurston County). No information available.

Neely-O'Brien School, Kent School District (King County). No information available.

Gaylord Nelson Gymnasium (See Lake Roosevelt High School.)

Nelson-Crane SDA School, Seventh Day Adventist, 904 Shaw Rd., Puyallup, Grades 1-8 (Pierce County). This school was named in 1960 in honor of two lay members of the Puyallup Seventh Day Adventist Church: J. Clyde Nelson and Eugene Crane. The school began operation in the 1920s as the Puyallup Seventh Day Adventist School. Miss Luella Crane was a teacher at the school in the 1950s. At the time the school was on East Main adjacent to the golf course. When the school was moved to a new building on Shaw Road, it was named Nelson-Crane. Mr. Nelson was, among other things, a church historian. Mr. Crane was another active layman and the father of Teacher Luella Crane. Miss Crane declined to have the new school named for her but agreed to having it named for her father.

Fred Nelsen Middle School, 2403 Jones Ave. S., Renton School District (King County). Fred Nelsen (1872-1964) was a pioneer valley dairyman and civic leader in the Renton area. He was active in Grange and served as master of the state Grange at one time. The school was built in 1963 and named for Mr. Nelsen at a dedicatory ceremony in 1964, the year of his death.

Ness Elementary School, E. 9612 Cataldo, Spokane, West Valley School District (Spokane County). Named in 1954 for former West Valley Superintendent Arthur B. Ness.

New Market Vocational Skills Center, 7299 Armstrong Lane, Tumwater School District (Thurston County). This school name was selected for two reasons: (1) New Market was the original name of the settlement that later became known as Tumwater. Thus this school name is a way of preserving a part of the community's history. (2) The educational philosophy of this school is to prepare students for a new job market, to train them for entry-level jobs where they can expect to receive additional on-the-job training.

New Oklahoma School, Entiat (Chelan County). In September of 1917 a school was opened in the home of Herman Miller for the children of the Miller family and two other families in the area. By mid-October the school was completed and being used. It was named for the plateau on which it was situated which, in turn, had been named by a settler from Oklahoma. The lumber for the school came from the Gordon Mill on the stream below the school. It is not recorded when the school was closed but the building still stood in 1989 and was being used for hay storage.

Nile Christian School/Hope Academy, Traditional Christian, 11180 Nile Rd., Naches, Grades K-12 (Yakima County). A co-educational school started in 1984 at the Flying H Ranch. Hope Academy moved from Mabton in 1985 and covers Grades 7-12 for boys only. The Flying H Ranch and the schools were started by The Reverend Allen Hires. They are non-denominational. The name Nile comes from the road on which the school is situated.

Ninth Street Elementary School, 825 Commercial St., Raymond School District (Pacific County). No information available.

Noble Field, Centralia School District (Lewis County). A high school athletic field was dedicated to the memory of Elmer Noble in 1922. Noble had been an outstanding Centralia High School athlete and one of the first Central-ians killed in France during World War 1. Noble Field is now a part of the Centralia Community College campus. A new college building was under construction on part of the former athletic field in 1990.

Northern Lights School, at intersection of Independence Road with Garrard Creek Road, near Oakville (Grays Harbor County). The name of the school is said to have originated with its builder. He claimed he could see the Northern Lights while working on the building at night. It is not known when the school—an eight-grade grammar school—was built, but it was closed in 1933 and used for several years as a chicken house. It has since been torn down, and a house and large storage building occupied the site in 1990.

North Wall Primary School, Unaffiliated, N. 9408 Wall St., Spokane, Grades K-3 (Spokane County). Opened in 1983 as a child development center. In 1990, North Wall was a school for kindergarten through Grade 3. It was named for the street on which it is situated.

Northwest Yeshiva High School, Jewish, P.O. Box 1834, Seattle, Grades 9-12 (King County). No information available.

NOVA Alternative School, 2410 E. Cherry St., Seattle School District (King County). No information available.

O

Okanogan School District No. 73, also known as Ellisforde School, was just one of many country schools in that county in the early part of this century. The name came from G.H. Ellis and J.E. Forde, business partners in the area. (Photo from Henry Gilbert via Mildred Marchesseau)

O'Brien Elementary School, 6804 S. 212th, Kent School District (King County). In 1870 M.B. Maddox, who came to the Kent Valley in 1860, donated a school site at a point a quarter of a mile south of the O'Brien Bridge on the east side of the Green River, then known as the White River. A one-room school was built on the Maddox property, but it was not be be known as the Maddox School. Morgan and Terrance O'Brien—the O'Brien brothers—had arrived in the same part of the Kent Valley from Ireland in 1868. The school and townsite were both named for the O'Briens.

O'Dea High School, Roman Catholic, 802 Terry Ave., Seattle Archdiocese (King County). Opened in 1923 and named for Bishop Edward O'Dea of Seattle who was bishop at the time the school opened.

O'Dell School District No. 92 (Whitman County). Named for W. O'Dell, the first clerk of the school board. This is one of the 180 country schools started in Whitman County between 1872 and 1918. All have since been consolidated into other districts.

Odle Middle School, 14401 N.E. Eighth, Bellevue School District (King County). When M. Frank Odle retired in 1968 after 50 years as teacher, principal, and superintendent in Bellevue, the school board named a new junior high school in his honor. Mr. Odle, who was 80 years old when he retired, died a year later. The school has since been reorganized into a middle school.

Peter S. Ogden Elementary School, 8100 N.E. 28th St., Vancouver School District (Clark County). The present Ogden School is the second building to carry this name. The first one was occupied in 1955 but at a different location. On April 5, 1972, at about 12:45 p.m., a tornado demolished the old Ogden School. Although some students and teachers required hospitalization, none was fatally injured. In November 1973, the new Ogden School was opened. The schools were named for Peter Skene Ogden (1794-1854), a native of Quebec, the son of a Canadian chief justice. He studied law for awhile but gave it up. He worked in John Jacob Astor's New York office for a short period before deciding to take up the occupation of fur trader in the wilderness West. Ogden was the first white man to see the Great Salt Lake. He explored much of Idaho, Utah, Nevada, and northern California. He was very successful as a fur trader for the Hudson's Bay Company working out of their Fort Vancouver site. In 1847 he led a rescue party from Fort Vancouver to Fort Walla Walla to help the remaining whites still alive at the Whitman Mission after the massacre.

O.K. School, Toledo area (Lewis County). Closed for decades. Existed for many years as a residence. In 1989 Evelyn Hurd said that when she was on the O.K. School staff, she was the only teacher there. Her husband, Harvey Hurd, was Lewis County superintendent of schools in the 1940s. Origin of name is unknown to current local historians.

Okanogan County Schools (Okanogan County). Like most western counties in the settlement days, Okanogan pioneers formed a school wherever there were a dozen or so children in a five-mile square area. The names of these schools often reflect experiences of the times or the names of families instrumental in founding the schools. Among those names were Anderson (also known as Ellisforde), Balky Hill, Boston Heights (aka Pleasant Valley), Brewster Flat (aka Virginia City), Carlton, Cherokee, Chesaw, Chewiliken, Chiliwist, Circle, College Flat, Creveling, Culbertson, Cunningham, Disautel, Ellemeham, Ellisforde, Ferry, Fields, Frazier (or Frazer) Creek, French, Golden, Hasson (aka Beeman), Jaquish, Kipling, Knob Hill, Knowlton, Leese (aka Aeneas Valley), Monse, North Star, Olema, Pat Miller (aka Lower Pine Creek, and as Fate), Pogue Prairie, Poland China, Pontiac Ridge, Rader, St. Mary's Mission, Basin, Stokely, Sonnyslope, Synarep, Watson Draw, Windy Hill, Pig Liver, Brown (aka Bench Creek), Chewuch, Flour Mill, Siwash, Aeaneas (later called San Poil), Cummings, Bell-Pugh, Grafford Hall, Porter, Revard, Log School, Pasley, Hetch, Kartar Morris, Bedard B&O, O'Keefe, Sherman, Elbow Canyon. (Also see Tonasket.)

O'Keefe Primary School, Okanogan School District (Okanogan County). Named for Eliza O'Keefe, an early teacher in the Okanogan area. No dates were provided.

Robert L. Olds Junior High School, Connell (Franklin County). When a new junior high school was nearing completion in Connell, a contest was held to name the new school. A Mrs. Welch (no first name nor dates provided), who was a school library aide at the time, submitted the name of Robert L. Olds, who had helped in the establishment of the first school in the area many years earlier. Mr. Olds was born July 24, 1864, and died May 29, 1946. Many of his line still live in the Connell area. An election was held and Mr. Olds' name was selected for the school.

Ontario School District No. 129 (Whitman County). No reason given for naming this early Whitman County rural school. It may have been named for someone's hometown or home Canadian province. The school no longer exists.

Open Window School, Unaffiliated, 5225 119th S.E., Bellevue (King County). No information available.

Orchard Ridges School, corner of Radar and Franks Roads, Sunnyside School District (Yakima County). Built in 1915 and named Orchard Ridges because of the nearby orchards in the valley. The school was closed in 1926 and sold in 1932 to The Church of Christ. In 1989 the building was a part of The Church of Christ at 13th and Edison.

Ordway Elementary School, 8555 Madison Ave. N.E., Bainbridge Island School District (Kitsap County). Ordway Elementary School opened its doors in 1978. It was named for Elizabeth Ordway, one of the women brought to Seattle from Lowell, Massachusetts, by Asa Mercer in 1864. The 11 young women who became known as the "Mercer girls" were welcomed in the female-scarce early days of Seattle. Most became school teachers and all but one married in Seattle. That one was

Lizzie Ordway. Instead of homemaker, she became a moving force in public education in the Washington Territory. She first taught in a school in Coupeville, then Port Madison, Seattle, Port Gamble, and Port Blakely. In 1881 she ran for Kitsap County school superintendent and won 244 to 165. The Seattle *Post-Intelligencer* opposed her election editorially, remarking "It may be a good joke to put a woman in nomination, but I do not regard the office of school superintendent of so little importance as to vote for a woman at the polls." In 1891 she returned to Seattle and assisted in the preparation of the state's educational exhibit at the Chicago Fair of 1893. She died in 1897 and is buried in Seattle.

John A. Osborn Elementary School, 225 Central Ave., Leavenworth, Cascade School District (Chelan County). John A. Osborn was a teacher, coach, and later superintendent from 1914 to 1937. The school was named for him in 1952 when the building was dedicated.

Osceola School in Lewis county in about 1890. (Photo from Lewis County Historical Museum via Elizabeth Wedin, Lewis County Retired Teachers Association)

Osceola School, on Cowlitz Prairie midway between Toledo and Vader (Lewis County). An early school now closed. It was consolidated with the O.K. School and the Turner School, dates uncertain. Origin of the name was not recorded.

Our Lady of Fatima School, Roman Catholic, 3301 W. Dravus, Seattle Archdiocese, Grades 1-8 (King County). No information available.

Our Lady of Guadalupe School, Roman Catholic, 3401 S.W. Myrtle St., Seattle Archdiocese, Grades K-8 (King County). The church was named in 1960 by then Seattle Archbishiop Thomas A. Connolly. The school was dedicated in March of 1963. Our Lady of Guadalupe is the Patroness of the Americas. For more than 400 years the story of how she appeared to a humble Mexican peasant on Mount Tepeyac has been a cherished tradition of the Catholic Faith. *Lives of the Saints* identifies Our Lady of Guadalupe as an apparition of Mary, mother of Jesus, to Juan Diego, an Indian convert. The event took place near Mexico City on December 9, 1531. There is a shrine marking the place.

Our Lady of the Lake School, Roman Catholic, 3520 N.E. 89th St., Seattle Archdiocese, Grades K-8 (King County). Opened in 1949. In 1990 Sister Dolores Crosby, principal, said of the school's name, "The history of its name goes back many centuries in the Catholic Church and spans every continent where people have sought to honor the Mother of Jesus with a title proclaiming her a patroness of their particular area—obviously one near a lake." She noted that the full name of Notre Dame University was Notre Dame du Lac (Our Lady of the Lake).

Our Lady of Lourdes School, Roman Catholic, 10211 12th Ave. S., Seattle Archdiocese, Grades K-8 (King County). No longer listed in the Washington Education Directory.

Our Lady of Lourdes School-St. James School, Roman Catholic, 4701 Franklin, Vancouver, Seattle Archdiocese (Clark County). This school traces its history back to the beginning of Catholic education in the Vancouver area. In 1856 Mother Joseph and her four Sisters of Providence began a day school, an orphanage, and a hospital. In 1956 Our Lady of Lourdes-St. James School opened, representing two parishes and named for both. The name Our Lady of Lourdes refers to St. Bernadette's visions of Mary at Lourdes, France. There are three different St. James listed in *Lives of the Saints.* Which St. James the school was named for was not identified by school authorities.

Our Lady of Perpetual Help School, Roman Catholic, 2617 Cedar St., Everett, Seattle Archdiocese, Grades K-8 (Snohomish County). No information available.

Our Lady of the Sacred Heart School, Roman Catholic (Cowlitz County). Operated by the Sisters of Providence from September 12, 1876, to June 16, 1889. The sisters came to the school in response to a plea to staff a small mission day school originally taught by a lay teacher. The school later had to be closed for lack of enrollment and financial support. It was named for the heart of Mary, the mother of Jesus, as a symbol of her love for humankind.

Our Lady of Seven Dolors School, Roman Catholic, Tulalip (Snohomish County). The school was operated by the Sisters of Providence from August 11, 1868, to July 16, 1901. It was established on the Tulalip Indian Reservation as a mission school for Indian girls. Although classified as an "industrial school," Our Lady offered a liberal education curriculum. A federal law abolishing all sectarian schools on Indian reservations caused the school to close in 1901. The school's name, "Our Lady of Seven Dolors," recalls the seven sorrows experienced by Mary as the mother of Jesus.

Our Lady Star of the Sea School, Roman Catholic, 1513 Sixth St., Bremerton, Seattle Archdiocese, Grades K-8 (Kitsap County). Founded in 1926 by the Sisters of St. Dominic, Dominicans of Edmonds. No explanation of the name was provided.

Our Redeemer Lutheran School, 805 Yelm Ave. E., Yelm, Grades K-8 (Thurston County). No information available.

Outlook Elementary School, Van Belle and North Outlook Roads (Yakima County). The origin of the name Outlook is in doubt. One version is that parents in the area named their local school Outlook at the turn of the century to depict the school's vision of a glorious future. Another version is that a Mr. Granger, a pioneer settler, stood on Snipes Mountain and looked out over the land and proclaimed the area Outlook. A third version is that the view from the ranch of another pioneer—E.W. Dooley—was an expanse of sage brush, an "outlook" used by the railroad to identify its nearby rail siding. Perhaps the school's most illustrious eighth-grade graduate was Bonnie Dunbar, one of the first female astronauts in the U.S. space program. The school was consolidated into the Sunnyside School District in 1944 and was still in use in 1989.

Overlake School, Independent, 20301 N.E. 108th, Redmond, Grades 6-12 (King County). No information available.

Morgen Owings Elementary School, 407 E. Woodin Ave., Chelan School District (Chelan County). Morgen Owings served as superintendent of the Chelan School District from 1944 to 1952. He was superintendent through the planning and building of the school named for him in 1948.

The first Packwood School in Lewis County opened in 1890. (Photo from Lewis County Historical Museum via Elizabeth Wedin, Lewis County Retired Teachers Association)

P

Packwood School, up Hanaford Creek near Centralia (Lewis County). Built in 1875 in part by David Hilpert, this was a log cabin school. Who Packwood was or why the school was named for him or her is not known. However, this is a different Packwood School than the one in the town of Packwood in eastern Lewis County. In 1911 the log cabin Packwood School was sold to a Rheinholt Hilpert, likely a relative of David Hilpert. Rheinholt lived in the old schoolhouse for many years. In 1989 the building still existed but not on the same site.

Paine School, S. Fourth St., Walla Walla School District (Walla Walla County). Built in 1928 and named for F.W. Paine, a member of the first consolidated Walla

Walla School District board of directors in 1880. Today's Paine School is a center for alternative education programs for persons from preschool ages to adults. The first Paine School was built on the present site in 1888. The top floor of that school became Walla Walla High School in 1890. In 1902 Paine was renamed Lincoln School and continued under that name until the building was torn down in 1927 and replaced with the present building.

Pampa School District No. 84 (Whitman County). No reason given for this name. This was one of the early Whitman County rural schools that has since been consolidated with a larger district.

Pan Terra Alternative School, 2800 Stapleton Rd., Vancouver School District (Clark County). Pan Terra comes from the Greek word pan, meaning "all," and the Latin word terra meaning "earth" or "environment." In September 1974, this alternative school became a reality, as envisioned by the Clark County Juvenile Justice Planning Commission, under the sponsorship of the Vancouver School District. It has occupied the present site since 1978. The first high school graduation commencement was held in 1975.

Floyd Paxton Elementary School, Unaffiliated, 1340 Avon Allen Rd., Mount Vernon, Grades K-9 (Skagit County). Founded in 1976 by Mrs. Joan Bogensberger, the school was closed in 1989. In 1990 the school was operating as a private educational resource center under the name Mrs. B's Educational Service. Paxton School was named for the late Floyd Paxton, resident of Yakima and inventor of the plastic fastener (Kwik Lock) used to keep plastic bread wrappers and other plastic bags closed. Mrs. Bogensberger admired Mr. Paxton for his success under the American free enterprise system and his political support of issues he felt promoted the republican form of government. The lessons at the Paxton School often stressed patriotism. Special student-performed musical programs were offered at Thanksgiving, Christmas, and Easter.

Hilder Pearson Elementary School, 15650 Central Valley Rd. N.W., Poulsbo, North Kitsap School District (Kitsap County). Built in 1952 and named for Hilder Pearson Johnson, daughter of John Pearson, Swedish immigrant and head of a prominent family in the Keyport area. The family's immediate community became known as Pearson. Daughter Hilder attended Broadway High School in Seattle and Bellingham Normal School. She taught school in Yelm and Poulsbo during the 1940s and '50s. She became principal of an elementary school that was later to be given her name at the suggestion of former pupils. She later served on the North Kitsap School Board.

Perkins Elementary School, Unaffiliated, 4649 Sunnyside Ave. N., Seattle, Grades 1-6 (King County). Perkins Musical Kindergarten was started by Mrs. E. Louise Perkins in 1946. In the 1970s Mrs. Perkins retired and her business partner continued to run the operation

under the name Perkins School for Children. The elementary school began in 1976 and became a non-profit organization for Grades 1-6. In 1989, Perkins School for Children was also a privately owned preschool, kindergarten, and daycare center.

Penewawa School District No. 30 (Whitman County). Another of the early rural schools in Whitman County; this one was given an Indian name but no translation.

Phillips Building, Aberdeen School District (Grays Harbor County). Judge James Marston Phillips of Aberdeen served his community as secretary of the Grays Harbor Labor Council, mayor, police judge, superior court judge, and state legislator. Judge Phillips was born in Colletsville, North Carolina, a Cherokee Indian. He attended Dickinson Law School and Carlisle Indian School in Pennsylvania where he played football. He also played football at Northwestern University, earning a place on the All-Star Western Team, predecessor of All-American honors. He came West in 1904 and coached football at Whitworth College when that school was in Tacoma. Shortly thereafter he and his wife moved to Aberdeen where he lived until his death in 1959. A school building in Aberdeen, a part of the Weatherwax High School campus, was named for him in 1963.

Wendell Phillips School, southwest of Sunnyside, School District No. 92, Yakima Valley (Yakima County). The first unit of this school was built in 1905. School board minutes of February and March of 1911 show that bids were let for a new concrete block structure. Another unit was built in 1919 and another in 1921. The name change from Central to Wendell Phillips was voted at the school board meeting of March 2, 1912. That name was selected over two other names suggested: Green Valley and Riverside. The Wendell Phillips School served as grade and high school through 1920 and continued as a grade school until 1966. In 1967 the school and grounds were sold and the buildings dismantled; and now private dwellings share the area. The school was named for Wendell Phillips (1811-1884), an American reformer born in

Boston. He is ranked with Edward Everett and Daniel Webster as an orator. He was a delegate to the World Anti-Slavery Convention in London in 1840. He opposed the Mexican War and the annexation of Texas. He advocated dissolution of the Union and denounced slaveholding. He believed that the government owed to the black slaves not only freedom but land, education, and full civil rights. Phillips also advocated prohibition of alcoholic beverages, equal voting rights for women, abolition of capital punishment, reform of currency, and recognition of organized labor.

Phoenix Center for Individual Education, 3516 Rucker Ave., Everett School District (Snohomish County). An alternative school for students who might otherwise drop out of school. This program was organized in 1971 under the name "alternative education." It was housed in the old Roosevelt School until 1981. That year it moved to another old school formerly known as South Junior High and then as Port Gardner Middle School. Students in "alternative education" renamed the building and the program Phoenix Center for Individual Education. The name Phoenix connotes a new beginning. It comes from an ancient legend about a huge bird that lived 500 years and then burned itself on a pyre, arising from the ashes as a new, young Phoenix.

Franklin Pierce High School, 11002 18th Ave. E., Tacoma, Franklin Pierce School District (Pierce County). The school was constructed in 1952 and named for Franklin Pierce, the 14th president of the United States (1853-1857) who was in office when the Washington Territory was formed.

Pietrzycki High School, 614 S. Third, Dayton School District (Columbia County). On April 20, 1923, the cornerstone was laid for a new high school in Dayton. The name of the new school honored Marcellus Marcus Pietrzycki, M.D. and community benefactor, whose interest in educating youth led him to bequeath about $140,000 to the school district to establish a "trade" school. Dr. Pietrzycki (1843-1910), an Austrian native of

Polish descent, came to the United States in 1866. Trained as an apothecary, Pietrzycki completed medical school in the United States. In April, 1880, he brought his family to Dayton, Washington Territory, and established a medical-surgical practice. As county health officer, Dr. Pietrzycki was instrumental in subduing the smallpox epidemic of 1881. In 1984 the high school bearing his name was completely refurbished inside. The original exterior architecture was preserved, the cornerstone and portico still bearing the Pietrzycki name even though the school is more familiarly known in the community as Dayton High School.

Pilchuck School District No. 9, Lake Stevens (Snohomish County). Established on April 14, 1879, the district was named for an Indian word for red water, as was the Pilchuck River and Mount Pilchuck. In 1882 a board of teacher examiners was created. That board hired Lizzie Anderson, the first teacher in that district to have graduated from a normal school. Today in the Lake Stevens School District there is a Mount Pilchuck Elementary School at 11806 20th Street N.E. The original Pilchuck School existed as early as 1877, but no records have been found that locate the site of that early school.

Pitt School District No. 55 (Whitman County). Another of the late 19th Century and early 20th Century schools in Whitman County. This one was named for William R. Pitt, who owned the land on which the school was built. He also had a local post office named for him. The school no longer exists.

Pope Elementary School, 15102 122nd Ave. E., Puyallup School District (Pierce County). Built in 1979, this school was named for Florence Pope, director of elementary schools in Puyallup for more than 20 years. She retired in the mid-1970s.

Pratt Elementary School, E. 6903 Fourth Ave., Spokane School District (Spokane County). Opened in 1948 and originally called Edgecliff Elementary, this school was later renamed Pratt Elementary after O.C. Pratt, superintendent of schools in Spokane from 1916 to

1943. In 1958 a new building replaced the original school.

Praxel Alternative School, a home school, Mile Marker, Queets, Queets-Clearwater School District (Jefferson County). Praxel Alternative School was established in 1985 by Edward Praxel, a teacher in the Queets-Clearwater School District. Mr. Praxel is certified by the state to teach his younger daughter in their home. In 1989, his daughter, a victim of cerebral palsy, was being taught in the Praxel home. The local school district did not have the resources to teach this special child. Mrs. Praxel is a physical therapist. Several other district children having special educational or therapy needs also have been served by the Praxel School.

Providence Academy, Roman Catholic, Vancouver (Clark County). Often identified as the "first permanent school in the Pacific Northwest" since the earlier school established at Monticello was swept away by floods in 1867. Providence Academy was established in 1856 by the Sisters of Providence, a community of "women religious" founded in 1843 by Emilie Tavernier Gamelin in Montreal, Canada. The school was in operation from December 8, 1856, to August 4, 1966. The present academy building was designed and built by Mother Joseph of the Sacred Heart, Sisters of Providence, in 1873. The building is on the National Register of Historic Places. It is currently used for offices, shops, and a restaurant.

The first Providence Academy in Vancouver was opened in 1856 in a rude but practical small building. (Photo from Sisters of Providence Archives, Seattle)

Mary Purcell School in Sedro-Woolley had been just completed when this photo was taken in 1952. (Photo from Eloise Stendal, Skagit-Island-San Juan Counties Retired Teachers Association)

Proyecto Saber School, 2600 S.W. Thistle St., Seattle School District (King County). No information available.

Carl Puckett Junior High School, Academy Street, Kelso School District (Cowlitz County). The first Kelso Junior High School was built in 1928 and named Puckett for a former school principal in the district. Puckett Junior High was built on the site of the old Presbyterian Academy. The school has since been torn down.

Mary Purcell School, Seventh and Bennett Streets, Sedro-Woolley School District (Skagit County). Mary Purcell Elementary School was completed in 1951 and named for a long-time teacher and principal of the area. Miss Purcell was born in St. Alfonse, Quebec, in 1873. She came to Skagit County at the turn of the century and to Sedro-Woolley in 1902 as a teacher at Franklin School. She became the school's principal in 1909. In 1925 she was named principal of both Franklin and Irving Schools, neither of which is still in existence. She retired in 1947

and died in 1957 after an active life as teacher, principal, member of Immaculate Heart of Mary Catholic Church, member of the Washington State Retired Teachers Association, and member of Skagit County Board of Education.

Purdy School District No. 103 (Whitman County). Also called Union School District. No reason given for either name. This school no longer exists.

Quakerville School District No. 63, Entiat (Chelan County). In 1906 business enterprises seeking settlers in central Washington organized as the Company Ranch and secured financing from the Waterville Bank. The group advertised in the eastern United States extolling the fruit-growing opportunities on land near Entiat. About 100 followers of the Society of Friends, a religious sect commonly called Quakers, responded. Soon after their arrival, they built a school and meeting hall. The school was closed in 1909 and consolidated with Harris Mill

School District No. 21. It is not known whether these settlers called their school and settlement Quakerville but it became known by that name. In 1991 a remodeled Quakerville School was being used as a private residence.

Queen of Angels, Roman Catholic, 1007 S. Oak St., Port Angeles, Seattle Archdiocese, Grades K-8 (Clallam County). Established in 1926, the school originally was staff by Sisters of St. Anne of Victoria, B.C. In the 1950s the teachers were Sisters of St. Joseph. By 1989 the school was staffed by lay teachers. Queen of Angels is a reference to Mary, mother of Jesus.

Quileute Tribal School, Unaffiliated, LaPush, Grades K-8 (Clallam County). No information available.

Irene S. Reed High School of Shelton was torn down in 1986 and is now the site of a public library. (Photo from Lorna Dayton, Mason County Retired Teachers Association)

Ray's Ferry - Hackaberry Hollow School, (Asotin County). Also known as District No. 5, Hackaberry Hollow School was sited in the rugged and remote Grande Ronde River areas of south central Asotin County. The school district was organized in May 1885. Access to the area was by horseback or foot only for many years. The Hackaberry Hollow School was replaced by a new building in 1927 and renamed Ray's Ferry School to honor Charles A. Ray, a pioneer settler who had built and operated a ferry boat on the Grande Ronde. The school was closed for lack of students in 1942. In 1983 the building was moved 30 miles to the town of Asotin. Its new site is next to the Asotin County Historical Museum. The school

has been restored and in 1991 was still a popular attraction for visitors and residents.

Irene S. Reed High School, Seventh and Alder, Shelton School District (Mason County). Irene Simpson was born on March 18, 1877, in Carson City, Nevada, the eldest daughter of Sol G. and Mary Simpson. The Simpson family moved to Mason County in 1888, living in New Kamilche. Sol Simpson organized the Simpson Logging Company. In 1901, Irene married Mark E. Reed, a Simpson Company employee. Irene became a Shelton School Board member in 1909 and remained on the board until her death in 1940. In 1922, when a high school was badly needed in Shelton, Mark Reed made a gift of the school to the city in honor of his wife. The new two-story brick building was dedicated on January 12, 1924. It was used as a high school and later as a warehouse for school purposes until 1975. In 1986 the building was torn down, the stones bearing the school name being saved and re-erected in the parking lot of a new library built on the site in 1989.

Reed Elementary School, 1802 S. 36th St., Tacoma School District (Pierce County). Named in 1951 for Dr. Jennie Reed, long-time teacher, principal, and director of educational research. She was noted throughout the Northwest for the psychological testing program she developed in the 1920s and 1930s. She began her career in Tacoma in 1910. She retired in 1941 but returned in 1945 for one year as a principal.

Reese School District No. 177 (Whitman County). An early rural school named for the school board's first clerk, H.S. Reese. No longer in operation.

Reeves Middle School, 2200 N. Quince, Olympia School District (Thurston County). In 1968 the Northeast Junior High was renamed as a memorial to Wilfred L. Reeves, who for more than 40 years was an educator in the Olympia schools. He was a teacher and had served as principal at McKinley, Roosevelt, and Washington Schools. In 1969 the new Reeves School opened.

Regal Elementary School, E. 2707 Rich Ave., Spokane School District (Spokane County). Despite its current address, Regal School is also situated on Regal Street and in 1915 was named for that street. The school was built and opened in 1907 and bore only the name "High School" for the first year. In 1908 it was named Hillyard High School after the township it served. Hillyard was named after the rail yards and shops of the Great Northern Railroad and its president, J.J. Hill. In 1915 the high school was renamed South Regal and turned into an elementary school. In 1912 a new Hillyard High School was built nearby and, in 1932, another new high school was built, this one named John Rogers High. In 1924 the citizens of Hillyard had voted to annex to the city of Spokane. Their schools became a part of the Spokane School District. In 1926 the word "South" was dropped from the name of South Regal Elementary School.

Robert W. Reid Laboratory School, 210 Seventh St., Cheney School District (Spokane County). When the Washington State legislature created Cheney Normal School, a teacher-training institution, in 1890, a campus elementary school was planned to give student teachers practical experience in the classroom. That training school was opened in 1892 in the old Pomeroy Building on First Street in Cheney. It was moved several times before 1897, the year the normal school (and its campus training school) were closed for lack of funds. The legislature had failed to appropriate any money for the school's operation. It was to remain closed until 1899 when the legislature again found support money. The training school also reopened that year in a building of its own. The training school was separated from the normal school in 1911 and operated as an independent school. It became part of Cheney Public Schools in 1921. A new training school was built in 1933. In 1937 Cheney Normal School became Eastern Washington College of Education and the elementary training school became known as a laboratory school. Robert W. Reid became principal in 1953 and, with the school staff, developed a building plan designed to be an ideal laboratory school. The new building was completed in 1959. In 1977 the school was renamed Robert W. Reid Laboratory School.

Irene Reither Primary School, 954 E. Hemmi Rd., Everson, Meridian School District (Whatcom County). Irene Reither was born in Whatcom County in 1915 and, after being trained at Bellingham Normal School, began teaching at Beach School, Lummi Island, in 1935. She taught for 41 years, 40 of them in the first grade in the Meridian School District. Upon her retirement from Meridian Primary School in 1976, the school board renamed the building for her. In 1989 she was still serving as a school volunteer at Reither School every Thursday.

Gildo Rey Elementary School, 1005 37th St. S.E., Auburn School District (King County). Originally this school was named South Auburn Elementary when it was opened in 1969. It was renamed in 1978 for its first principal, a man who served as an educator for more than 40 years and who helped design this school's original floor plan.

Ricketts Elementary School, 9816 N.E. 183rd St, Bothell, Northshore School District (King County). Built in 1949 and named for Dr. George Ricketts, a dentist and Bothell resident for 35 years. Dr. Ricketts was elected to the Bothell School Board in 1948 when the district began building its first primary school. The Ricketts Building was being used for the district's administrative offices in 1990.

Riffe School (Lewis County). Established sometime before 1898 at which time the community was named for the school. The school was named for Floyd L. Riffe, not further identified but likely a farmer who gave land for the school.

Riggs School District No. 128 (Whitman County). This early rural school was named for one of the first school directors, S.H. Riggs.

Borghild Ringdall Middle School, 11650 S.E. 60th, Bellevue School District (King County). Norwegian-born Borghild Ringdall was a founding director of the Overlake School District, predecessor to the Bellevue School District. As a member of the Parent-Teacher Association, she organized a hot lunch program in the schools. When the school district took over operation of the food service program in 1947, Mrs. Ringdall was hired as its director. She retired from the school district in 1968, and a school was named for her in 1970. She died in 1979. In 1989, Ringdall School was no longer in use as a school.

Robertson Elementary School, 2807 W. Lincoln, Yakima School District (Yakima County). Built in 1958, this school was named for W.W. Robertson, owner and editor of the Yakima Herald and Republic newspapers.

Hamlin Robinson School, Unaffiliated, 10211 12th Ave. S., Seattle, Grades 1-6 (King County). An independent elementary school for children having difficulty with reading, writing, and spelling (dyslexia). Founded in 1983 and named for Hamlin Robinson. Mr. Robinson was a native of Yakima and a graduate of the University of Washington in 1937, with a masters degree from Columbia University in 1939. He spent most of his career working for the federal government in the Treasury and State Departments. His wife, a teacher and psychologist, was one of the founders of the Hamlin Robinson School soon after his death in 1982. Mr. Robinson was the first chairman of the Slingerland Institute founded in Seattle in 1978 to train public and private school teachers in the Slingerland technique of instructing dyslexic children.

Ron Robinson Field, Oakesdale High School, Oakesdale School District (Whitman County). The high school athletic field at Oakesdale was named for Ron Robinson in 1973. Robinson was an excellent student and athlete at Oakesdale. He was killed in a farm machinery accident the summer before his senior year.

Norman Rockwell Elementary School, 11125 162nd Ave. N.E., Redmond, Lake Washington School District (King County). Named in 1981 for Norman Rockwell (1894-1978), American illustrator especially remembered for depicting small-town America on the cover of the *Saturday Evening Post* magazine.

Roeder School, 1306 Dupont St., Bellingham School District (Whatcom County). Named after Captain Henry Roeder, who, with Russell Peabody, landed on the shores of Bellingham Bay in 1892. They settled at the mouth of Whatcom Creek where they built a sawmill. Roeder took claim to land which later became the town of Sehome. There has been a school at this site for many years; the building still there in 1990 opened as an elementary school in 1908. It also served briefly as a junior high school and in 1990 was being used for district administrative offices. Dr. James Roberts, retired superintendent of Bellingham Schools, once was a student at Roeder and later a teacher at the same school.

Clara E. Rogers Elementary School, Seventh-Day Adventist, Fourth and Bade Streets, College Place (Walla Walla County). Named sometime between 1945 and 1951 for Clara E. Rogers, born in Waitsburg in 1877 and a long-time teacher at Walla Walla College. The Rogers School is on the campus of the college. Miss Rogers was a graduate of and a teacher at the college from 1906 to 1941 and served as a tutor until her death in 1951. As both student and teacher, she spent 55 years at Walla Walla College. In 1945 she was married to Birdette Wilson.

John Rogers Elementary School, 200 Norris Rd., Vancouver School District (Clark County). John Rankin Rogers (1838-1901) was a newspaperman, state legislator, and governor of the state of Washington. He is often remembered for having sponsored a bill which became the "Barefoot School Boy" law. This statute provided tax dollars to support country schools and made education available to children living in rural areas. When this Rogers Elementary School opened its doors in 1945, it was known as Fourth Plain Village School (named for a wartime housing project built for shipyard workers' families). Principal Gordon Gardner immediately applied to the superintendent of schools to have the name changed to either John Ball (the first teacher at Fort Vancouver) or John Rogers.

John Rogers Elementary School, 4030 N.E. 109th St., Seattle School District (King County). The first school in the area now served by Rogers School was the Pontiac School, built in 1890. It served the Pontiac community located not far south of Matthews Beach. Matthews School, the forerunner of Rogers School, opened in October, 1953, on a nine-acre site that had once been a hog farm. In 1954 the name of Matthews School was changed to Rogers to honor an early state governor. The change caused some local controversy.

Rogers Elementary School, 1301 E. 34th, Tacoma School District (Pierce County). Named for John R. Rogers, an early governor who died in office. McKinley School, built by District No. 93, was annexed to Tacoma School District in 1904. In 1906 its name was changed to Rogers. In 1907 a new school was built at the present site

and opened for classes in February, 1908. The widow of Governor Rogers attended the opening ceremonies of the new school.

Governor John Rogers High School, 12801 86th Ave. E., Puyallup School District (Pierce County). Named in 1968 for a former state governor, John R. Rogers. Governor Rogers is buried in a Puyallup cemetery. His association with state support for education probably accounts for why so many schools in Washington State were named for him. Mr. Rogers was a legislator from Puyallup when elected governor in 1896.

John R. Rogers High School, E. 1622 Wellesley, Spokane School District (Spokane County). Opened in 1932 and named for early Governor John Rogers. Only one other Washington State governor, Ernest Lister (1912 to 1920), has a school named for him, and he shares the honor with his brother. Territorial Governor Stevens, however, has several schools named for him. Rogers High School replaced the old Hillyard High School.

Rogers Elementary School, 2001 26th Ave. N.E., Olympia School District (Thurston County). John Rankin Rogers was the third governor of the state of Washington serving from 1897 to 1901. As a senator, he wrote and worked for the passage of the "Barefoot School Boy" law, which provided state support for public schools on a per-pupil-served basis. There is a statue of Rogers in the park at Sixth and Capitol Way in Olympia. This school was named in 1955.

Roosevelt Middle School, 400 S. Monroe Rd., Port Angeles School District (Clallam County). Named for former President Theodore Roosevelt in 1978 because he was instrumental in the establishment of the Olympic National Park.

Roosevelt Elementary School, 6915 E. Fourth Plain Blvd., Vancouver School District (Clark County). When the McCarty and Vancouver School Districts consolidated in 1918, the McCarty School was renamed Roosevelt, presumably for former President Theodore Roosevelt. The origin of the name McCarty is not known at this writing.

That school district was in operation as early as 1876, according to a report by then Clark County Superintendent W. Bryan Daniels. As late as 1930 the one-room school was in use for the first four grades. The building no longer exists.

Lake Roosevelt High School, Civic Way, Coulee Dam, Grand Coulee Dam School District (Grant County). Originally called Coulee Dam High School of the Coulee Dam School District, this school was built in 1951 by the federal government. The building was modernized in 1979. The high school students renamed the building Lake Roosevelt High School in the fall of 1971 when the Coulee Dam and Grand Coulee School Districts consolidated. Lake Roosevelt is the man-made body of water behind Grand Coulee Dam. The lake was named for President Franklin Roosevelt. The high school, housing Grades 10-12, is actually sited in Okanogan County.

Roosevelt High School, 1410 N.E. 66th St., Seattle School District (King County). Roosevelt High School's first students, freshmen and transfers from Lincoln High School, crossed the Cowen Park foot bridge on opening day, September 12, 1922. The school was named for Theodore Roosevelt.

Roosevelt Elementary School, Centralia School District (Lewis County). Built in 1923 and named for former President Theodore Roosevelt. From 1930 to 1937, Roosevelt was a primary school (Grades 1-4) and Jefferson an intermediate school (Grades 5-8). Roosevelt was closed in 1937 and its students transferred to Lincoln. The structure was used as the maintenance building and bus garage office for some years before being razed in 1981 to make way for the then-new Centralia-Chehalis Pupil Transportation Cooperative.

Roosevelt Elementary School, 3550 E. Roosevelt Ave., Tacoma School District (Pierce County). When School District No. 93 lost Rogers School to Tacoma through annexation in 1904, it built another school which also became part of the Tacoma School District on June 5, 1905. It was named Roosevelt School for Theodore Roosevelt, then in office. A newly built Roosevelt School was opened in 1922 on a site south of the older school.

Roosevelt School, 124 Lawrence St., Mount Vernon School District (Skagit County). The school was built and dedicated in 1907. As was traditional at that time, the school board selected the name from a list of presidents, choosing Theodore Roosevelt, president from 1901 to 1909. The building was first used as a high school. It later housed Skagit Valley Junior College (now a community college separate from the school district) and then was converted to an elementary school and was used as such until 1972. In 1990, it housed the central office school district administrators.

Roosevelt Elementary School, W. 333 14th Ave, Spokane School District (Spokane County). Opened in 1906 during the presidency of its namesake, Theodore Roosevelt. The school's motto is "We Bears Care," a reference to the Teddy bear, also named for Theodore Roosevelt. In 1908 Miss Lena Witt began a 32-year career as principal of Roosevelt. A distinguished alumnus of Roosevelt was Walter Brattain, who won the 1956 Nobel Prize in physics for his work on the transistor. Roosevelt was the last of 13 schools to be rebuilt in the district's building program of 1981. In 1988 Roosevelt was one of 10 Washington schools chosen by the state superintendent of public instruction for the U.S. Department of Education's Exceptional Elementary Schools Program.

Roosevelt Elementary School, 1417 San Francisco, Olympia School District (Thurston County). Named in 1908 for Theodore Roosevelt, 26th president of the United States. New Roosevelt Schools were built in 1923 and 1949. In 1989 students moved into the fourth new Roosevelt School.

Roosevelt Elementary School, 2900 Yew St., Bellingham School District (Whatcom County). The original school near this site (between Alabama and Texas Streets) was called Eureka School, built in 1902. In 1927 the name was changed to honor former U.S. President Theodore Roosevelt. A new school was built nearby in 1972, and the Roosevelt name was transferred to that school.

Roosevelt Elementary School, Box 400, Granger School District (Yakima County). Opened in 1938 after the condemnation of the Central School. Named for Franklin D. Roosevelt, U.S. president at the time. This is the only school in the state directly named for FDR.

Roosevelt Elementary School, 120 N. 16th Ave., Yakima School District (Yakima County). In 1903 a school was built on the corner of 16th and Summitview and was named Summitview School. In 1921 the school board changed the name of the school to Roosevelt to honor Theodore Roosevelt, 26th president of the United States. In 1937 a new building was constructed alongside the older building to house cafeteria, classrooms, and gymnasium. The old building was torn down in 1954. The "new" building was scheduled to be replaced by a new plant in 1990.

Rosehill Elementary School, Third and Lincoln, Mukilteo School District (Snohomish County). Built in 1893 at the site of a treaty signed in 1855 by Territorial Governor Isaac Stevens and Indian tribal representatives giving the United States control of coastal lands between Seattle and Canada. A historic marker is at the site. Mukilteo School District No. 6 was established in 1874, but no school was built until 1882. By 1905 the district had a population of 200 whites, 150 Japanese, and an uncounted number of Indians. The Japanese had been recruited from Japan to work in the Crown Lumber Mill. Mukilteo teachers tutored the Japanese adults and children in English after regular school hours. As an expression of appreciation, the Japanese parents helped landscape a school whose grounds were overrun with wild roses. The school became known in the community as the Rosehill School. The original building burned on March 19, 1928. The new building was constructed by parents and towns-people over a six-month period. In 1973 the school was converted to a community center housing a history

This is Ruark School in Garfield County as it appeared in 1931. The parents and students in the photo are, from left, Mrs. George Bailess, Nora Childers, Mrs. Alva Ruark, Mrs. Virginia Reavis, Eloise Bailess, Susan Ruark, and Mrs. Gale Weatherly, the teacher. (Photo from collection of R.P. Weatherly)

museum, public library, performing arts center, day care center, thrift store, city offices, and a senior citizens' center.

Ross School, North Queen Anne Hill, Seattle School District (King County). John Ross was an early Seattle settler who took up homesteading north of Queen Anne Hill in 1853. The original Ross School was annexed to the Seattle School District in 1891. The school was first opened in 1873 when Mrs. John Ross insisted that some provision be made for the education of her children. The first Ross School was on the second floor of the Ross home. A two-room frame school was opened in 1903. The Ross School was torn down in 1940.

Ruark School, N.W. Quarter, Section 16, Township 12 N. Range 44 E. W.M. (Garfield County). Named for Thomas Ruark who came to the Garfield County area of Washington Territory in 1878 and settled in the upper Deadman country in the northeastern part of the county. School was held in private homes for several years but finally the community built a schoolhouse on Morrissey Road near the original Ruark homestead. Ruark School

was consolidated into Pomeroy School District in February, 1944. Later the schoolhouse was moved a few miles to the farm of Frederick Ruark, descendant of homesteader Thomas Ruark. In 1991 the school was still on the Ruark property serving as a farm shop.

Paul Rumberg Elementary School, Entiat School District (Chelan County). Named for Paul Rumberg, former superintendent of schools in Entiat. No other information available.

Benjamin Rush Elementary School, 6101 152nd N.E., Redmond, Lake Washington School District (King County). Named in 1970 for Benjamin Rush (1745-1813), American physician, the first professor of chemistry in the colonies, and a signer of the Declaration of Independence. He also organized the first American anti-slavery society.

Russell School, Dayton (Columbia County). James A. Russell came to Columbia County in a covered wagon in 1878 from Coffee County, Kansas. Mr. and Mrs. Russell had 10 children. One son, Jack, married Catherine Frey who was a teacher at Russell School. One of their sons, Murphy Russell, still lived on the Russell property in

Russell School in Columbia County was built in 1895 and used until 1944. (Photo from Charlotte Hutchens, Dayton)

1990. The school was named for the Russell family because it was situated on Russell land. It was built in 1895 and continued in operation until 1944. The old school was moved to the foot of Blind Grade and in 1990 was part of a trapper's residence there.

Russell School District No. 144 (Whitman County). Another of the early Whitman County country schools. Who it was named for is not recorded.

Ryan School, three miles south of Toledo (Lewis County). Joe Ryan homesteaded in the Salmon Creek area in about 1883. Ryan came with his family from Missouri. He gave land for the Ryan School which his children and the children of others attended. The school was built in 1884 or 1885 and is no longer in use as a school.

St. Joseph School of Sunnyside. (Photo from Diocese of Yakima Education Center)

Sacajawea Elementary School, 518 Catskill, Richland School District (Benton County). Built and named in the 1944-45 school year. By the end of the first school year, enrollment was 1,521, requiring double shifting of students and staff. In 1970 a new Sacajawea Elementary School was occupied, this one called Sacajawea II. Sacajawea I in 1989 was being leased by the Washington Association of Retarded Citizens. These Sacajawea schools, as were four others throughout the state, were named for a guide and interpreter for the Lewis and Clark expedition to the Pacific Northwest (1804-1806). She was a Shoshone Indian born in what is now Idaho probably in about 1787. Some sources give her estimated year of death as 1884, which would make her nearly 100 years old at death. Some historians believe she died in 1812. Her husband, who met her while on the Lewis and Clark trip, was a French-speaking woodsman, fur-trader, and interpreter Toussaint Charbonneau.

Sacajawea Elementary School, 700 N.E. 112th St., Vancouver School District (Clark County). Named as soon as it was ready for occupancy in 1977. The Lewis and Clark Expedition passed through this area, making it an especially important episode in local history. (See Benton County Sacajawea, above.)

Sacajawea Junior High School, 1101 S. Dash Point Rd., Federal Way School District (King County). No information available.

Sacajawea Elementary School, 9501 20th Ave. N.E., Seattle School District (King County). In September, 1959, the new Sacajawea Elementary School opened for the first time. A school on the same site made up of portable classrooms had been in operation since 1955. That school was called Victory Heights. (See Benton County Sacajawea, above.)

Sacajawea Middle School, E. 401 33rd Ave., Spokane School District (Spokane County). Opened in 1960. Students chose the Thunderbird, prominent in Pacific Northwest Indian culture, as the school's symbol to complement the name Bird Woman by which Sacajawea also was known. Built as a junior high, the school became, along with other junior highs in Spokane, a middle school in 1986. (See Benton County Sacajawea, above.)

Sacred Heart School, Roman Catholic, Fort Colville, Ward Mission, Kettle Falls (Stevens County). Operated by the Sisters of Providence from September 26, 1873, until July 30, 1921. The Sisters taught the local girls and Colville Indian girls. The name is taken from the heart of Christ as the symbol of his love for humanity. A log building, believed to be an original part of the school, still stood on the property of what in 1991 was the home of Steve and Jeanne Pratt of Kettle Falls.

John Sager Middle School, 1755 S. College Ave., College Place School District (Walla Walla County). John Sager Middle School's name was chosen as the result of a student contest in 1965, shortly after the school was completed. At the time the name was selected, the reason given was that "John Sager's courage, intelligence, and character represented what all student body members can hope to achieve while enrolled in his namesake, John Sager School." John Sager and his five sisters and a brother were left orphans when their parents died on the way to Oregon from Missouri by wagon on the Oregon Trail. On October 17, 1844, the Sager children arrived at the Whitman Mission. John, the oldest, was 14. All seven children were adopted by Marcus and Narcissa Whitman. On November 29, 1847, John, his brother, Francis, and Dr. and Mrs. Whitman were killed by Cayuse Indians. So were nine other settlers at the mission. The carnage has become known as the Whitman Massacre. The Indians had been alarmed over the deaths of their own children from diseases brought to them by settlers. John Sager is credited with attempting to save the life of Dr. Whitman at the expense of his own life.

Sahalee School, Unaffiliated, 20101 66th Pl. W., Lynnwood, Grades 1-12 (Snohomish County). No information available.

Sain School District No. 98 (Whitman County). Named for the D. Sain family. An early school no longer in existence.

St. Aloysius School, Roman Catholic, E. 611 Mission Ave., Spokane Diocese, Grades K-8 plus Montessori preschool and, in 1990, an Educare daycare program (Spokane County). Named for St. Aloysius Gonzaga, the same saint for whom Gonzaga High School and University are named. Of noble Italian family and born in 1568, Aloysius Gonzaga devoted himself to the service of others.

St. Alphonsus School, Roman Catholic, 5816 15th N.W., Seattle Archdiocese, Grades K-8 (King County). This school opened in 1908 with Holy Angel High School housed in the same building. The high school was closed in the early 1970s. Named for St. Alphonsus Liguori, who was born in the village of Marianella, Italy, in 1696. An outstanding student, he completed studies in law by the age of 16 and was admitted to the bar in Naples. He became an ordained priest in 1726 and was named Bishop of St. Agatha Diocese in 1756, where he governed until 1775. He died in 1787.

St. Andrews School, 12 miles west of Coulee City, N.W. Corner of Section 3, T25N, R27E (Douglas County). Despite its name, this school was named, not for St. Andrew, but for Captain James Andrews, an early settler in the area and a Civil War veteran. The school actually was named for a post office located in Captain Andrews' home. Captain Andrews wanted to have the post office named Andrews but the U.S. Post Office Department objected. Perhaps there already was a post office with that name. So Captain Andrews somewhat impishly suggested "Saint Andrews," an idea readily accepted. St. Andrews School opened in 1889 (but was not named until sometime after 1890) and continued in operation until 1952. The schoolhouse is now gone and a Grange Hall located on its site. St. Andrews was the first school between Hartline and Waterville, and, at its demise, was the oldest school in that area.

St. Anne School, Roman Catholic, 101 W. Lee St., Seattle Archdiocese, Grades K-8 (King County). Founded in 1923 by Bishop Edward O'Dea with a faculty of Holy

Names Sisters. The school was named for St. Anne, identified as the mother of Mary, the mother of Jesus.

St. Anthony School, Roman Catholic, 336 Shattuck Ave. S., Renton, Grades K-8, Seattle Archdiocese (King County). Founded in 1927 by Father Carey. Originally staffed by the Sisters of Charity, Halifax. The school is named for St. Anthony of Padua, remembered as a saint to whom prayers are addressed when articles are lost. Born in Lisbon, Portugal, in 1195, he joined a community of Augustinian canons when he was 15. In his own day he was noted as an inspiring preacher.

St. Benedict School, Roman Catholic, 4811 Wallingford Ave. N., Seattle Archdiocese, Grades K-8 (King County). Founded in 1906 and named for the patriarch of western monasticism. St. Benedict was born in Nursia, Italy, in about 480. In his youth he left home to live a hermit's life. He gathered disciples for whom he erected monasteries in which they lived a community life under strict rules of behavior including silence, obedience, prayer, humility, and detachment from the world.

St. Bernadette School, Roman Catholic, 1028 S.W. 128th, Seattle Archdiocese, Grades K-8 (King County). Opened in 1960 by Franciscan Sisters. In 1990 there were no longer any Franciscan Sisters on the staff. Named for a French peasant girl, St. Bernadette Soubirous (1844-1879), who saw 18 visions of Mary, mother of Jesus, at Lourdes beginning in 1858. Bernadette was received by the Sisters of Notre Dame de Nevers in Lourdes, where she lived until her death.

St. Boniface School (See Guardian Angel.)

St. Brendan School, Roman Catholic, 10049 N.E. 195th, Bothell, Seattle Archdiocese, Grades 1-8 (King County). Opened in 1960 by Franciscan Sisters, St. Brendan was named for an Irish saint. Although little of St. Brendan's history can be known for sure, he is believed to have been born in Tralee, in Kerry, probably in the year 484. The most spectacular event in Brendan's life was his expedition with 60 chosen companions to discover the legendary Island of the Blessed. They sailed the Atlantic Ocean in two hide-covered boats, taking with them sufficient provisions for a month's journey. The monks came back with tales of incredible adventure and their odyssey became one of the most popular Christian stories told in Europe.

St. Catherine School, Roman Catholic, 8524 Eighth Ave. N.E., Seattle Archdiocese (King County). The school was built in 1941 and originally staffed by Dominican Sisters. Now staffed by lay Catholics, St. Catherine School was named for St. Catherine of Siena, Italy, who lived from 1347 to 1380. She became a Dominican tertiary at age 16. She is renown for her skills at nursing the ill, particularly lepers and those with the plague, and for settling disputes.

St. Charles Borromeo School, Roman Catholic, 7112 S. 12th, Tacoma, Seattle Archdiocese (Pierce County). St. Charles Borromeo lived from 1538 to 1584. He was a nobleman and an archbishop in Milan, Italy, who used his own money to feed the poor during the plague of 1576. He later died of hunger at 46. The school and the parish were named for St. Charles in 1958 by Father Edward McCallion.

St. Charles School, Roman Catholic, N. 4515 Alberta, Spokane Diocese, Grades K-8 (Spokane County). The school was named for St. Charles Borromeo, an Italian Bishop who was one of the reformers of the church in the 16th Century. He was the patron saint of The Most Reverend Charles D. White, Bishop of Spokane at the time of the school's opening in 1951.

St. Edward School, Roman Catholic, 4212 S. Mead St., Seattle Archdiocese, Grades K-8 (King County). Founded in 1911 by the Sisters of St. Dominic. Named for St. Edward, king of the English (1042-1066). His piety caused him to be called "the confessor." He was canonized in the 12th Century.

St. Frances Cabrini School, Roman Catholic, 5621 108th S.W., Tacoma, Seattle Archdiocese, Grades K-8 (Pierce County). The school was opened in 1953 by the Sisters of the Holy Names and Father Squier. It is named for Frances Xavier Cabrini, born in Lombardy, Italy, in 1850. She came to the United States in 1889 to work among Italian immigrants. She founded schools, hospitals, and orphanages around the world. She became a U.S. citizen and died in Chicago in 1917. In 1946 she became the first American citizen to be canonized.

St. Francis of Assisi School, Roman Catholic, 15216 21st Ave. S.W., Seahurst, Seattle Archdiocese, Grades K-8 (King County). Established in 1953 and named for Francis Bernardone, the founder of the Franciscan Order. He was born in Assisi, Italy, in 1181. At 25 he abandoned his affluent way of life and began living a life of radical poverty. He organized a band of roving preachers called the Friars Minor to spread the gospel.

St. Francis Xavier/Assisi School, Roman Catholic, E. 544 Providence, Spokane, Grades K-8 (Spokane County). Opened in 1910. No other information available.

St. George School, Roman Catholic, 5117 13th Ave. S., Seattle Archdiocese, Grades K-8 (King County). No information available.

St. George's School, Independent, W. 2929 Waikiki Rd., Spokane, Grades K-12 (Spokane County). No information available.

St. James of Thomas School, Episcopal, 8207 S. 280th St., Kent, Grades P-9 (King County). No information available.

St. John School, Roman Catholic, 120 N. 79th St., Seattle Archdiocese, Grades P-8 (King County). Founded in 1923 and named for the parish which in turn was named for St. John the Apostle and Evangelist. He is credited with writing the fourth Gospel, three Epistles, and the Book of Revelation. He was the youngest of the Apostles and the last of them to die.

St. John Vianney School, Roman Catholic, N. 501 Walnut Rd., Spokane Diocese, Grades P-8 (Spokane County). Opened in 1953. St. John Vianney was ordained a priest in 815. Three years later he was made parish

priest of Ars, a remote French village. Patron of parish priests. Little else is known of his life.

St. Joseph School, Roman Catholic, 901 W. Fourth Ave., Kennewick, Yakima Diocese, Grades P-8 (Benton County). Opened in 1964, St. Joseph was named for the patron saint of the Universal Church, foster father of Jesus.

St. Joseph School, Roman Catholic, 600 St. Joseph Pl., Wenatchee, Yakima Diocese, Grades P-5 (Chelan County). Joseph's parish was named by Father Joseph Caruana, a Jesuit priest who had spent his religious life in the Indian missions of the Pacific Northwest. The parish is named for Jesus' foster father. Father Caruana was born on the Island of Malta, August 28, 1836. He entered the Society of Jesus and volunteered for the Indian missions of the Rocky Mountains. He was the first Jesuit on the Ahtanum near Yakima. He conducted the first recorded Christian ceremony in the Wenatchee Valley in 1871 when he baptized eight Indian children. The school was built in 1955 and named by Father P.J. O'Sullivan, parish pastor. The school opened under the direction of the Sisters of St. Joseph of Peace.

St. Joseph School of Wenatchee was completed in 1955. (Photo from St. Joseph School via Mary Louise Schneider, Chelan-Douglas Counties Retired Teachers Association)

St. Joseph School, Roman Catholic, 6500 Highland Dr., Vancouver, Seattle Archdiocese, Grades K-8 (Clark County). Opened in 1954. A new wing was built in 1961.

St. Joseph School, Roman Catholic, 700 18th Ave. E., Seattle Archdiocese, Grades K-8 (King County). Founded by the Holy Names Sisters in 1908.

St. Joseph Academy, Roman Catholic, Sprague (Lincoln County). Opened December 28, 1886, by the Sisters of Providence. The school was named for St. Joseph, foster father of Jesus, in recognition of his intercession to get a religious order to accept the school. After 79 years the school closed due to lack of sister faculty personnel.

St. Joseph School, Roman Catholic, 123 S.W. Sixth, Chehalis, Seattle Archdiocese (Lewis County). The school lists its founding year as 1923. It was originally staffed by Dominican Sisters of Edmonds who had established a school in Chehalis in 1895. The parish of St. Mary's in Centralia was created from a portion of the parish of St. John's in Chehalis, according to *A History of St. Mary's Catholic Church 1910 to 1986* by Dr. James Vosper. At some later date and for reasons not clear, the St. John parish became St. Joseph, including the St. Joseph School. A historical paragraph distributed by the school does not identify its namesake. It likely is Joseph, husband of Mary and foster father of Jesus Christ. There are four St. Josephs listed in *Lives of the Saints.*

St. Joseph School, Roman Catholic, Steilacoom (Pierce County). The school was opened in 1863 by the Sisters of Providence in response to petitions from missionary priests in the Northwest. Several factors contributed to the closing of the school in 1875, including the closing of Fort Steilacoom and subsequent loss of personnel, relocation of the federal prison, selection of Tacoma (instead of Steilacoom) as the railroad terminal. These events all decreased the number of students at St. Joseph School, which was named for the husband of Mary, mother of Jesus.

St. Joseph School, Roman Catholic, 907 S. Sixth St., Sunnyside, Yakima Diocese, Grades P-8 (Yakima County). Built in 1964, the school has existed since 1962, meeting for the first two years in temporary quarters. The school is a function of St. Joseph Parish in Sunnyside,

founded in 1925. It is likely the school was named for Jesus' foster father, known as the patron saint of the Universal Church.

St. Joseph Academy, Roman Catholic, Yakima Diocese (Yakima County). From November 6, 1875, to June 21, 1969, the Sisters of Providence operated this school, named for the principal patron of the Sisters of Providence. Since so many schools were founded by this order, it can be understood why St. Joseph is the most used name for Catholic schools in Washington State, perhaps in the nation. The academy's high school was consolidated in 1969 with two other Catholic high schools to become Carroll High School.

St. Joseph Elementary School, Roman Catholic, 212 N. Fourth St., Yakima, Yakima Diocese, Grades P-5 (Yakima County). Established by Jesuits in 1887 as an Indian School. Closed as an Indian School in 1896 when the U.S. government severed contracts with private educational institutions. This school has been a Roman Catholic elementary school since 1897. It was named for the convent that housed the Sisters of Providence. The convent was named for the earthly father of Jesus.

St. Joseph Elementary School and Marquette Middle School of Yakima occupy the same school plant. (Photo from Diocese of Yakima Education Center)

St. Leo School, Roman Catholic, 1323 S. Yakima, Tacoma, Seattle Archdiocese (Pierce County). St. Leo opened as a high school in 1912 and was named for the parish which already existed. When Bellarmine Preparatory School opened as a boys' high school, St. Leo became a girls' high school and elementary school. When it was closed in 1976 due to lack of enrollment, it was a Grades 1-8 elementary school. St. Leo was a pope in the Fifth Century who is credited with persuading Atilla, the Hun, to spare Italy. St. Leo School was being used in 1990 as a food bank, a theater for a local actors' company, and a hospitality kitchen for the homeless and needy.

St. Louise School, Roman Catholic, 133 156th S.E., Bellevue, Seattle Archdiocese, Grades K-8 (King County). Founded in 1961 and named for St. Louise de Marillac, who was widowed with a young son in 1625, became a nun, and chose St. Vincent de Paul as her spiritual director. She established the Daughters of Charity. She died in 1660 and was canonized in 1934.

St. Luke School, Roman Catholic, 17533 St. Luke Pl. N., Seattle Archdiocese, Grades P-8 (King County). Opened in 1957 under the direction of the Dominican Sisters of Edmonds. Named for St. Luke, a physician, an early convert to Christianity, and missionary companion of St. Paul. He is credited with writing the third Gospel and the Acts of the Apostles as well as many epistles.

St. Mark School, Roman Catholic, 18033 15th Pl. N.E., Seattle Archdiocese, Grades K-8 (King County). The school was founded in 1955 and named for St. Mark, the evangelist, believed to be the author of the Gospel bearing his name.

St. Mary Magdalen School, Roman Catholic, 8615 Seventh Ave. S.E., Everett, Seattle Archdiocese, Grades K-8 (Snohomish County). Started in 1960 with Grades 1-5, the school was named for Mary of Magdala in Galilee, who stood beside the cross of Jesus, assisted at his burial, found the empty tomb, and was the first to behold the risen Christ.

St. Mary School, Roman Catholic, 518 N. "H" St., Aberdeen, Seattle Archdiocese, Grades K-8 (Grays Harbor County). Started by the Sisters of St. Dominic in 1890 or 1891 under the name Academy of St. Rose. In 1926 the name was changed to St. Mary School.

St. Mary School, Roman Catholic, 225 N. Washington, Centralia (Lewis County). Built in 1917. In November, 1943, the school was severely damaged by fire. For several months classes were held in temporary quarters while repairs were made. In 1968 the school was closed permanently. Named for the mother of Jesus.

St. Mary School, Roman Catholic, E. 14601 Fourth Ave., Spokane Diocese, Grades 1-8 (Spokane County). Opened in 1958.

St. Matthew School, Roman Catholic, 1230 N.E. 127th, Seattle Archdiocese, Grades K-8 (King County). Opened in 1955. Named for one of the 12 Apostles, who is credited with writing the First Gospel.

St. Matthew's Lutheran School, N. 6917 Country Home Blvd., Spokane, Grades K-8 (Spokane County). Opened in 1971. Named for the Apostle Matthew, the tax collector.

St. Michael School in Olympia was preceded by this Providence Academy, which had been earlier called St. Amable, founded in 1881. (Photo from Sisters of Providence Archives, Seattle)

St. Michael Parish School, Roman Catholic, 1203 E. 10th Ave., Olympia, Seattle Archdiocese, Grades K-8 (Thurston County). Organized as a private school by the Sisters of Providence. Founded on August 22, 1881, the boarding school and high school were known as St. Amable Academy. It was later known as Providence Academy. In 1926, St. Michael Parish bought the school, closing the high school and boarding school but operating the grade school as St. Michael Parochial School. St. Amable is the patron saint of compassion for the unfortunate and protection against fire. St. Michael is one of the archangels honored by the Roman Catholic Church. This school is believed to be the oldest operating parochial school in the state.

St. Monica School, Roman Catholic, 4320 87th S.E., Mercer Island, Seattle Archdiocese, Grades K-8 (King County). Founded in 1960 and named for the mother of St. Augustine. St. Monica lived from 333 to 387.

St. Paschal School, Roman Catholic, N. 2521 Park Rd., Spokane Diocese, Grades P-8 (Spokane County). Opened in 1940. No reason was given for the school's name. *Lives of the Saints* lists a St. Paschal Baylon born in the kingdom of Aragon in 1540.

St. Patrick School, Roman Catholic, 1016 N. 14th Ave., Pasco, Spokane Diocese, Grades P-7 (Franklin County). Opened in 1951 as the first parochial school in the Tri-Cities. By 1960 a junior high building was opened. In 1984 the junior high was closed and a Montessori Preschool Educare and after-school care program started soon thereafter. In 1991 a seventh grade was added. The school is named for St. Patrick (387-461) in honor of his Christian stewardship and missionary work.

St. Patrick School, Roman Catholic, 1112 N. "G" St., Tacoma, Seattle Archdiocese, Grades K-8 (Pierce County). St. Patrick was born in Roman Britain in 387. At 16 he was captured by pirates and sold into slavery in Ireland where he tended a chieftain's cattle. Six years later he escaped to a monastery in France. At 43, now a bishop, he returned with monks to bring the faith to Ireland. This school was named for St. Patrick in 1893 by Bishop Shaughnessy. Father W.J. Emonds, parish pastor, petitioned Mother Tomasina for teachers. Two sisters were sent and the school was opened on September 7, 1893. This was the first free parochial school west of the Mississippi. On August 15, 1905, the school was consumed by fire. It was not rebuilt and reopened until October 11, 1919. Until 1940 the Sisters of St. Dominic staffed St. Patrick School. They were housed at Aquinas Convent nearby. St. Patrick School is now located in the old Aquinas Building where it has been since the early 1970s.

St. Patrick School, Roman Catholic, E. 2706 Queen, Spokane Diocese, Grades 1-8 (Spokane County). Opened in 1914.

St. Patrick School, Walla Walla, Spokane Diocese (Walla Walla County). Opened and named in 1928. Closed in 1959.

St. Paul Cathedral School, Roman Catholic, 1214 W. Chestnut, Yakima Diocese, Grades P-8 (Yakima County). The land for this school was purchased by Father Armstrong (no first name given) on April 23, 1914. By October 2, 1914, there was an operating school on the site, and it is still in operation. The name of the cathedral and school are from the Apostle Paul who started out as Saul, persecutor of Christians, and became Paul, preeminent in spreading the new religion—Christianity—among non-Jews.

St. Paul's Lutheran School, Palouse and Buchanan Streets, Wenatchee (Chelan County). Opened in 1907 and named for the local church serving a largely German-speaking congregation. The church in turn was named for the Apostle Paul. The school, under the direction of Pastor Schreiber, began daily at 8 a.m. and concluded at 4:30 p.m. The school day opened with religious instruction for one hour followed by an hour of English. Other basic subjects filled the rest of the day. English was of particular importance because many of the children came from German-speaking homes. The school was closed in 1936.

St. Paul School, Roman Catholic, 10001 57th S., Seattle Archdiocese, Grades K-8 (King County). Established in 1954 by the Holy Cross Sisters. Named for St. Paul, writer of many of the epistles of the New Testament.

St. Philomena School, Roman Catholic, 1815 S. 220th, Des Moines, Seattle Archdiocese, Grades K-8 (King County). Opened in September, 1963, by the Sisters of Notre Dame. In 1802 the bones of a young girl were discovered in a wall cavity in Rome's catacomb of

St. Priscilla. Three tiles on the outside of the cavity were construed to mean "Peace be with you, Philomena." A devotion arose to a St. Philomena, supposedly a virgin martyr of the second century.

St. Pius X School, Roman Catholic, 22105 58th Ave. W., Mountlake Terrace, Seattle Archdiocese, Grades K-8 (Snohomish County). Established in 1957. Joseph Sarto, son of an Italian shoemaker and the oldest of eight children, became a priest, then a bishop, then a cardinal, and, when Pope Leo XIII died in 1903, Joseph Sarto was selected as his replacement and took the name Pope Pius X. He died in 1914, having emphasized frequent holy communion. He was to become known as the pope of the Blessed Sacrament.

St. Rose School, Roman Catholic, 25th and Nichols Blvd., Seattle Archdiocese, Longview, Grades P-5 (Cowlitz County). The school was built in 1950, opened in 1951, and originally housed Grades 1 through 8. It is operated by the St. Rose Parish Church, established in 1927 and named for St. Rose of Viterbo. Before the city of Longview was incorporated, the church was a mission. It is believed the parish was named by The Reverend Edward O'Dea, who was the bishop of Seattle at the time. St. Rose of Viterbo is an obscure saint whose life is not well documented. She lived in Italy in the 13th Century and came from a poor family. She was refused entry into religious life because of her poor health and lack of a dowry. She nevertheless lived a life of holiness filled with acts of penance and was declared a saint in 1457.

St. Rose of Lima, Roman Catholic, Yakima Diocese, Ephrata, Grades K-6 (Grant County). Mrs. Fabiola Torrisn spearheaded the movement that was responsible for the opening of St. Rose of Lima School in 1959. The school is named for Isabel de Flores y Del Oliva, called Rose by her mother and confirmed with that name. Born in Lima, Peru, in 1586, she became a Dominican Tertiary at 20, modeling her life on that of St. Catherine of Siena. In her short life (she died at age 31), St. Rose worked with the poor and ill and is regarded as the originator of social

service in Peru. She was the first person in the Americas to be canonized.

St. Therese, Roman Catholic, 900 35th Ave., Seattle Archdiocese, Grades K-8 (King County). Opened in 1927 by Sisters of St. Joseph with an enrollment of 85. No further information provided. St. Therese is not listed with that spelling in *Lives of the Saints.*

St. Thomas More, Roman Catholic, 6511 176th S.W. Seattle Archdiocese, Lynnwood, Grades K-8 (Snohomish County). Opened in September, 1966, with three grades. Gradually grew to full elementary offering by 1980. Named for Sir Thomas More, English statesman martyred in 1535 for his religious convictions. The play "A Man for All Seasons" is based on his life.

St. Thomas More, Roman Catholic, W. 515 St. Thomas More Way, Spokane Diocese (Spokane County). St. Thomas More School opened its doors in September of 1962. It was originally operated by the Dominican Sisters of Spokane. Since 1979 it has been staffed by lay educators but maintains its Catholic identity. The school was named for St. Thomas More, an English author, statesman, and scholar. He served as Lord Chancellor, the highest judicial post in England, from 1529 to 1532. He resigned because he opposed the plan of King Henry the Eighth to divorce his queen when the Pope refused to grant an annulment. Sir Thomas was beheaded in 1535 for refusing to accept the king as head of the English church. The Roman Catholic Church proclaimed him a saint in 1935.

St. Thomas School, Episcopal, 8300 N.E. 12th, Bellevue, Grades P-6 (King County). No information available.

St. Urban School, Roman Catholic, near Winlock (Lewis County). Established in 1886. St. Urban I was the 18th Pope, who died in 233. The church and school also served the community as a Grange Hall.

St. Vincent de Paul School, Roman Catholic, 30527 Eighth Ave. S., Seattle Archdiocese, Federal Way,

Grades 1-8 (King County). The school was opened in September, 1965, by the Sisters of Notre Dame. In 1990 it was completely staffed by lay teachers. The seventh and eighth grades were dropped in 1971 but were reinstated, one grade at a time, in 1989 and 1990. St. Vincent was born of poor parents in Gascony, France, about 1580. In 1596 he entered the University of Toulouse for theological studies. While he worked in many fields, charity was his predominant interest. He died at age 80 in 1660.

St. Vincent Academy, Roman Catholic, Walla Walla (Walla Walla County). Opened by the Sisters of Providence on February 18, 1864, this school was closed in 1932. The academy was named for St. Vincent de Paul, the apostle of charity.

James Sales Elementary School, 11213 S. Sheridan, Tacoma, Franklin Pierce School District (Pierce County). The original structure of this school was built in 1953 and named for an infant, James Sales, the first white baby born in Pierce County, a member of a pioneer family whose descendents still reside in the Parkland area.

Salk Middle School, N. 6411 Alberta St., Spokane School District (Spokane County). Named in 1961 for Jonas Salk, American physician and microbiologist. In the 1950s he developed a killed-virus vaccine against poliomyelitis.

Salnave Elementary School, 1015 Salnave Rd., Cheney School District (Spokane County). Salnave School derives its name from the road which forms the northern border of the school property. One source said the name Salnave came from the name of an Indian chief of a local tribe. The school was built in 1972.

Sanislo Elementary School, 1812 S.W. Myrtle, Seattle School District (King County). Opened in 1970 and named for Captain Stephen Sanislo of the Seattle Fire Department. His widow attended the ground-breaking for the new school. Captain Sanislo was noted for his special fire-safety program aimed at children. He visited classrooms throughout the district in the 1930s and '40s.

Sartori Elementary School, 315 Garden Ave. N., Renton School District (King County). When the Renton School Board decided in 1907 it needed an elementary school in the north end of town, it purchased some parcels of land from the La Franc estate and from a Dr. Ignazio Sartori of San Rafael, California. Still more land was needed for a suitable playground. Dr. Sartori agreed to donate the additional land in return for the school being named for him. The school was built that same year (1907). A sign reading "Sartori School" was posted over the door, and a photograph taken and sent to Dr. Sartori. It is not known whether he ever actually saw the school. The source of his income is not given, but his resources were plentiful. He also donated land for Liberty Park and for the first Renton Public Library. A new brick structure was built on the school site in 1939. The school no longer serves as an elementary school but in 1989 was a satellite building of the Renton Vocational-Technical Institute. Walter Dale, who served as custodian at Sartori Elementary School, painted a portrait of Dr. Sartori from a photograph. The painting hung in Sartori School for several years.

Satellite School, 440 S. 186th St., Seattle, Highline School District (King County). In June of 1979 Manhattan Elementary School, named for the community, was closed. The following fall Satellite Alternative High School opened in the same building. An alternative middle school was added some years later. Barbara Birch, the founding principal, was still principal in 1990. She cannot recall where the name Satellite came from. It may have been prompted by the U.S. space program. It may have been an allusion to a school program that was in a sense a spin-off of the traditional school. Or it may have been selected simply because it was a non-judgmental name.

Satus School, Granger School District (Yakima County). Built in the early 1900s to serve the first eight grades. Closed between 1929 and 1932 after consolidation with Granger and improved school bus service. The Indian word "shatush" is said to mean "stopping ground." The school was named for this word as was the creek, a meadow, and a nearby mountain pass. The area was a favorite camping ground for Indians and settlers. It was also called Ben Snipes' Camp. Snipes used the area for camping while he ran cattle in the 1850s. In 1989 Satus School was a burned-out hulk standing forlornly by Satus Creek.

Peter G. Schmidt Elementary School, 6600 Capitol Blvd., Tumwater School District (Thurston County). The school was named in 1957 for Peter G. Schmidt, son of Leopold Schmidt, founder of the Olympia Brewing Company located in Tumwater. Peter was president of the brewing company from 1933 to 1953.

Schmitz Park Elementary, 5000 S.W. Spokane St., Seattle School District (King County). Opened in 1953 adjacent to Schmitz Park. The park site was donated to the city in parcels in 1908 and 1912 by Ferdinand Schmitz. Dietrich Schmitz, son of Mr. and Mrs. Ferdinand Schmitz, was appointed to the school board in 1928. He served until 1961. A new Schmitz Park School building was opened in the fall of 1962.

Morris Schott Middle School, Mattawa, Wahluke School District (Grant County). The town of Mattawa was built for construction workers and their families during the building of the Wanapum Dam on the Columbia River. Morris Schott was the owner of the land on which the town was situated. He was a leader in the effort to get irrigation to the area. His name was selected by a committee to give to its new middle school in 1977.

Schroll School District No. 40 (also called **Risbeck School**) (Whitman County). No reason given for either name. The school is long-gone.

Dick Scobee Elementary School, 1031 14th St. N.E., Auburn School District (King County). On April 27, 1986, the Auburn School Board renamed North Auburn Elementary School for Dick Scobee, commander of the space shuttle Challenger which exploded shortly after launch on January 28, 1986. Commander Scobee attended Auburn schools from kindergarten through Grade 12, graduating in 1957. Attending the school renaming cere-

monies were Commander Scobee's widow, his parents, two children, a brother, and a grandchild.

Seabloom Field, 1727 N.E. 104th, Redmond, Lake Washington School District (King County). The athletic field at Redmond High School was dedicated to the memory of Walter Seabloom, who had been a principal at the high school. The field was named in the 1960s after Seabloom suffered a fatal heart attack.

Chief Sealth High School, 2600 S.W. Thistle, Seattle School District (King County). Seattle is a mispronunciation of an Indian chief's name. Sealth is believed to be more closely representative of its original sound. The high school was opened in 1957. It is, of course, named for the Puget Sound Indian Chief so influential in the lives of early settlers and for whom the city of Seattle was named.

Seats School District No. 54 (also called **Davis School),** (Whitman County). Another early country school, this one named for a Seats family who owned the property at the time the school was built. Later that property was owned by W.J. Davis.

John Sedgwick Junior High School, 8995 S.E. Sedgwick Rd., Port Orchard, South Kitsap School District (Kitsap County). This school was named in 1981 for General John Sedgwick who served the Union forces under General George McClellan. After the Civil War, the wives of former Union Army members formed an organization to develop and care for the cemeteries. One of the cemeteries in South Kitsap was named for the popular General Sedgwick. Since the school is on Sedgwick Road and is close to Sedgwick cemetery, it also was named for General John Sedgwick. A distant relative—Marbeth Sedgwick Powell, a member of the school board—made the motion to name the school.

Seward Elementary School, 2515 Boyleston Ave. E., Seattle School District (King County). Seward School consists of three buildings constructed during periods of community growth: 1893, 1905, and 1917. The site was acquired in 1892. The original one-story frame structure was called Denny-Fuhrman. Seward School was named for William Seward, U.S. secretary of state from 1861 to 1869.

Seward Elementary School, 4902 S. Alaska, Tacoma School District (Pierce County). Opened in 1962 and named for William Henry Seward, secretary of state in the Lincoln and Johnson administrations, who negotiated the purchase of Alaska from Russia in 1867. He earlier had served as governor of New York and as a U.S. senator.

Shadle Park High School, N. 4327 Ash, Spokane School District (Spokane County). The school was named in 1954 for Eugene A. Shadle, a local civic leader and philanthropist. His wife, Josie, donated land to the city for a park. Land from the park was given for the school site. On September 4, 1957, Shadle Park opened its doors to welcome 1,331 students.

Shanghai School, rural upper Coweeman Road, Kelso (Cowlitz County). Built in 1873, this was the first school in the logging community of the upper Coweeman River east of Kelso. The school was named by the residents near the school. The name is said to have come from a flock of Shanghai chickens owned by a nearby farmer. However, another nearby school was named Pekin, giving rise to the supposition that both schools were named for cities in China. Neither school now exists.

Sharples Junior High School, 3928 S. Graham St., Seattle School District (King County). Opened in 1952 and named for Dr. Caspar W. Sharples, one of nine physicians who took the first medical examination given in the state of Washington. In 1894 he married Anne Goodrell, a physical education supervisor in the Seattle schools. Dr. Sharples served as a Seattle school director for nine years from 1922 to 1931. In 1990 the Sharples School was being used as an alternative high school.

Sharpstein Elementary School, 410 Howard St., Walla Walla School District (Walla Walla County). Named in 1898 for B.L. Sharpstein, a member of the school board in the early days of consolidation in the 1870s.

John Shaw Middle School, N. 4106 Cook St., Spokane School District (Spokane County). Opened as a junior high school in the fall of 1959, this school was named for a former teacher and long-time superintendent of schools in Spokane whose public school career extended from 1921 to 1959.

Shearer School, at Satus on the Plank Road near Bank Road and Tulle Road (Yakima County). The school building, made of brick, still stands on land given to the school district by a Mr. Shearer, of whom nothing else is known at this writing. The school was built in 1922 and closed in 1935. It may have been a part of the Granger School District. After it was closed as a school, the building was used as a community center, a Grange Hall, polling place, and, most recently, a residence for itinerant farm laborers.

Sheridan Elementary School, 5217 McKinley Ave., Tacoma School District (Pierce County). Built in 1889 by School District No. 53, Bismark School became part of the Tacoma School District when the area was annexed to the city of Tacoma in 1890. That same year the Tacoma School Board changed the school's name to Sheridan to honor Philip H. Sheridan (1831-1888), Civil War Union general.

Sheridan Elementary School, 3737 E. Fifth, Spokane School District (Spokane County). Named in 1908 for General Philip Henry Sheridan, U.S. Army officer on the Union side in the Civil War as well as western territories army officer. In 1978 a new building replaced the historic old Sheridan School.

Paschal Sherman Indian School, Unaffiliated, Omak, Grades P-8 (Okanogan County). Now operated by the leaders of the Colville Indian Reservation, this school was founded in 1886 by a Jesuit priest, Father Etienne de Rouge, on Indian land above Omak Creek eight miles south of the city of Omak. The school was part of a mission later called St. Mary's. Frank Wapato's widowed mother brought her sons from Chelan to the Okanogan country in 1907. She enrolled her boys in the St. Mary's mission school. At 15, already a promising artist, Frank Wapato (the surname is said to be an Indian word for potato) changed his name to Paschal Sherman at the suggestion of his mission priest, Father de Rouge, an admirer of General William Tecumseh Sherman. Paschal Sherman (the "Paschal" was for a Catholic saint) later was graduated from St. Martin's College in Olympia, took a doctorate in constitutional history from Catholic University in Washington, D.C., and a law degree from the Washington College of Law. For 43 years he was an attorney for the Veterans Bureau in Washington, D.C. The Indian school near Omak was renamed for Paschal Sherman in 1973, the year the Colville Indians took over its operation from the Jesuits.

The Indian School at St. Mary Mission near Omak Creek in Okanogan County was founded in 1886. In 1973 its name became Paschal Sherman Indian School. (Photo from Okanogan County Historical Society)

Sherman Elementary School, 4502 N. 39th, Tacoma School District (Pierce County). Named for William Tecumseh Sherman, Union Army general during the Civil War. The original Sherman School was built in 1891 and replaced with a new building on the same site in 1953.

Shine School (Jefferson County). Bob Slyter had a horse he dearly loved named Cheyenne. He rode that horse to bring back mail from Port Townsend to the citizens of what was known as Squamish Bay. In 1912 the community built a new school. The school likely would have been called Squamish Bay but that name did not suit Bob Slyter. It was too easily confused with Suquamish on the east side of the Kitsap Peninsula. So Bob named the new school for his horse. He wasn't the world's best speller but no one challenged his phonetic rendering of Cheyenne. So he wrote the new school name as Shine. In 1991 the Shine Schoolhouse was serving as a private residence for Mr. and Mrs. Leroy Pettersen. Mrs. Pettersen is a retired schoolteacher.

Shorts School (Snohomish County). The Shorts School was started in 1884. The building was located about one and a half miles southeast of Snohomish on the old road to Monroe. By 1889 there were 45 pupils, and school was held during the three months of summer only. In 1907 a new two-room building was constructed. At this writing the origin of the name Shorts is not known.

Showalter Middle School, 4628 S. 144th, South Central School District, Seattle (King County). Built in 1938 as a junior high school and named for Noah D. Showalter, state superintendent of public instruction from 1929 to 1937. He also had served as president of the normal school at Cheney, as a member of the state board of education, and was the author of *The Handbook for Rural Officers.* He had been a teacher and a county school superintendent in years past. The Showalter Bill of 1933 (also called the "New Barefoot School Boy" law), established the basic state school support at 25 cents per day per pupil in attendance.

Shumway Middle School, 3201 Main St., Vancouver School District (Clark County). Shumway Junior High was constructed in 1928. It was one of the earliest junior high schools in the state of Washington. It was named for Charles Wesley Shumway, whose career in Vancouver schools spanned 1895 to 1930. He was superintendent at the time Shumway Junior High was built. Mr. Shumway, often called Professor Shumway, attributed his long career as superintendent to two practices: "avoiding spectacular plays," and "showing appreciation to personnel." The name of the new school caught Professor Shumway by complete surprise at the dedication ceremonies.

Shumway Junior High School (now a middle school) of Vancouver. (Photo from Gertrude Stendal, Washington State Retired Teachers Association)

Sidney Glen Elementary School, 500 S.W. Birch Rd., Port Orchard, South Kitsap School District (Kitsap County). This school opened September 5, 1990. It is named for Sidney Stevens, a founding father of Port Orchard. The original name of Port Orchard was Sidney, also named for Mr. Stevens.

Sightly School, 5050 Spirit Lake Memorial Highway, Toutle, Toutle Lake School District (Cowlitz County). In 1936 three country schools were consolidated: Toutle, Silver Lake, and Sightly. The resulting school district was named Toutle Lake for two of the three schools. The Sightly School was so named because it was on Sightly Road. The origin of the road's name was undiscovered by our researchers.

Michael T. Simmons Elementary School, 1205 Second Ave., Tumwater School District (Thurston County). The original Simmons School was built in 1937. It was named for Michael T. Simmons, an early pioneer who, in 1845, came with the Bush party to the Pacific Northwest. Simmons was second in command of the wagon train. He settled at the falls called Tum Water (English representation of an Indian name). Simmons called his settlement New Market.

Simpson Avenue Elementary School, 519 Simpson Ave. W., Montesano School District (Grays Harbor County). Built in 1958 and opened in 1959, the school was named for its street address. The street was named for the Simpson Logging Company, principal employer in the area. Sol G. Simpson founded the Simpson Logging Company in 1895. The company was a dominant employer in Montesano, McCleary, and Shelton for many years. Sol Simpson's daughter, Irene, became Irene S. Reed, for whom a school in Shelton was named.

Small School District No. 100 (Whitman County). Named for school director J. Small. This is another of the 180 rural schools founded in Whitman County between 1872 and 1918. It and the others have since been consolidated into larger districts.

Smelter Elementary School, 515 E. Marine Dr. (or intersection of Highway 99 and Walnut Street), Everett School District (Snohomish County). Built in early or middle 1890s and named for the metal smelter, an important source of employment at that time in Everett. Guggenheim interests are reported to have purchased the smelter and moved its operations to Tacoma in the early part of the 20th Century. The Smelter School structure still survived in 1990 but at some time had been moved from its original site at Butler and Pilchuck Path to its present location on the southwest corner of Ninth Street and East Marine View Drive. In 1990 it served as an apartment house under the name Eastview Apartments. It is believed to be the oldest surviving structure in Everett built originally for use as a school.

J.J. Smith Elementary School, 1640 Fell, Enumclaw School District (King County). No information available.

Samantha Smith Elementary School, 23305 N.E. 14th, Redmond, Lake Washington School District (King County). Samantha Smith Elementary School was opened on September 6, 1988, with 546 students and 26 teachers. It was officially dedicated on November 10, 1988, when Jane Smith, Samantha's mother, flew out from New England to participate in the dedication ceremonies. Three students—first grader Ryan Stanley, kindergartner Heather Edwards, and fourth grader Erin Mulligan—had submitted the name Samantha Smith for the new school. In an election the spring before the school opened, held among students who were to attend the school, the name Samantha Smith was chosen. Samantha Smith was 10 in 1983 when she wrote to the then-premier of the Union of Socialist Soviet Republics, Yuri Andropov, asking for his support of world peace. The Soviet leader answered her letter and invited her to visit the Soviet Union and meet its people. The visit of this New England schoolgirl became a symbol of new hope for understanding among various peoples of the world. In 1985 Samantha and her father were killed in a plane crash.

Smith School, on Jones Road out of Winlock (Lewis County). In 1908 a one-room school was established on the Jones Road on the Rowland Smith property. Rowland Smith came to Winlock in a covered wagon in 1879 and served as mayor beginning in 1894.

Arthur H. Smith Elementary School, 205 Fir Ave., Grandview School District (Yakima County). Named in 1954 for a long-time teacher, coach, and principal in the Grandview school system. At the time the Smith School was dedicated, Smith was principal of the junior high school. He retired from the school district in 1961 and went into fruit farming. He died in 1981 at 79.

C.O. Sorenson School, 13209 N.E. 175th, Woodinville, Northshore School District (King County). This special education center was opened in 1972 and was named at that time for a school board member—Chris O. Sorenson—who had advocated the center. He served on the board from 1959 until 1967.

Martin Sortun Elementary School, 12711 S.E. 248th, Kent School District (King County). Opened in the fall of 1987 after students destined to attend the school had voted to name it for a farmer who had once owned the land on which the new school sat. Martin Sortun was a Norwegian immigrant who raised 12 children on his Kent

Valley farm. As a young man he worked as a logger in 1889 near Enumclaw, returning to Norway after four years. In 1929 he brought his wife and 10 children to America where he added two more children to his family. An article in the first issue of the Martin Sortun School newsletter states: "It is fitting that the new Kent central site elementary school be named Martin Sortun Elementary, not only because the school is being built on land that once was owned and farmed by Martin Sortun, but also because he was a man who strongly believed that education was a way to achieve your dreams and aspirations." Martin Sortun died working on his farm in 1981 at the age of 92.

Southworth Elementary School, Yelm Community Schools (Thurston County). No information available.

Spalding Elementary School, 1301 Sacramento, Richland School District (Benton County). Built and opened in 1948, this school was named for The Reverend Henry Spalding (1803-1874), a Presbyterian missionary who, with his wife, started the Lapwai Mission among Nez Perce Indians in Idaho in 1836. He and his wife also were associated with the Waiilatpu Mission near Walla Walla started by Marcus and Narcissa Whitman. The Spalding School was closed in 1982 and in 1989 was being used as a food bank, a Head Start preschool, a private Montessori preschool, the Shudokan Karate School, and some classes from the nearby Liberty Christian School.

Spinning Elementary School, 1306 Pioneer E., Puyallup School District (Pierce County). The building existing in 1990 was built in the early 1930s. A previous Spinning School at that site existed sometime before 1918. The school is named for Frank R. Spinning, an early Puyallup Valley pioneer.

Spruce Street School, Unaffiliated, 411 Yale Ave. N., Seattle, Grades K-4 (King County). No information available.

Squires School District No. 90 (Whitman County). Source of school name not given. This is another one of

180 early Whitman County schools. There were several Squires families in this area of the territory before 1889.

Stadium High School, 111 N. "E" St., Tacoma School District (Pierce County). In 1891 construction began by Northern Pacific Railroad on a tourist hotel in Tacoma. The railroad failed in the Panic of 1893 and work on the hotel ceased. The unfinished hotel was damaged by fire in 1899. In 1903 an agreement was reached with the Tacoma School Board to buy the remains of the hotel and convert it into a high school. The conversion was completed in 1906, and the hotel became Tacoma High School. In 1908 plans were submitted to build a stadium in the gulch just north of the school. The new stadium was dedicated in 1910. The name of Tacoma High School was changed to Stadium High School in 1913.

Stahlville School, Unaffiliated, Route 1, Box 78, Odessa, Grades K-9 (Lincoln County). No information available.

Stanford Middle School, Unaffiliated, 6818 124th Ave. N.E., Kirkland, Grades 4-9 (King County). Opened in 1965 under the name Adaptive Learning Center, this school specializes in helping students who are experiencing learning difficulties. The students wanted a school name other than Adaptive Learning and, in 1972, suggested naming the school Stanford after Stanford Denton, the school's founder.

Stanley Elementary School, 1712 S. 17th, Tacoma School District (Pierce County). Named in 1925 for George A. Stanley, a principal in the district for 27 years. He helped develop the junior high program and headed the district's normal school program from 1896 to 1901. In 1983 the main part of the building was closed. The building was rebuilt and reopened in 1988.

Stanton Elementary School, 901 W. Whitman, Yakima School District (Yakima County). Built in 1955 by the Broadway School District and named for one of that district's most distinguished teachers—Florence Stanton, who died in 1955. Mrs. Stanton came to the Yakima

Valley from Wisconsin with her parents in 1889, the year Washington became a state. She attended Woodcock Academy in Ahtanum and Ellensburg Normal School. Mrs. Stanton was active in several historical interest societies. The school became part of the Yakima School District which has used it as an alternative secondary school since 1988.

Star School of Columbia County was named for the Starr family but an "r" in the school name was dropped in later years. (Photo from Charlotte Hutchens, Dayton)

Star School, Dayton (Columbia County). Built on ground owned by the Starr family in 1874. The school's name over the years was shortened from Starr to Star. The building was moved across the Touche River once because more students lived on the other side and there was no bridge. The school served Grades 1-8 until 1951. It is now a residence.

The Stein School, Unaffiliated, 7218 208th S.W., Edmonds, Grades P-6 (Snohomish County). No information available.

Vivian M. Sterling Middle School, 600 N. James St., East Wenatchee, Eastmont School District (Douglas County). The new junior high school in the Eastmont School District was dedicated as the Vivian M. Sterling Junior High on September 24, 1961. The building was rededicated to Ms. Sterling in 1979 when it was changed to a sixth and seventh grade middle school. She was present for the ceremony. She died July 12, 1984. Ms. Sterling had been a teacher and administrator in the district for 42 years, the last 12 of which she was director of libraries.

Stevens Elementary School, 200 Block on South Chelan Street, Wenatchee School District (Chelan County). The first Stevens School was built in Wenatchee in 1893 and originally called the Wenatchee School. It was renamed in 1904 by the board of education after soliciting suggestions from students. The name was in honor of Isaac Stevens, first governor of Washington Territory from 1853 to 1857 who was later named territorial representative to Congress. Mr. Stevens was killed at Chantilly in 1862 while serving as a Union officer in the Civil War. The first Stevens School was replaced by a new building in 1925 which was in use until 1963. From 1964 to 1970 the building was used as a maintenance shop, warehouse, and central library storage. In 1970 the building and site were sold to the federal government. The school has been torn down and replaced by a post office and other government offices.

Stevens Middle School, 1139 W. 14th St., Port Angeles School District (Clallam County). Built in 1961 and named in honor of Isaac Stevens, first governor of the Washington Territory.

Stevens Junior High School, 1120 N. 22nd, Pasco School District (Franklin County). Built in 1961 and named for Isaac Stevens, first territorial governor of Washington.

Stevens School of Wenatchee was one of at least six schools in the state named for Isaac Stevens, governor of the Washington Territory while in his 20s. (Photo from North Central Washington Museum, Wenatchee, via Mary Louise Schneider, Chelan-Douglas Counties Retired Teachers Association)

Stevens Elementary School, 301 S. Farragut, Aberdeen School District (Grays Harbor County). This school was named for Isaac Stevens, first governor of the Washington Territory, in 1907. The original Stevens School building was at the corner of Curtis and Evans Streets. A graduate of West Point, Stevens served as a member of General Winfield Scott's staff during the Mexican War and as a colonel in the Union Army during the Civil War. He died at the Battle of Chantilly.

Stevens Elementary School, 1242 18th Ave. E., Seattle School District (King County). Property for this school (north Capitol Hill site) was purchased in 1904. In 1906 the school board named the new school for Isaac I. Stevens, first territorial governor of Washington.

Stevens Elementary School, E. 1815 Sinto Ave., Spokane School District (Spokane County). Built in 1909 and named for Isaac I. Stevens, the first governor of the Washington Territory. Stevens Elementary School was first built as a two-room school in the early 1850s for the Nash and Stevens children. This first building was actually a frame portable. Mr. Nash was a judge in the Washington Territory at that time. Mr. Stevens was governor. Judge Nash's home still stands directly north of the Stevens complex and can be visited by students. The Stevens home is located midway up the Sharp Street hill in the East 1700 block. It has been restored by the Harriton family. Stevens School also served as a night school for immigrant families from 1901 to 1916, offering courses in English, Swedish, and German. Longtime residents of the neighborhood still consider the 1909 building "the new school."

Stevenson Elementary School, 14220 N.E. Eighth, Bellevue School District (King County). In May of 1964, shortly before he retired as principal, the Highland Elementary School was renamed in honor of Walter S. Stevenson. Mr. Stevenson came to what was then known as the Highland School District in 1932. That district later became a part of the Overlake School District which, in turn, became the Bellevue School District.

James Stewart Playfield, Aberdeen School District (Grays Harbor County). Stewart Field was named in 1902 for a pioneer who came to the community in 1873 as a member of the second family to reside in the area. He was from Aberdeen, Scotland, and suggested that his new home city be named Aberdeen. The playfield and Robert Gray Elementary School are on land formerly owned by the Stewart family. Stewart was a stonemason by trade. Among projects he worked on was the first stone building in Seattle—the Dexter Horton Building.

Stewart Elementary School, 426 Fourth Ave. N.E., Puyallup School District (Pierce County). The current Stewart School, built in 1962, is the second Puyallup school to be named for this Puyallup Valley pioneer and the third school to be named for him in Pierce County. He is described in the paragraph on Tacoma's Stewart School below.

Stewart Middle School, 5010 Pacific Ave., Tacoma School District (Pierce County). Opened in 1925 as James P. Stewart Intermediate School. The name was suggested by William P. Bonney, long-time secretary of the Washington Historical Society. He wanted to honor Tacoma's first teacher. Stewart taught classes in Tacoma from 1869 to 1870. He then became a Puyallup Valley hop farmer, first mayor of Puyallup, and an organizer of Pacific National Bank of Tacoma. In 1886 he was elected to the territorial legislature.

Strohm School District No. 156 (Whitman County). No reason given for this name. This is another of the early-day Whitman County country schools no longer in existence.

Walter Strom Junior High, 20 Idaho Ave., Cle Elum-Roslyn School District (Kittitas County). Named in 1968 for C. Walter Strom, long-time educator and public servant in the Roslyn area and in Kittitas County in general. He was a classroom teacher from 1929 to 1934 and a school administrator in Roslyn from 1934 to 1944 and (interrupted by war service) 1946 to 1967. He also served in many community organizations and governmental functions such as the city park board, Kittitas County Civil Service Board, county fair board, and as a county port district commissioner.

Gael Stuart Buildlng, 1610 Blaine St., Port Townsend School District (Jefferson County). This building houses both classrooms and district offices. It was built in 1952 and renamed in 1974 at the retirement of Gael Stuart, superintendent of schools. Mr. Stuart had come to the Port Townsend School District in 1948 as an elementary school principal. He was chosen superintendent of schools in 1955. After retirement, Mr. and Mrs. Stuart continued to live in Port Townsend and to serve that community. In 1988 and 1989 Mr. Stuart assisted with the establishment of a performing arts complex at Fort Worden State Park. He also spearheaded a drive to raise funds for the restoration and enlargement of the Port Townsend Library. He wrote a history of the Jefferson County schools which is now on file in the Jefferson County Museum in Port Townsend. He also was the author of the segment "Educational Trends" in the book *With Pride in Heritage, a History of Jefferson County,* published in 1966.

Sunset School District No. 126 (Whitman County). Said to be a site picked by early settlers at sunset. Another early rural Whitman County school, long since merged into another district.

Swan School, Unaffiliated, 2345 Kuhn St., Port Townsend (Jefferson County). Swan School is a parent-administered, cooperative school covering preschool through Grade 5. It was established in 1983 and at this 1989 writing is overseen by Aaron Carver, who teaches Grades 1-5, and Hilary Carver, who teaches the preschool. The 1989 enrollment was 34. Swan School is named for James G. Swan, Washington Territory pioneer historian, particularly noted for his book *The North Coast or Three Years Residence in Washington Territory.* Born in Massachusetts in 1818, Mr. Swan came to the Pacific Northwest in 1852. He served at various times as teacher, naturalist, lawyer, probate judge, and consul for Hawaii. Judge Swan served in the appointed position of Jefferson County Superintendent of Schools in 1869. He lived out his life in Port Townsend where he died on May 19, 1900, at the age of 82.

Swan's Trail School (Snohomish County). The first school was in 1890 with three pupils. The next building was constructed on land that had been cleared by the parents and relatives of potential students. Origin of the name is not known at this writing.

Sylvan Way Christian School, Traditional Christian, 900 Sylvan Way, Bremerton, Grades K-6 (Kitsap County). No information available.

Sylvester Middle School, 16222 Sylvester Rd. S.W., Burien, Highline School District (King County). Named in 1954 for Sylvester Road on which the school is situated. The road was cut through a dense forest to Three-Tree Point on Puget Sound in 1919. It was named for the two Sylvester brothers who were among the early developers and promoters of the Three-Tree Point residential and vacation cabin area.

Syre Elementary School, 19545 12th Ave. N.W., Seattle, Shoreline School District (King County). Opened in 1964 at a dedicatory ceremony attended by then Senator Henry Jackson, a friend of the man for whom the school was named. Melvin G. Syre was a former teacher, coach, principal, and superintendent in rural Whatcom and King County school districts. He became deputy superintendent in the Shoreline School District in 1944, the year that district was formed by consolidations of smaller districts. He served in that capacity until 1952 when he died at age 48. He also was one of the organizers of Northwest Hospital, a member of the ration board during World War 2, a Boy Scout leader, and a member of his church's board of trustees.

Truman Junior High School of Tacoma typifies the lower rooflines of schools built in the 1960s. (Photo from Pat Flynn, Community Relations, Tacoma School District)

T

Tahoma School District No. 409, 23015 S.E. 216th Way, Maple Valley (King County). Contrary to popular belief, this school district was not named for the mountain that looms over Maple Valley—the one we call Mount Rainier but the Indians called Tahoma or Tacoma, depending on your source. It's easy to believe that the namers of this school district knew that the word they were coining coincided with the Indian word. Tahoma School District in King County was formed in 1943 through a merger of Taylor, Ravensdale, Barneston, Hobart and Maple Valley Schools. At first the district name was capitalized TaHoMa, an acronym encompassing TAylor, HObart, and MAple Valley. Other predecessor schools, some of them going back to the 1880s, include Crosson, Cedar Mountain, Sherwood, Eddyville, Kerriston, Walsh Lake, and Arthur Schools. Taylor was named for a company town producing clay products, mostly brick. Crosson was named for a family who owned the property on which an early school was built. The Arthur School was named for the first voter precinct (and later a post office of the same name) in Maple Valley which, in turn, was named for Arthur Albert Russell, first-born son of the C.O. Russell family, who lived on Hobart Road. Other predecessor schools were named for communities.

Mount Tahoma High School, 6229 S. Tyler, Tacoma School District (Pierce County). A new high school for the south end of Tacoma was built in 1961 and bore the Indian name Tahoma. It was the district's first "all electric" school. It also was the first school designed around a complete set of educational specifications written before the architect began work. Mount Tahoma is another name for Mount Rainier.

Tapteal Elementary School, 705 N. 62nd Ave., West Richland, Richland School District (Benton County). The school opened on September 5, 1978, and was dedicated on April 18, 1979. The name was selected in a contest involving citizens of West Richland and school staff members. The name chosen is an Indian word which has several interpretations: two rivers, or a bend in the river, or a narrow river. Tapteal was an early name of what is now known as the Yakima River.

Tayet School, 5030 E. Roosevelt, Tacoma School District (Pierce County). Fritz Tayet, a native Tacoman, was a popular principal at Mason Junior High when, along with family members, he drowned in a tragic boating accident. At the time of his death in 1959 he was president of the Washington State Principals' Association. He had been a teacher and principal in Tacoma since 1936. In 1964 Salishan Teenage Development Center was renamed to honor Fritz Tayet. The Tayet facility was destroyed by fire in 1971 and replaced by 10 portable buildings. In 1972 the school was closed.

Harriet Taylor Elementary School, 510 Chambers, Steilacoom School District (Pierce County). The name of the McNeil Island Elementary School was changed by action of the Steilacoom School Board on July 27, 1988, to the Harriet Taylor Elementary School. Mrs. Taylor and her family resided on McNeil Island for 17 years, during which time she was a cook at the McNeil Island Elementary School. She later was employed by the McNeil Island prison as a switchboard operator. Mrs. Taylor died in 1988. The elementary school where she once cooked was renamed for her because, in the words of the board's petition, "Mrs. Taylor was loved and respected by all who had contact with her."

Taylor School, North Wenas Road, Selah School District (Yakima County). In 1866 George Taylor, 20 years old, and his wife settled on a homestead in the Selah area after migrating from Indiana. The Taylors became cattle ranchers. In the 1880s the Selah Ditch Company, involved in an irrigation project, brought more people into the area and, with them, the need for a school. George Taylor gave the land for the school, which eventually grew to three rooms and covered all grades through the freshman year of high school. In 1990 the building still existed at its original site, converted to a residence.

Terminal Park Elementary School, 1101 "D" St. S.W., Auburn School District (King County). Named in 1946 for the railroad influence in Auburn's economy. Auburn once was primarily a railroad town. The roundhouse and the terminals were located two blocks from the school's present site.

Texas Draw School District No. 121 (Whitman County). A displaced Texan must have named this early rural school. No record remains of the origin of the name. It may refer to a nearby shallow gully that carries off water after a heavy rain. In topography, Whitman County is not too different from north central Texas cow country. If this is the origin of the name, it does not qualify as historic under our definition. However, it also is possible the name is for a man's ability to quick-draw his holstered pistol in the manner of some Texas cowhands. If that is the origin of the school's name, it qualifies as a bit of cultural history.

Chester Thompson Elementary School, 15605 E. "B" St., Tacoma, Bethel School District (Pierce County). A new school when it was named in 1968 for Chester Thompson, a Spanaway pioneer who served on the Pierce County Planning Commission from its inception in 1940 until his death in 1967 at the age of 81. He was a leader in school, Grange, church, and other organizations. He operated a resort on Harts Lake and, according to an editorial January 9, 1968, in the Tacoma *News Tribune,* was "a strong voice for the rural community."

David Thompson High School, Colville (Stevens County). Opened September 14, 1926, David Thompson High School was named for an early explorer who worked for the North West Company, an English trading company in competition with the Hudson's Bay Company to set up trade with the Indians. David Thompson kept good journals of his travels and they became the earliest written history of what is now called the Pacific Northwest. His travels took him to Kettle Falls in 1811. The school no longer exists.

Harriet Thompson Elementary School, 114 Euclid, Grandview School District (Yakima County). In 1911, N.H. Thompson of Mayville, North Dakota, came west to Grandview, Washington, to find a more rewarding life for himself and his family. Both he and his wife, Harriet, were trained to be school teachers. Mrs. Thompson had taught for several years before her marriage and the birth of three daughters. In Grandview, Mr. Thompson gave up teaching for full-time farming. In the mid-1920s Mrs. Thompson went back into teaching, taking a position in the Grandview High School as science teacher and student counselor. She was also active in her church, taught Sunday School, and worked for the success of Republican candidates. In 1949 the Grandview School Board named a new school for Mrs. Thompson. She attended the dedication ceremonies. She died in 1953.

Thomson School, 7812 S. 124th St., Seattle, Renton School District (King County). Skyway Elementary School was opened in 1949 and closed in June, 1972, for lack of enrollment. It reopened as a special education school in the fall of 1972, a role it was continuing in 1990. It was renamed to honor John and Marian Thomson, a husband and wife special education team. John Thomson began his career as an elementary teacher in the 1930s, eventually becoming an elementary school principal. His interest and activity in special education lead to his eventual appointment as director of the Renton special education program. Marian Thomson worked in special education as a home tutor for many years.

R.H. Thomson Elementary School (See Broadview-Thomson.)

Henry David Thoreau Elementary School, 8224 N.E. 138th St., Kirkland, Lake Washington School District (King County). Named in 1964 for the noted

American philosopher, naturalist, social critic, and essayist who lived from 1817 to 1862.

Thorndyke Elementary School, 4415 S. 150th St., Tukwila, South Central School District (King County). George Lorenzo Thorndike owned six acres of land between what is now South 148th and South 150th. He sold about one square acre to the Foster School District in 1905. The first Thorndyke School, a one-room structure, was built on the property in 1908, housing the first eight grades. Why the spelling of the school's name is different from the spelling of the original property owner's name is not recorded.

J. Thornton Lane School, Dungeness Valley, Clallam County School District No. 1, Sequim (Clallam County). District and school were established in 1862 on land given by John Thornton, a farmer. In 1896 the school was closed and relocated on the Lotzgezell farm and renamed the Lotzgezell School. In 1912 the Lotzgezell School was closed and consolidated into the Macleay School.

Tillicum Middle School, 16020 S.E. 16th, Bellevue School District (King County). No information available.

Tonasket Schools, Tonasket School District (Okanogan County). Since Tonasket schools are named for the city of Tonasket rather than directly for a historic person, event, entity, or man-made landmark, Tonasket does not qualify as a historic school name under our working definition. However, many predecessor schools consolidated into the Tonasket School District do qualify as historic school names and are dealt with here. The Tonasket School District now covers some 1,600 square miles. The city and river were named for Chief Tonasket of the Colville Indians, an influential Indian leader in territorial days. He is credited with getting federal approval for a Government School, established in 1885 near Tonasket, which burned in 1895 and was not replaced. In 1911, E.B. Grinnell organized Consolidated School District No. 100 including such schools, many of them taught in private homes, as Miller, Burbery, Schwartz, Chewilliken, Anglin, Mountain View, and Central. Mr.

Grinnell also started a high school and became superintendent of the collection of schools from 1911 until 1914. Other early schools preceding the consolidation into the Tonasket School District included Ellisforde, Brittain Flats, Whitestone, Horsespring Coulee, Bungalow, Carter, King, Oakes, Flanagan, Loomis, Chopaka, Nighthawk, Palmer Mountain, Huntley, Cummings, Synarep, Lower Synarep, Tunk Valley, Taroda Meadow, Bell, Wauconda, Davis, Blevins, Bodie, Fate, Pine Creek, Beeman, Lemanasky, Havillah, Bonaparte, Mount Hull, Rubert, Sunnyslope, Rockview, Curry, San Poil, Frosty Creek, and Cape LaBelle.

Eugene P. Tone School Project, Young Women's Christian Association, 405 Broadway, Tacoma School District (Pierce County). In the early 1980s a Tacoma School District teacher—Tina Foss—volunteered in the battered women program at the Tacoma YWCA. She instituted a program of having retired teachers read to or listen to the reading of children of battered women temporarily housed at the YWCA. Ms. Foss talked to YWCA staff members about the need for a school program for these children. Dr. Eugene Tone, a Tacoma school district administrator in charge of student and community services, became interested in the plight of these children and helped sell the school district on organizing an instructional program at the YWCA. In 1988 such a school program was established. In recognition of his efforts to start the project, it was named for Eugene Tone.

Totem Junior High, 26630 40th Ave. S., Kent, Federal Way School District (King County). No information available.

Traceyton Elementary School, 5550 Traceyton Blvd. N.W., Bremerton, Central Kitsap School District (Kitsap County). No information available.

Trafton School, Highway 30 and Jim Creek Road, Arlington School District (Snohomish County). Built in 1912, this school was in continuous use through the 1989 school year. Source of the school's name is obscure. It was named Trafton by a pioneer settler named Thomas

Jefferson, who had no known connection to the Jeffersons of Virginia. Where he got the name Trafton and why he was empowered to name the school is unrecorded.

Trent Elementary School, N. 330th Pines Rd., Spokane, East Valley School District (Spokane County). No information available.

Harry S. Truman Elementary School, 4505 N.E. 42nd Ave., Vancouver School District (Clark County). An open-concept school, Truman Elementary was beset with construction problems. It was not ready for its first occupants (primary pupils and teachers) until October 22, 1970, well after the beginning of the school year. The rest of the students and staff could not move in until January of 1971. One of the first school events was the dedication ceremony April 25, 1971, naming the school for the 33rd president of the United States.

Truman Middle School, 6501 N. 23rd, Tacoma School District (Pierce County). In 1961 the Tacoma School Board appointed a name-selection committee from the community to name a new elementary school. That committee recommended that the school be named for Isaac Stevens, first Washington Territory governor. The board ignored that recommendation and, instead, named the school Truman. Former President Truman had already been invited to the dedication ceremonies. He did not attend. In 1962 Truman School opened as an elementary school. By 1963 junior high classes were meeting in another building of the complex. In 1978 the elementary building was renamed Skyline Elementary and Truman became a junior high, later a middle school.

Tualco Valley School District No. 7, near Monroe (Snohomish County). Above the fork joining the Snoqualmie and Skykomish Rivers to form the Snohomish River is a valley once named Qualco by the native American Indians. White settlers mispronounced the name as Tualco Valley, a community that became one of the first voting precincts in Snohomish County in 1865. These citizens also formed a school district at about that same time and built a log-cabin school back in the woods. In 1878 a

frame, one-room school replaced the log cabin school. A second room was added in 1902. This building is now used as an outbuilding on a Tualco Valley farm. A new school was built in 1907. That building is now used as a Grange Hall. In 1953 the Tualco Valley School was consolidated with the Monroe School District and children bussed to Monroe.

Tulalip Elementary School, 7730 36th Ave. N.W., Marysville School District (Snohomish County). This school was built in 1958 on land sold to the district for one dollar by the Tulalip Tribe Inc., on a part of the tribal reservation. The school serves all children of that general community.

Tulalip Indian School, Tulalip Bay (Snohomish County). In 1857 Father Chirouse started a mission school near the mouth of the Quil Ceda River. In 1864 the mission school was moved to the south of Tulalip Bay. After 1868 the school was run by the Catholic Sisters of Charity under contract to the federal Bureau of Indian Affairs. It is believed to have been the first contract Indian school in the United States. Among its students were the grandchildren and great grandchildren of Chief Seattle and descendents of signers of the Tulalip Treaty agreed to at Mukilteo in 1855.

Turnbow School District No. 19 (Whitman County). This early rural school was named for the owner of the land on which the school was built—I.P. Turnbow.

Turner School District No. 8 (Columbia County). B.M. Turner filed a homestead claim in 1874. He later gave land for a school. In 1903 two districts were consolidated and became District No. 8. A two-room school was built and C.H. Strupp named principal. The new school was named Turner. In 1914 a third room was added for high school students. The high school was closed in 1924; the rest of the school in 1941 when it was consolidated with the Dayton School District.

Turner School in Columbia County lasted from 1908 until 1941. (Photo from Charlotte Hutchens, Dayton)

Turner School District No. 168 (Whitman County). Named for H. Turner, one of the first school directors of this early school district.

Mark Twain Elementary School, 1801 Rd. 40, Pasco School District (Franklin County). Built and named in 1955 for the best-read American writer of the 19th Century.

Mark Twain Elementary School, Star Lake Rd., Federal Way School District (King County). Opened in 1968. Closed in 1974. Reopened in 1990. Named for Samuel L. Clemens who wrote under the name Mark Twain.

Mark Twain Elementary School, 9525 130th Ave. N.E., Kirkland, Lake Washington School District (King County). Opened in 1963 and named for the famous Missouri-born American writer and humorist who lived between 1835 and 1910. Twain's real name was Samuel L. Clemens.

Tyee Middle School, 13630 S.E. Allen Rd., Bellevue School District (King County). No information available.

Tyee High School, 4424 S. 188th St., SeaTac, Highline School District (King County). The school was opened in 1963. The name was chosen by the school board from a list of recommended names provided by a citizens' committee. Tyee is a Chinook jargon word for a chief or anyone of superior status.

U

Lucille Umbarger Elementary School, 820 S. Skagit St., Burlington-Edison School District (Skagit County). Named in 1958 for a long-time elementary teacher in the district who died in 1956. Born in 1907, Mrs. Umbarger first taught in a one-room school in Nevada before coming to Burlington with her husband, who operated a berry farm there. She taught in Lincoln and Roosevelt Schools in the district as well as Sunday School at the Burlington Lutheran Church. In 1989 Mrs. Umbarger was again honored at the school named for her at a special Spirit Day assembly. Patty Martin, mother of an Umbarger student, researched Mrs. Umbarger's life and presented the information at the assembly.

Chief Umtuch Elementary School, Battle Ground School District (Clark County). The first Clark County school to be named for a local Indian chief of the 1850s was Kumtux School, built in 1914. Kumtux was one of some 13 spellings of the chief's name. The present spelling—Umtuch—was given by a now-forgotten government employee on an early Bureau of Indian Affairs document. The current Chief Umtuch Elementary School in Battle Ground was built in 1973. The name of the new school was recommended to the school board by the Silver Star Junior Women's Club, a local service club. The city of Battle Ground got its name as a sarcastic joke by white settlers who wanted the Army to force the local Indians to winter at Fort Vancouver in 1854. Some settlers blamed Indians for their loss of horses and other property. Indeed Captain William Strong and his troop of volunteer soldiers had overtaken Chief Umtuch's hunting party and negotiated their return to the fort. However, a shot was fired by an unidentified assailant and the chief fell dead. Captain Strong, a judge in civilian life, deferred to the Indians' wishes to mourn their chief, and granted them ample time to return to the fort. Some angry settlers, frightened by reports of Indian attacks led by Chief Kamiakin of the Yakimas to the east, were furious about the Captain's agreement with Umtuch's followers. They derisively named the area of ground on which the non-confrontation took place as Strong's Battle Ground, since shortened to Battle Ground.

Utsalady School, Camano Island (Island County). Founded in 1862, this was the first school on Camano Island. It was named for an Indian word meaning "place of many berries." The school was organized by Thomas Cranney with the help of the Crennan Lumber Mill. The mill provided the building, desks, blackboards, and other equipment. It was a subscription school. The first term was four months long instructed by a James M. Kennedy. R.B. Estes was clerk of the school board. By 1863 enrollment ranged from 10 to 14 youngsters aged 4 to 21. Its last year of operation is not known at this writing.

V

Vale Elementary School, 101 Pioneer Ave., Cashmere School District (Chelan County). The town of Cashmere was named for the Vale of Kashmir in India (but contested by Pakistan), the heartland of wheat and rice agriculture in that region. In 1903 the town of Old Mission was renamed Vale of Kashmir by Judge J.H. Chase, who had visited that part of Asia and found it beautiful. The spelling of Kashmir was changed. The first Vale Elementary School was built in 1952. On June 19, 1990, the old Vale School was demolished to make way for a playground for the new Vale Elementary School opened that fall.

Van Asselt Elementary School, 7201 Beacon Ave. S., Seattle School District (King County). Henry Van Asselt, together with Luther Collins and Jacob and Samuel Maple, staked claims to land in the Duwamish Valley on September 14, 1851, preceding the arrival of the Denny party by several weeks. In 1860 these early Duwamish settlers established the first school in King County. The school's first class consisted of nine pupils: Addie Van Asselt, Lissa Mercer, Tabitha Cavanaugh, Warren Maple, Samuel Maple, Mary Snyder, William Snyder, and Lucy Byrd. It was known as the Van Asselt School and was used until about 1865. The present Van Asselt School is located on land donated for that purpose by Henry Van Asselt. It is a part of the original 300-acre homestead. In 1907 the first Van Asselt School was built on that site. Many additions and remodelings have increased the size of the school since then.

Vaness School, south of Winlock (Lewis County). This school, now long-gone, was named for J.A. Vaness who came to the area already a rich man. He opened two sawmills near Winlock, the first in 1888. The school presumably opened shortly afterward. Vaness served a term in the state's first House of Representatives and began his first term in the State Senate in 1904.

Victor Falls Elementary School, 18605 Rhodes Lake E., Sumner School District (Pierce County). When 14-year-old Victor Johns and his family settled in Pierce County around the turn of the century, there was a beautiful little falls on their homestead. When Victor did not live through that first winter, folks decided to call the falls Victor in his memory. The Victor Falls School was completed in 1982. A citizen-staff committee recommended the name because of its local historical significance.

Victoria School (Snohomish County). Opened in about 1906 on the highlands east of Stanwood and was named after the Victoria Shingle Mill which donated the lumber used to build the school. The school has been closed for many years. Children of the area are now bussed to Stanwood.

Villa Academy, Independent Roman Catholic, 5001 N.E. 50th St., Seattle, Grades K-8 (King County). Founded by Mother Cabrini and the Sisters of the Sacred Heart, the school became independent in 1977 with the approval of the Archdiocese of Seattle. No original founding date nor explanation of the school's name is given in the parent handbook nor was it provided by the school administration.

Virden School District No. 15 (Kittitas County). Built in 1890, this country school was named for George Virden, not otherwise identified but likely a school director or the farmer on whose land the school was built. The building no longer exists.

Voyager Junior High School, 18002 "B" St., Spanaway, Bethel School District (Pierce County). Named in 1988 for the Voyager unmanned spaceship of the U.S. space exploration program. This school is also a part of the Bethel District's Schools for the 21st Century Project.

Built in the early 1920s, this Ellensburg elementary school is one of at least 25 Washington Schools in the state. This building was preceded in 1891 by another Washington School. (Photo from Verna Watson, Kittitas County Retired Teachers Association)

Frank Wagner Intermediate School, W. Main Street, and **Frank Wagner Primary School,** Dickinson Road, Monroe School District (Snohomish County). Frank Wagner was the logger-entrepreneur who donated the land on which these schools were built. The Wagner family operated a sawmill in 1906 and a lumber company from 1911 until 1930. In 1906 a Wagner School was built and served until 1953. The Frank Wagner Primary School was built in 1955 on Wagner land. In 1989 this school was torn down and a larger plant incorporating both primary and intermediate grades was built on the same site. In 1939 the Wagner Memorial Auditorium and Monroe Junior High School were built. Frank Wagner, Jr. had donated the funds for the auditorium within the school as a memorial to his father.

Wa He Lut Indian School, Unaffiliated, 11110 Conine Ave. S.E., Olympia, Grades P-8 (Thurston County). A school for children of Indian communities of South Puget Sound. The school's name—Wa He Lut—comes from a Nisqually warrior and medicine man whose power flowed from thunder and lightning "who still signify their sacred blessing." The Wa He Lut School began in 1974 on land owned by Willie Frank, prominent Indian leader in the area. In 1980 Senator Warren Magnuson secured lands from the U.S. Army on which to locate a new school. Wa He Lut is an independent day school funded by the U.S. Bureau of Indian Affairs.

Wainwright Elementary School, 130 Alameda Ave., Tacoma School District (Pierce County). In 1911 this school was known as Regents Park, a one-room building serving the three primary grades. A new building was erected in 1924 and renamed Fircrest. After considerable remodeling in 1948, the building was again renamed, this time for General Jonathan Wainwright, hero of World War 2 who surrendered to overwhelming odds at Corregidor in the Philippines in the early days of the war with Japan, survived the Bataan Death March, spent the rest of the war in prisoner-of-war camps, and was present on the battleship *Missouri* at the signing of the Japanese surrender.

Waldorf Schools, Unaffiliated. In the 1989-90 school year, there were four Waldorf Schools in the state: Chinook Waldorf of Clinton (Island County), Morning Star Waldorf of Gig Harbor (Pierce County), Olympia Waldorf of Olympia (Thurston County), and Whatcom Hills Waldorf of Bellingham (Whatcom County). No information available.

Mary Walker School District, and **Mary Walker Senior High School,** Springdale (Stevens County). Among early residents of the Whitman Mission at Waiilatpu in the 1830s were Mary and Elkhana Walker, newly commissioned missionaries to the Spokane Indians. Like Narcissa and Marcus Whitman, Mary and Elkhana had been married a short time before leaving on the year-long trip to the West. Mary had been allowed to sit in on the seminary classes in Maine and was unusually well-educated for a woman of those times—education ordinarily being a male preserve. In the spring of 1839 the Walkers and The Reverend Cushing Eels and his wife, Myra, pressed on to a new mission near Ford, about 25 miles north of present-day Spokane. The mission was called Tshimakain. Mary Walker had six children over the next few years (the first having been born while the Walkers were still at Waiilatpu). She started a school in her home at the mission both for her own children and for Indian children. After the Whitman massacre in 1847, the mission board in Boston closed the mission at Tshimakain, and the Walkers moved to the Willamette Valley of Oregon. The school district and the high school now serving the area once served by Mary Walker's school was named for her in 1960.

Pat Wall Memorial Field, Tekoa School District (Whitman County). The school district baseball field in Tekoa was named for Pat Wall in a dedication ceremony in April of 1981, a few months after his death. A memorial fund established by the Wall family was used to renovate the baseball field and to build new dugouts. Mr. Wall was a Tekoa High School graduate of 1975. He was an excellent athlete, especially in baseball. During his college vacation summers he helped coach the youth Little League and Babe Ruth League teams. He was killed in an automobile accident while returning to Spokane after playing in a softball game in Tekoa. Mr. Wall was graduated from Washington State University with a degree in business administration and at the time of his death was employed as a commercial casualty underwriter with United Pacific Insurance Company of Spokane.

Wallace Elementary School, 410 Elm St., Kelso School District (Cowlitz County). Built in 1912 and rebuilt in 1942, the school is named for Victor Wallace, early-day pioneer who took out the donation land claim in 1849 that later was sold to the Kelso School Board by Victor's two sons.

Waller Road Elementary School, 6312 Waller Rd. E., Tacoma, Puyallup School District (Pierce County). Waller Road Elementary School consists of a single complex of buildings constructed in the early 1920s with an addition in 1953 and 1960. The entire plant was remodeled in 1980. The school was named for the road outside its doors. Origin of that name was not given.

Walters School District 151 (Whitman County). No records left of where this school got its name. It no longer exists.

Waneta School, Waneta Road, Sunnyside (Yakima County). In the late 19th Century, blacks were recruited to work in northern coal mines, including those in the Pacific Northwest. Some of those recruits left the mines of Roslyn, Washington, after about two years and, with their families, took out homestead claims around Sunnyside in Yakima County. In 1901 they built a school on land donated by Ole and Lucy Washington, black homesteaders. When school opened in the fall, it was called Sage Valley School for the copious amounts of sage brush in the area. In 1908 the name of the school was changed to honor the infant daughter of one of the school board members. The baby's first name was Juanita, last name unrecorded. The spelling of the school's name, however, was recorded as Waneta, a phonetic rendering of Juanita. Another account of the naming of the school relates that the name came from the first white child to attend the school. Both stories could be true. In 1944 the Waneta School was closed. In 1989 the school was being used as a residence.

Warren Avenue School, Seattle School District (King County). No information available.

Washington Elementary School, 105 W. 21st Ave., Kennewick School District (Benton County). Built and named in 1957 for the first U.S. president.

Washington Street School, Washington Street at Kennewick Avenue, Kennewick School District (Benton County). Built in 1904 and named for the street. Was used as a school until 1935 and later as a school bus depot.

Washington Elementary School, 112 Elliott St., Wenatchee School District (Chelan County). In 1951 the Wenatchee School District purchased a 10-acre site on the corner of Washington Street and Elliott Street. A new school was completed in 1953 and named for the first president of the United States.

Washington Elementary School, First and Vine, Port Angeles School District (Clallam County). Built and named for the first U.S. president in 1922 near the old Central School. Washington was closed in 1975. It has since been razed and a U.S. Post Office occupies the site.

Washington Elementary School, 2908 "S" St., Vancouver School District (Clark County). It is assumed, but not verified, that when it was built in 1911, the school was named for George Washington, first president of the

United States. The school opened for business in a one-room portable classroom in 1912, closed for two years during World War 1, reopened in 1918, and soon had a permanent structure. Another "permanent" structure was added in 1926, found unsafe and closed in 1965, replaced with another building in 1966. The new Washington School was re-dedicated in 1967 with Miss Elsie Johnson in attendance. Miss Johnson had been the principal of the old Washington School for 35 years. Washington is the oldest continuous school name among all of Vancouver's schools.

Washington School, Columbia Street and Sixth Avenue, Kelso School District (Cowlitz County). Originally called the Columbia Building when constructed in 1892, the name was changed to Washington when an addition was built in 1917. The school was closed in 1922 and its name transferred to a new brick elementary school built nearby. This Washington School was demolished in 1980. It is presumed the school was named either for George Washington or for the state.

Washington High School, North Third Street, Pasco School District (Franklin County). Built in 1921. The Washington name did not stick. This building soon became known as Pasco High School and, later when a new high school was built, as McLoughlin Junior High.

Washington Elementary School, 200 S. Boone, Aberdeen School District (Grays Harbor County). This school was built and named for the first U.S. president in 1922. It was closed in 1976, later demolished, and in 1990 the property was used by an automobile sales company.

Washington Elementary School, 3003 Cherry Ave., Hoquiam School District (Grays Harbor County). Originally Washington School was on Simpson Avenue between 25th and Ontario Streets. It was completed in 1907 and named for the first president of the United States. That school was destroyed by fire in 1972 and a new school built at the address given above in 1973.

Washington Elementary School, 20 "E" St. N.E., Auburn School District (King County). No information available.

Washington High School, Seattle School District (King County). (See Broadway High School.)

Washington Middle School, 2101 S. Jackson St., Seattle School District (King County). An annex to the Seattle High School opened at the above address in 1907. It was called Franklin High School. But in 1912 when a new high school was opened in the Mount Baker District, that school was named Franklin and the former Franklin School became Washington Elementary School (presumably for former President George Washington), which it remained until 1938. That year it became a center for Grades 7 and 8. In 1945 the school became a Grades 7, 8, and 9 junior high. A new building was constructed in 1964. The school became a part of Garfield High School in the late 1960s, its name changing to Garfield "B." It now exists again under its own name as Washington Middle School.

Martha Washington School, 57th and South Holly, Seattle School District (King County). This parental or truancy boarding school served "indigent" children at several sites in the Seattle area from 1900 to the 1950s. The first parental school was a contract school founded by Major and Mrs. Cicero Newell in the basement of an old rooming house a block north of the Warren Avenue School. The parental school occupied several other sites, eventually becoming a girls' parental school to complement the boys' parental school called Luther Burbank. In 1919 the school was relocated to nine acres of land on 57th and South Holly on Lake Washington. It is believed that it received the name Martha Washington at that time, named for the wife of George Washington, first U.S. president. In 1957 the state took over operation of all parental schools. Martha Washington School is no longer in operation.

Washington Elementary School, 306 N. Sprague, Ellensburg School District (Kittitas County). Built and named in 1925 for the first president of the United States. There have been at least 25 pre-college schools in the state named Washington.

Washington Elementary School, Field and Spruce Streets, Centralia School District (Lewis County). A new Washington Elementary School was built and opened in 1950 for sixth, seventh, and eighth grades. The school was remodeled and updated in 1977. Centralia has more reason than most cities in the state for naming a school for George Washington. The city was founded by a George Washington, a pioneer settler, "man of color," born in 1817 in Frederick County, Virginia. His father was a slave, his mother a white woman of English descent. He was raised by white friends of his mother whom he came to regard as his parents. He started toward the Oregon Country in 1850, staked a squatter's claim in 1852 to land now the site of Centralia. Washington Elementary School serves now to honor the state, the first president of the United States, and a local settler who founded the city of Centralia.

Washington High School, 12420 Ainsworth Ave. S., Tacoma, Franklin Pierce School District (Pierce County). Constructed in 1969, the school actually opened the year before with sophomores attending classes at Keithley Junior High School. The school was named for the state of Washington rather than for the first U.S. president. At the time the school was named, one of the justifications for naming it Washington was that there was no other Washington High School in the state.

Washington Elementary School, 3701 N. 26th, Tacoma School District (Pierce County). Built in 1901 and named for George Washington, first president of the U.S. There have been many additions and improvements to the school.

Washington Elementary School, 1020 McLean Rd., Mount Vernon School District (Skagit County). The original school was built in 1905, a two-story structure with four large classrooms and a full basement. The present school was built and dedicated in 1951. The school is named for George Washington, first president of the U.S. Several wings have been added to the school and, in 1982, it was completely modernized.

Washington Elementary School, 1715 Rockefeller, Everett School District (Snohomish County). Original building constructed either in 1902 or 1907, depending on source. Named for George Washington. Closed in 1972 as a school but used for various temporary classes until 1981. Sold in 1985 and later remodeled into a retirement apartment complex named Washington Oakes.

Washington Elementary School, W. 1617 Riverside Ave., Spokane School District (Spokane County). Opened in 1896, closed in 1962. Named for the first U.S. president. From 1967 to 1973 the building served as a second campus for the Continuation High School. In 1973 the original brick building was demolished, leaving only the relatively new multipurpose unit. That was used from 1980 to 1982 as the district's Teacher Center. The building was later sold and in 1990 was owned by the Washington School Partnership.

Washington Middle School, 3100 Cain Rd., Olympia School District (Thurston County). The first Washington School in Olympia was built in 1890. A new school was built in 1924. It eventually became known as "Old Washington" and in 1970 became the district's administration building. In 1987 "Old Washington" was renamed Esther R. Knox Administrative Service Center in honor of the district's longest-serving school board member, 1952 to 1983. In 1969 the school board transferred the Washington name to a new junior high in the southeast area of the district. That junior high has since been changed to a middle school.

Washington School, Bellingham School District (Whatcom County). The original Washington School, built in 1891, was two stories high, made of brick and topped by a bell tower and spire. The school was closed in October, 1958, and demolished immediately.

In 1990 Washington Square occupied the lot where the school had been.

Washington School, rural grade school on Factory Road near Sunnyside (Yakima County). Built in 1894, this school served the first eight grades until 1929, the first six grades until 1930 when it was closed. The local Grange bought the building in 1935. In 1982 the old school was being prepared for a fireman's ball when it caught fire and burned to the ground. As a school, it was named for George Washington, first president of the United States. His picture hung in every classroom.

Washington Middle School, 501 S. Seventh, Yakima School District (Yakima County). The original structure was built in 1923 and named for the first U.S. president. This school is believed to be the first in the state to be built as a junior high school. In 1988 it became a middle school.

Camp Waskowitz, North Bend, Highline School District (King County). Purchased by the Highline School District in 1957, Camp Waskowitz was originally a federally operated Civilian Conservation Corps camp in the early 1930s. Young unemployed men were stationed at the camp and worked for the government to improve and preserve public land. After World War 2, the camp (by then a Seattle Police Department training facility) was named after Fritz Waskowitz, an American B-17 pilot who was shot down in the Philippines in the early days of World War 2. Waskowitz also had been a football star at the University of Washington in the late 1930s under Coach Jimmy Phelan. The Highline School District borrowed (and repaid with interest) funds to buy the camp from the Seattle Police Department in 1957. It was then transformed into an outdoor education camp. Most of the original CCC Camp buildings remain, and the Waskowitz name was retained.

Waterman School (Columbia County). C.H. Waterman, a homesteader, donated the land for this school. His daughter, Miss Ethel Waterman, was the first teacher. The school was named in 1897. The original building burned

in 1921. A new school was built on land donated by Frank Robinson, but it retained the name Waterman School. The school was closed in 1929. Logs from the building were moved to Eckler Mountain where they were used in the construction of a summer home still in use in 1990.

Watson-Groen Christian School, Traditional Christian, 2400 N.E. 147th St., Seattle, Grades P-12 (King County). No information available.

Waverly Hall, Lake Washington School District (King County). In the 1940s this was a junior high school but was changed to an intermediate school (Grades 5, 6, and 7). No other information available.

Wawawai School District No. 86 (Whitman County). An early-day country school named for an Indian word said to mean "council grounds."

Weatherly School, S.W. Quarter of Section 5, Township 9 N., Range 43 E., W.M. (Garfield County). Organized in 1890, the school served the area on the northern edge of the Blue Mountains bordering on Asotin County. The winters were and are relatively severe at this 4,500-foot altitude of timbered terrain. The J.H. Weatherly family farm was central to several homesteads, so the first school was held there in a back bedroom until a small schoolhouse was built in 1897. The building served also as a community center. Weatherly School District No. 42 consolidated with the Peola School District in 1919. The schoolhouse stood for many years in deteriorating condition until 1940 when members of the Weatherly family tore it down.

Weatherwax High School, 414 N. "I" St., Aberdeen School District (Grays Harbor County). Opened in 1909, the building was named for John M. Weatherwax, pioneer lumberman and early mayor of Aberdeen. Mr. Weatherwax died in 1896. Four of his descendents served, at various times, on the Aberdeen School Board.

Webster Elementary School, 3014 N.W. 67th, Seattle School District (King County). Built in 1907 to replace the Ferry Street School and the Bayview School. Named for Daniel Webster (1782-1852), representative from New Hampshire, senator from Massachusetts, secretary of state under William Henry Harrison, and noted orator. No current information on this school was made available.

Webster Elementary School, E. 615 Sharp Ave., Spokane School District (Spokane County). Opened in 1900, closed in 1940. This school was named for both Daniel Webster, the congressman and orator, and Noah Webster, the compiler of an American dictionary. After the school closed in 1940, it was rented by Gonzaga University and housed Gonzaga High School. In 1951 the school board offered to sell the old school, but there were no offers. So it was used for administrative offices and special education classes for a number of years, finally being sold at auction in 1962.

Opened in 1900, this Webster School in Spokane was named both for American dictionary compiler Noah Webster and Congressional orator Daniel Webster. (Photo from Eastern Washington State Historical Society, Spokane)

Julius A. Wendt Elementary School, Cathlamet, Wahkiakum School District (Wahkiakum County). Built in 1952 as Cathlamet Elementary School, its name was changed in 1968 upon the retirement of Julius A. Wendt, superintendent of schools. Mr. Wendt had served the schools as coach, teacher, principal, and superintendent since 1929 soon after his graduation from Montana University. He died in 1969. A memorial service was held at the elementary school bearing his name.

Weppler Outdoor Education Classroom, Camp Waskowitz, North Bend, Highline School District (King County). Built in 1988 and named for Bill Weppler, who served as camp site director for 17 years, to "acknowledge the years of dedicated service that Bill Weppler gave to students and teachers who participated in ... outdoor education at Camp Waskowitz."

Wesleyan Christian School, P.O. Box 668, Vashon Island, Grades 1-8 (King County). No information available.

A.J. West Elementary School, 1801 Bay Ave., Aberdeen School District (Grays Harbor County). The first section of this school was opened in 1952 and named for A.J. West, pioneer lumberman and sawmill operator. Between 1885 and 1903 he served three separated terms on the Aberdeen School Board. The first A.J. West School was at Second and Conger Streets, so named in 1917. That school had been built in 1914 and named for Samuel Benn, another local pioneer. But a new school on former Benn property was named for him in 1917, leaving the old Benn School in need of a new name. A.J. West was the new name selected.

W.F. West High School, 342 S.W. 16th, Chehalis School District (Lewis County). In 1947 William F. and Blanch West donated 18 acres of undeveloped land on the edge of Chehalis as a new high school site. Two years later an earthquake destroyed the existing high school in town and a new one was built on the West property. Mr. West, a land developer, was the son of a Chehalis pioneer family. He died in 1963 and his wife in 1969, after which, by their wills, the West estate established the West Foundation, a million-dollar scholarship fund for needy students. The name of Chehalis High School was changed to W.F. West High School in 1957. The school's athletic field had already been named W.F. West in 1953.

Western Camp School, between Wildwood and Winlock (Lewis County). This school existed from 1922 through 1924. School was held in a logging camp building. A photo of the building is in the Lewis County Historical Museum at the old railroad station in Chehalis.

Weyerhaeuser Elementary School, 6105 356th St. E., Eatonville School District (Pierce County). The Weyerhaeuser Timber Company built a school serving all grade levels for children of its employees and other children in the Eatonville area in 1904. A new elementary school was built by Eatonville School District at another site in 1980. Title to the site of the earlier school reverted to other owners. A poll of the community determined that the new school should continue use of the name of the Weyerhaeuser Timber Company.

Wheatland School District No. 82, rural district northeast of Sunnyside (Yakima County). It is not recorded when this school was built, but the date probably was between 1910 and 1920. It was named by patron parents for the wheat fields that surrounded the school. In 1926 the Sunnyside School District was formed, and Wheatland patrons voted to consolidate with that district. Consequently, their school building was moved from its wheat field into Sunnyside. Records of later remodeling work on the building refer to it as "Arcadia" without explanation. The school is now closed.

Wheeler Building, a junior-senior high school at Spruce and Church Streets, Montesano School District (Grays Harbor County). Dedication ceremonies for this school were held on September 5, 1913. Named the Wheeler Building in honor of Prof. Eldridge Wheeler, who was first elected head of the Montesano Schools in 1896. When he retired in 1935, he had the longest continuous service of any city superintendent in the state of Washington. The school was scheduled for closure and replacement in 1991.

Whetstone School (Columbia County). Thomas Whetstone filed for the first homestead in Columbia County in 1867. His patent was granted in 1872. He not

only built the first house between Wallula and Lewiston, but set up a trading post just off the stagecoach route. No starting date for the school is given, but it closed in 1944.

Whetstone School, Columbia County, one of many rural schools in the area. (Photo from Charlotte Hutchens, Dayton)

The building was then used as a meeting place for the Grange, Farm Bureau, and home economics club. The building was torn down by Guy Wiles some years later. He used the materials to build a home in Dayton.

Whiskey Creek School District No. 30 (Columbia County). This elementary school was built in the summer of 1878 on the site of an old Indian camp. The school was named for trading that went on at that site, principally the sale of whiskey.

Whispering Winds SDA School, Seventh-Day Adventist, Route 1, 540 Road K N.W., Quincy, Grades 1-8 (Grant County). No information available.

White Bird School (Columbia County). An elementary school of uncertain date. Originally this rural school was called Delaney for the man who donated the land, Bert Delaney. Later the school was moved to a new site. A literary society, calling itself White Bird, used the school as a meeting place. The society's name eventually became the name of the school. It later became a Grange Hall and was torn down sometime in the 1980s.

White Bird School of Columbia County was named for a literary society that met at the school. It had formerly been called Delaney School. (Photo from Charlotte Hutchens, Dayton)

The White School, shore of Lake Stevens, Lake Stevens School District (Snohomish County). The Rucker brothers of Everett built a large lumber mill on the shore of Lake Stevens in 1906. Workers and their families increased the population so fast that the local school was inadequate. Captain John Monslery sold an acre of land to the school district for $50 with the understanding that a new four-room school would be built to replace the two-room school then existing. A two-story wooden structure was constructed. The Rucker brothers took great pride in the appearance of their mill and painted all buildings and fences white, including the new school building. Having a beautiful white school was such a novelty the townspeople called it The White School, the only name it ever had. It served several generations of children and was torn down in 1956 to make way for a new school—the Mount Pilchuck Elementary School, built on the same site in 1957.

White School District No. 64 (Whitman County). Another early rural school, this one named for the first clerk of the school board, Mary White, and one of the first school directors, E. White—likely a husband and wife team.

Whitlock Field, St. John School District (Whitman County). Named for Melvin Whitlock, outstanding teacher in the St. John schools, in 1957. Mr. Whitlock had been a college athlete at Oregon State University and, from 1934 to 1957, a teacher in St. John. The district's athletic field was named for him soon after his death.

Marcus Whitman Elementary School, 1704 Gray St., Richland School District (Benton County). Built and named in 1944 for Dr. Marcus Whitman, medical missionary to the Indians in the 1830s and '40s in the Oregon Territory near Fort Walla Walla. A new Whitman School was built on the same site in 1970.

Whitman Elementary School, 301 N. Chelan St., Wenatchee School District (Chelan County). Built in 1903 and called "the High School" until 1904 when it was turned into an eight-grade elementary school and named Whitman for Marcus and Narcissa Whitman, medical missionaries in Washington Territory in the 1830s and '40s. A new Whitman School was built on the site in 1938 and used as an elementary school through Grade 6 until 1974. The building and site were sold, and the school was remodeled into the Central Washington Bank, which it still housed in 1989.

This Whitman School in Wenatchee was built in 1903, replaced by another Whitman School in 1938, and used until 1974. (Photo from North Central Washington Museum, Wenatchee, via Mary Louise Schneider, Chelan-Douglas Counties Retired Teachers Association)

Whitman Elementary School, 1001 Summit, Aberdeen School District (Grays Harbor County). Built and named in 1907 for Dr. Marcus Whitman (1802-1847), martyred missionary of territorial days. The school was closed at a date not known at this writing and in 1990 was being used for offices and warehouse of a construction company.

Whitman Middle School, 9021 15th Ave. N.W., Seattle School District (King County). This school opened in the fall of 1959 at the site of the former Olympic Golf Course. The Seattle School Board named the school for Dr. Marcus Whitman (1802-1847), medical missionary to the Cayuse Indians near what is now the city of Walla Walla.

Marcus Whitman Junior High School, 1887 Madrona Dr. S.E., Port Orchard, South Kitsap School District (Kitsap County). Dedicated on May 20, 1956, to the memory of Dr. Marcus Whitman, territorial pioneer and medical missionary. A booklet published for the dedication ceremony recounted the death of Dr. Whitman at the hands of Cayuse Indians in 1847. "Thus at the age of 45 this fine worker with high ideals was swept away from American society, a loss too great to measure. We take pride in naming our school for this martyred hero of our great state of Washington." The 1956 school was razed and a new Whitman School built in its place in 1981.

Whitman Elementary School, 1120 S. 39th St., Tacoma School District (Pierce County). Whitman School was built in 1892. Classes had been meeting for a year in a nearby Methodist church while the school was being readied. This building was damaged by the 1949 earthquake and completely rebuilt in 1952. Early school board records indicate that the building was one of those of the same vintage named for writers such as Bryant, Lowell, Emerson, Hawthorne, Whittier, and Irving. Thus Whitman was believed to have been named for Walt Whitman. In 1947, then Board President Fern Pratt, in the absence of any dissent, declared the school to have been named for Narcissa and Marcus Whitman. A portrait of Marcus

Whitman hangs in the school. Since there is no authenticated likeness of either Marcus or Narcissa Whitman in existence, the portrait is representational.

Whitman Elementary School, N. 5400 Helena St., Spokane School District (Spokane County). The early history of this school, named for Marcus Whitman, the missionary of territorial days, is sketchy. It was probably built before the turn of the century and was part of the Spokane School District in 1908. It was located on the corner of Wellesley Avenue (then called South Avenue) and Pittsburg Street. In 1913 a new Whitman School was opened a few blocks north of the original school. The use of ramps instead of stairs at the new school was a "first." The children marched in and out of the school to music played on a piano at the top of the ramp. Ground-breaking ceremonies for a newer Whitman School were held in 1980 at the address given at the top of this paragraph.

Marcus Whitman-Cowiche Elementary School, 1181 Thompson Rd., Highland School District, Cowiche (Yakima County). This school was formed in 1912 by petition of citizens. The first teacher, Miss Grace Curry (later Mrs. Frank Adams of Yakima), was given the honor of naming the new school. She named it for Dr. Marcus Whitman, early missionary in the Oregon country. A new schoolhouse was built in 1913. The school was closed in 1954 when a new school was built in Cowiche. The old Marcus Whitman schoolhouse was owned by the American Union Sunday School in 1990.

Whitney Elementary School, 12th and "M" Streets, Anacortes School District (Skagit County). Named for R.E. Whitney, an early settler in the area that became Anacortes. The original Whitney School was opened in 1910 and replaced by a new Whitney School in 1961.

Whitney Elementary School, 4411 W. Nob Hill Blvd., Yakima School District (Yakima County). Built in 1960 and named for two valued teachers, Anna and Frank Whitney, sister and brother, and F.C. Whitney, their father. The Whitney family came to Yakima in 1907 from Minnesota. The Reverend Mr. Whitney oversaw the building of the First Baptist Church, then on North Fourth Street. Mr. Whitney then went into orchard farming on reservation land. In 1912 F.C. Whitney took over operation of a weekly newspaper—*The Yakima Democrat*—whose name he changed to *The Independent*. In his newspaper Mr. Whitney consistently supported the cause of good schools. His older daughter, Anna, and one of his four sons, Frank, became teachers in Yakima schools. The Whitney School was remodeled in 1982.

Hulan Whitson Elementary School, 450 N. Main, White Salmon Valley School District (Klickitat County). In 1971 this elementary school was named for Mr. Whitson, long-time teacher and principal in the district. He had been a principal at the elementary, junior high, and high schools in White Salmon. He was an elementary principal at the time of his death in 1970.

Whitstran Elementary School, Prosser School District (Benton County). The name Whitstran comes from two Northern Pacific Railroad nurses—Laura Whitaker and Mary Strangways. They were cousins who retired to the area. The Northern Pacific siding was named for them, and the Whitstran Elementary School took that name when it was built in 1910. That school had been preceded by another school called Valley Heights, opened in 1909 in a homestead shack. In the early 1930s a new brick Whitstran School was built as a part of the Prosser school system.

Whittier Elementary School, east side of Pasco, Pasco School District (Franklin County). Built and named in 1911 for John Greenleaf Whittier (1807-1892), American poet and slavery abolitionist. The building was vacated in 1956. Some time later it was damaged by fire and subsequently demolished in 1979.

Whittier Elementary School, 7501 13th Ave. N.W., Seattle School District (King County). A school was built at the corner of Railroad and Schooner Streets in Ballard in 1905. It became known as the North End School. New buildings were constructed and the name changed by 1908 to Whittier School, honoring John Greenleaf Whittier, the American poet and abolitionist.

Whittier Elementary School, 777 Elm Tree Lane, Tacoma School District (Pierce County). Opened as Frace School in 1899. Later that year the name was changed to Whittier in honor of John Greenleaf Whittier, American poet listed in the American Hall of Fame from whose members many schools were named at the turn of the century. The building was closed in 1901, reopened in 1908. It burned in 1909. The present school dates from 1962, the name resurrected after a 53-year absence.

Whittier Elementary School, 916 Oakes Ave., Everett School District (Snohomish County). Opened in January, 1949; named the previous June for John Greenleaf Whittier, American poet. Whittier was chosen from a list of five names submitted by the North Washington PTA. In the planning stages the school had been called North Washington up until the selection of Whittier.

Whittier Elementary School, Seventh and "E" Streets, Spokane School District (Spokane County). The first Whittier School was opened in 1891. It was replaced by the "new" Whittier School in 1913. That school was closed in 1964; demolished in 1981. Both schools were named for John Greenleaf Whittier, American poet.

Whitworth Elementary School, 1810 N.W. 65th, Seattle School District (King County). Built in 1907 and named for The Reverend George Whitworth (1816-1907), English-born founder of the First Presbyterian Church in Seattle, one-time deputy U.S. surveyor, former superintendent of schools in both Thurston and King Counties, one-time president of the territorial university (now the University of Washington), and founder of Whitworth College in Tacoma (since moved to Spokane).

Whitworth Elementary School, W. 44 Hawthorne Rd., Spokane, Mead School District (Spokane County). This school carries the name of the Whitworth School District consolidated into Mead School District in 1942. The school opened in 1915 and closed in 1985. The school grounds bordered on the grounds of Whitworth

College, named for The Reverend George Whitworth, early territorial pioneer.

Wilder School, 2230 N.E. 133rd, Woodinville, Lake Washington School District (King County). Opened in 1989. This school was named for Laura Ingalls Wilder, author of children's books, often autobiographical, such as *Little House on the Prairie.*

Captain Charles Wilkes Elementary School, 12781 Madison Ave. N.E., Bainbridge Island School District (Kitsap County). Named for Charles Wilkes, commander of the United States Exploring Expedition of 1838-42. In just four years Captain Wilkes, with his flagship *Vincennes* and five other vessels, surveyed and charted hundreds of Pacific islands, the Oregon Territory, and the coast of Antarctica. In 1841 Captain Wilkes' party sailed into Puget Sound, charting and naming many of its islands, including Bainbridge Island.

Willard Elementary School, Cashmere School District (Chelan County). Frances Willard (1839-1898) was national president of the Women's Christian Temperance Union. She devoted most of her life to organizing women's pressure groups to prohibit the sale of alcoholic beverages. She effectively advocated women's right to vote and their right to education at all levels. She fought for public kindergartens and separate correctional institutions for women. This unusual woman may never have set foot in Washington State, but three schools here were named for her. The Cashmere Willard School was built in 1903. Willard School was torn down in 1952 after construction of the Vale Elementary School.

Willard Elementary School, 3201 S. "D" St., Tacoma School District (Pierce County). Built in 1899 and named for Frances E. Willard (1839-1898), a national leader of the women's suffrage and the temperance movements. The building was closed after the 1949 earthquake and rebuilt in 1952. It was closed again for lack of enrollment in 1987 and in 1989 was used for the L.H. Bates Vocational-Technical Institute Home and Family Life Training Program.

Willard Elementary School, W. 500 Longfellow Ave., Spokane School District (Spokane County). The first Willard School on this site was opened in 1908 and named for a famous woman activist who worked for women's right to vote and against the sale of spirits. In 1980 a new school of the same name was constructed at the same location.

Wilma School District No. 185 (Whitman County). No reason given for the name. This was the last of the 180 country school districts formed in Whitman County between 1872 and 1918. All of them have since been consolidated into larger districts. Few of the original school names survive.

Wilson-Pacific School, 1330 N. 90th St., Seattle School District (King County). In the fall of 1947 an essay contest was sponsored by the school board of the Shoreline School District and by the Shoreline Community Council. The student essays were on Americans who had won Nobel prizes. Darlene Taylor, a student at Lake City School, wrote an essay on Woodrow Wilson, 28th president of the United States. Thus in 1952 a new school was named Woodrow Wilson Junior High School. In 1954 Wilson Junior High was annexed into the Seattle School District. It was later merged with Pacific School for the developmentally disabled.

Wilson High School, 1202 N. Orchard, Tacoma School District (Pierce County). Named in 1958 for Woodrow Wilson, 28th president of the United States. When it was built, Wilson became Tacoma's first new high school in 44 years.

Wilson Elementary School, W. 911 25th Ave., Spokane School District (Spokane County). Opened in 1922. A new school was built in 1927. In 1941 a five-room wing was added. In 1961 a second wing, including a gymnasium, was added. The school was named for Woodrow Wilson, 28th president of the United States.

Wilson School, Tulle Road near Granger and Toppenish (Yakima County). Another country school whose origins are lost to memory. Sources in the area say the school was built in 1913 and closed in 1935. The building has been moved to another site which, in 1989, was still unidentified. Origin of the school's name has not yet been found in records.

Wilson Middle School, 902 S. 44th Ave., Yakima School District (Yakima County). Named for former President Woodrow Wilson. No other information available.

Windsor Elementary School, W. 5504 Hallett Rd., Spokane, Cheney School District (Spokane County). Built in 1959, the school was given the name of a pioneer farm family whose name already was being used to identify the area.

Winton Elementary School, Cascade School District, Leavenworth (Chelan County). Source of the name is not clear. Winton, the town, and the school were started at about the same time in the early 1890s. The name may have originated with the post office, as did the names of so many towns. In that case, it could be the name of the first town postmaster. The name also could have been given to the railspur by Great Northern Railroad, although the earlier name for that spur was Wood Spur. The first Winton School was replaced in 1924 by another one-room school, a school still in operation in 1990, one of six one-room schools in the state still open. In the early 1960s, Winton School consolidated with great reluctance with Leavenworth School District (now named Cascade School District).

Homer J. Wisner Field, LaCrosse School District (Whitman County). Homer Wisner was born in about 1900. He was graduated from Sunnyside High School in 1917 and from Washington State College in Pullman in 1925. From 1925 to 1948 Mr. Wisner was a teacher and later a superintendent in the LaCrosse School District and also was the football, baseball, and boxing coach. The Homer J. Wisner Field was dedicated at half-time of the LaCrosse-Rosalia football game on November 2, 1973. Mr. Wisner was present and was introduced to the crowd. He died in Tacoma in 1985.

Wivell School District No. 36, W. 5090 Cloquallum Rd. (Mason County). In 1887 Charles Wivell, his father J.T. Wivell, and his brother-in-law Charles Saeger, filed adjoining homesteads in upper Isabella Valley. Here they established one of the finest dairy farms in the state. In 1897 when a school district was formed, it was named for the Wivell family. The schoolhouse, built in 1898, was referred to as the Isabella Valley School. This schoolhouse was used until 1935. The building was being used as a residence in 1989.

Woldale School was built in 1905 several miles outside Ellensburg. The building to the right in this faded old photograph served as the school gymnasium as well as a community hall and polling place. (Photo from Verna Watson, Kittitas County Retired Teachers Association)

Woldale School, three and one-half miles west of Ellensburg (Kittitas County). Built in 1905, the school was named for Peter Wold, school board member and farmer of many acres. He came to the Kittitas Valley in the spring of 1871 from the Gilman Village area of Issaquah. Wold and A.A. Munson constructed a 15-mile-long irrigation ditch from First Creek to serve their farms. In 1990 the school still existed but was privately owned.

David Wolfle Elementary School, 27089 Highland Rd. N.E., Kingston, North Kitsap School District (Kitsap County). David Wolfle was Kitsap County superintendent of schools, an elective office, for 17 years between 1913 and 1952 with as long as 14 years between terms. This school was named for him in 1953. Mr. Wolfle was noted for visiting schools in the county regardless of the obstacles to transportation. In the early days of his office, to get from Port Orchard to Port Gamble, he had to go to Seattle and board a boat to Port Gamble. He would go on to visit Silverdale schools, and then row a boat or walk the beach to Bremerton. It was a healthy life.

A.D. Wood School, 626 Terrace Ave., Aberdeen School District (Grays Harbor County). Built in 1892 and first named for Alanson D. Wood, a prominent early-day lumberman, shipping executive, and school board member. The school later and unexplainedly became known as the Terrace Heights School. A.D. Wood School joined the Aberdeen School District in 1893, becoming one of three schools in the city system. From 1893 to 1910 Wood offered classes at all grade levels through high school.

A.D. Wood School was built as a high school, the first in Aberdeen. It later housed other class levels, including a junior college, before being demolished. (William Jones Historic Collection Photo from Rosalie Spellman, Grays Harbor County Retired Teachers Association)

With the completion of a new high school in 1910, Wood became an elementary school. By 1924 Wood School was generally known as Terrace Heights School. In 1930 the school was boarded up and then reopened in 1934. From 1935 and through World War 2 the building housed the Grays Harbor Junior College. The old school was torn down in 1945. The property on which it stood was sold to private parties in 1948.

Woodcock Academy, Unaffiliated, Ahtanum (Yakima County). Named in 1897 for Fenn and Frances Woodcock, husband and wife teachers who had founded the school perhaps 20 years earlier. Both were graduates of Hines College in Connecticut. Mr. Woodcock was a Civil War veteran, born in Massachusetts in 1834. The Woodcocks donated the land for the academy and, over the years, much of the monetary support for what was then called Ahtanum Academy. On Mr. Woodcock's death at 63, the board of trustees changed the school's name. By the early 1900s the academy apparently no longer existed. Its building was being used by the Red Cross Auxiliary. The structure still stood in the 1930s but is now gone.

Woodin Elementary School, 12950 N.E. 195th, Bothell, Northshore School District (King County). Named for Ira and Susan Woodin, who settled the area near Woodinville in 1871, and who hosted the first school classes in the area in their parlor in 1878. Ira Woodin was on the first school board of Woodinville School District No. 23, predecessor to Northshore School District.

Woodland Elementary School, 4630 Carpenter Rd. S.E., Lacey, North Thurston School District (Thurston County). Opened in 1981 and named by a panel of parents, students, and others for the original name of the community now called Lacey. The area was homesteaded in the 1850s by Isaac Wood and called Woodland until the early 1900s. A second name was given to the area when a post office was established and could not be named Woodland because such a post office and town already existed elsewhere in the state. A local real estate developer—P.C. Lacey—had been prominent in working

for the post office so the new post office was named for him. Woodland Elementary School preserves the older town name.

Salem Woods Elementary School, 12802 219th Ave. S.E., Monroe School District (Snohomish County). The school was named in 1981 for local pioneer Salem Woods who started a town called Park Place in 1878. Mr. Woods was the first sheriff of Snohomish County. Speaking of Salem Woods, another pioneer, H.E. Pearsall, said, "In the early days of my settling in the Woods Creek country, there were no early settlers that I respected more than Salem Woods. He settled on 100 acres in the middle of the forest called Woods Prairie.... He married a young Indian girl and raised a fine family."

Wright Elementary School, Crest Drive, Coulee Dam, Grand Coulee Dam School District (Grant County). Named for a retiring principal, Arthur "Bud" Wright, in 1980.

Annie Wright School, Independent, 827 N. Tacoma Ave., Tacoma (Pierce County). Annie Wright Seminary, a school for girls, was founded in 1884. The name was changed from seminary to school in 1970. Charles Wright, president of Union Pacific Railroad in the 1880s, donated an initial gift of $50,000 to establish the school. On the day the cornerstone was laid, one of Mr. Wright's daughters, Annie, was given the honor of sealing the stone. The school was named for her. On the same day St. Luke's Episcopal Church in Tacoma had its cornerstone laid. Mr. Wright had also endowed that institution. His daughter Kate laid the cornerstone at that ceremony. If Mr. Wright had asked Kate to help at the seminary and Annie to help at the church, Annie Wright School could well have been named Katy Wright instead.

Charles Wright Academy, Independent, 7723 Chambers Creek Rd., Tacoma (Pierce County). This boys' school first opened in 1957 in a remodeled restaurant and was named for Charles B. Wright, an Episcopal layman who had been president of the Union Pacific Railroad before the turn of the century as the company pushed across America establishing a major terminus in Tacoma. He is the second president of Union Pacific to have a school named for him in the state of Washington. The other is Charles Francis Adams High School in Clarkston. Charles Wright Academy was started in order to offer boys an educational program modeled after the program offered girls at Annie Wright Seminary (later Annie Wright School). Charles Wright Academy, now co-educational, is independent but associated with the Episcopal Diocese.

Wy'east Junior High School, 1112 S.E. 136th, Vancouver, Evergreen School District (Clark County). Opened in 1978 and given an Indian name also applied to Mount Hood, which is visible from the school site. No translation of the Indian name was provided.

Neal Wyer Memorial Field, Rosalia School District (Whitman County). Neal Wyer was hired in the summer of 1965 as bus maintenance mechanic and bus driver for Rosalia School District. In addition to keeping the buses in top shape, he also maintained the school district ball field. He not only drove his regular bus route, but also drove rooter buses, field trips, and sports teams until his death in 1977. Rosalia students raised funds to honor Mr. Wyer in 1980 by naming the district athletic field for him.

Y

Yakima County Schools, in addition to those already mentioned under their own names, also include many other rural schools no longer open. We have too little information on some of these schools to include them in separate listings but there are three on which we have some information at deadline: Cowan School was named after the John Cowan family, who were early settlers in the Wenas area. They farmed and raised stock on 160 acres they owned and where the school was built, dates uncertain. Marks School was located in the Ahtanum area. The Marks family raised stock on the 10 1/2 sections of land they purchased. John Marks taught school for several years. Elmer Marks served several terms as superintendent of Education for Yakima County. No dates for this school are available. Armstrong School was built on the Lower Ahtanum Road at an undetermined date. However, it was still in operation in the 1960s. The schoolhouse also has been used as a church and, in 1991, had been remodeled into a private home. Origin of the school's name had not been learned by deadline.

Yakima Tribal School, Unaffiliated, Toppenish, Preschool and Grades 7-12 (Yakima County). Founded in 1979. In 1855 Territorial Governor Isaac Stevens was busy making treaties with Northwest Indians—treaties that would promote settlement and development of the Washington Territory. On June 9, 1855, Governor Stevens concluded negotiations on the "Yakama Treaty" at Walla Walla. (After 1891 the spelling "Yakima" became standard.) The treaty of 1855 brought together as a nation 14 tribes and bands whose ancestral homeland comprised about 12 million acres in what is now central Washington. The legal name of the group is the "Confederacy of Tribes and Bands of the Yakima Indian Nation." The Yakima Tribal School is an approved, private school owned and operated by the Yakima Indian Nation. Its school board is composed of elected tribal council members. The majority of the students are Yakima tribal members; however, Indian students who are members of other federally recognized tribes may also enroll if space is available. To receive a high school diploma students must complete credits in Yakima Indian language and culture as well as the traditional high school courses.

Yale School, 11842 Lewis River Road, Ariel, Woodland School District (Cowlitz County). Dates of the first school in this remote area are not available. One predecessor to Yale School was called Cougar School. Origin of the present school name of Yale is unknown. Yale is a two-room school serving youngsters through the eighth grade. It is situated 33 miles up the Lewis River from Woodland. A post office was established in the area in 1898 and closed in 1941. The community as well as the school has come to be known as Yale.

Yoe School District No. 52 (Whitman County). One of the country schools founded between 1872 and 1918 in Whitman County. This one was named for R. Yoe, who was a school director and donated the land for the school site.

Alexander Young Elementary School, 1700 Cherry, Aberdeen School District (Grays Harbor County). Named in 1957 for an Aberdeen pioneer who served several terms on the school board beginning in 1884 and again beginning in 1892. An early settler, Mr. Young homesteaded north Aberdeen. The original Alexander Young Elementary School was a wooden building at the end of Thomas Street in north Aberdeen, built on Young land in 1922. It was the school board policy to name schools after Aberdeen pioneers.

Z

Zaring School District No. 138 (Whitman County). Originally named Horton after Andrew Horton, the man who established the school in 1899. The land on which the school was built was later sold to Mr. Zaring and the school's name changed.

James David Zellerbach Middle School, 841 N.E. 22nd Ave., Camas School District (Clark County). The school was named for J.D. Zellerbach in 1966. The Zellerbach family donated the land. The Zellerbachs owned and operated the largest paper specialty mill in the world at Camas until it was purchased by the James River Corporation in 1986. Most of the town's citizens depended directly or indirectly on the mill for their incomes. The Zellerbach family gave the mill good management and for many years the Zellerbach name was dominent in one segment of papermaking.

Zenkner Valley School, northeast of Waunch Prairie outside Centralia (Lewis County). "One day a Mrs. Matteson, teacher in the little valley school, wrote on the side of the building 'Zenkner Valley Schoolhouse.' Since then, this has been the name of the valley." So wrote Herndon Smith in her book, *Centralia, the First 50 Years.* Austin Zenkner came to Lewis County from Bohemia with his brother, mother, and sister in the 1880s. He and his brother, Anton, selected homesteads on the south side of Hanaford Creek, a swampy area northeast of Waunch Prairie. In 1893 Austin Zenkner was elected to the state legislature where he served one term. The Zenkner Valley School was closed and consolidated into the Centralia School District years ago, the exact date not recorded.

Zion Christian School, Traditional Christian, 620 20th Ave. S., Seattle, Grades P-12 (King County). Zion was the Biblical city of David and has become symbolic of The Promised Land. The exact location of the ancient city is in dispute, but it is somewhere within today's city of Jerusalem. Information on school not available.

Zion Educational Center, Unaffiliated, 1209 Minor Rd., Kelso, Grades K-12 (Cowlitz County). Started in 1981 under the sponsorship of the Zion Christian Church in Kelso. This private school offers the A.C.E. packaged instructional program designed for private Christian schools.

Zion Lutheran School, 3923 103rd Ave. S.E., Everett, Grades P-8 (Snohomish County). Zion Lutheran School was started in 1901 in a one-room wooden building behind the original Zion Lutheran Church in Snohomish. Blackboards and desks were homemade by parishioners. The teacher's desk was part of an old altar. In 1923 a new church and school combination building was completed on Union and Fourth Avenue in Snohomish. There was more expansion in 1962. An early teacher was Martin C. Kosche who started teaching in 1903 and taught until retirement in 1956. After retirement he was a substitute teacher for many years. He died in the 1980s at the age of 101. The classroom and campus at Zion Lutheran School were named for Mr. Kosche in 1979.

Index of School Names by County

McLoughlin
Ogden
Our Lady of Lourdes—
   St. James
Pan Terra
Providence
Rogers
Roosevelt
Sacajawea
St. Joseph
Shumway
Truman
Chief Umtuch
Washington
Wy'east
Zellerbach

COLUMBIA COUNTY

Baldwin
Bundy
Jackson
Pietrzycki
Russell
Star
Turner
Waterman
Whetstone
Whiskey Creek
White Bird

COWLITZ COUNTY

Barnes
Broadway
Butler Acres
Catlin
Columbia Valley Gardens
Coweeman
Crawford House
Freeport

Gray
Huntington
Kessler
Long
Our Lady of the Sacred Heart
Mint Valley
Monticello
Morris
Natural
Puckett
St. Rose
Shanghai
Sightly
Wallace
Washington
Yale
Zion

DOUGLAS COUNTY

Gilbert
Grant
Gribble
Kenroy
Lee
St. Andrews
Sterling

FERRY COUNTY

(No historic school
names submitted.)

FRANKLIN COUNTY

Emerson
Frost
Captain Gray
Livingston
Longfellow
Markham
McGee
McLoughlin

Olds
St. Patrick
Stevens
Twain
Washington
Whittier

GARFIELD COUNTY

Ruark
Weatherly

GRANT COUNTY

DeLancey-Houghton
Evans
Grand Coulee Dam
Grant
Keller
Loeffelbein
Morrison
Chief Moses
Lake Roosevelt
St. Rose of Lima
Schott
Whispering Winds
Wright

GRAYS HARBOR COUNTY

Benn
Emerson
Finch
Franklin
Gray
Grisdale
Hopkins
Humptulips
Huntley Building
Lincoln
McDermoth
McKinley
Miller

Northern Lights
Phillips Building
St. Mary
Simpson Avenue
Stevens
Stewart
Washington
Weatherwax
West
Wheeler Building
Whitman
Wood
Young

ISLAND COUNTY

Freeborn
Mabana
Utsalady

JEFFERSON COUNTY

Alpha Omega
Blevins Gym
Brinnon
Grant Street
Jefferson
Lincoln
Praxel
Shine
Stuart
Swan

KING COUNTY

Adams
Addams
Alcott
Allen
Anderson Building
Apollo
Audubon
Bagley

Ballard
Bell
Bennett
Bergh Field
Bertschi
Blaine
Blanchet
Boren
Brighton
Broadview-Thompson
Broadway
Bryant
Burbank
Bush
CAMPI
Challenger
Chinook
Christ the King
Chrysalis
Clark
Cleveland
Coe
Colman
Concord
Cooper
Day-Orca
Decatur
Denny
Dickinson
Dimmitt
Discovery
Dunlap
Dykeman
Eckstein
Edison
Einstein
El-Shadai
Emerson

Enatai
Federal Way
Fernwood
Ford
Foster
Franklin
Frost
Fulton
Garfield
Garvey
Gatzert
Gompers
Goodhue
Hale
Hamilton
Handy Center
Hauck
Hawthorne
Hay
Hazelwood
Hazen
Highline
Lea Hill
Holgate
Hughes
Illahee
Ingraham
Irving
Janikula Building
Jefferson
Jensen Shelter
Kamiakin
Keller
Kellogg
Mrs. Kelly's Kitchen
Kennedy
Kilo
Kimball

King
Kirk
LaEscuelita
Lafayette
Lakota
Lawton
Lee
Lemon Building
Leschi
Lincoln
Lindbergh
Love
Lowell
Luke
Mac Field
Madison
Mann
Maple
Market Street
Marshall
Mattson
McAuliffe
McClure
McDonald
McGilvra
McKnight
McMicken
McMurray
Mead
Meany
Meeker
Mercer
Meridian
Minor
Monroe
Montessori
Muckleshoot
Muir

Neely-O'Brien
Nelsen
Northwest Yeshiva
Nova
O'Brien
O'Dea
Odle
Open Window
Our Lady of Fatima
Our Lady of Guadalupe
Our Lady of the Lake
Our Lady of Lourdes
Overlake
Proyecto Saber
Perkins
Rey
Ricketts
Ringdall
Robinson
Rockwell
Rogers
Roosevelt
Ross
Rush
Sacajawea
St. Alphonsus
St. Anne
St. Anthony
St. Benedict
St. Bernadette
St. Brendan
St. Catherine
St. Edward
St. Francis
St. George
St. James of Thomas
St. John
St. Joseph

St. Louise
St. Luke
St. Mark
St. Matthew
St. Monica
St. Paul
St. Philomena
St. Therese
St. Thomas
St. Vincent de Paul
Sanislo
Sartori
Satellite
Seabloom Field
Schmitz Park
Scobee
Chief Sealth
Seward
Sharples
Showalter
Smith
Sorenson
Sortun
Spruce Street
Stanford
Stevens
Stevenson
Sylvester
Syre
Tahoma
Terminal Park
Thomson
Thoreau
Thorndyke
Tillicum
Totem
Twain
Tyee

Van Asselt
Villa
Warren Avenue
Washington
Martha Washington
Camp Waskowitz
Watson-Groen
Waverly Hall
Webster
Weppler Classroom
Wesleyan
Whitman
Whittier
Whitworth
Wilder
Wilson-Pacific
Wooden
Zion

KITSAP COUNTY

Bainbridge
Berg Building
Blakely
Breidablik
Christ The King
Givens
Haddon
Jahr
Jenne-Wright
Marion
Montessori
Morgan
Mullenix Ridge
Munger
Naval Avenue
Navy Yard City
Ordway
Our Lady Star of the Sea
Pearson

Sedgwick
Sidney Glen
Sylvan Way
Traceyton
Whitman
Wilkes
Wolfle

KITTITAS COUNTY

Ballard
Damman
Hebeler
Lincoln
Morgan
Strom
Virden
Washington
Woldale

KLICKITAT COUNTY

Henkle
Klickitat
Whitson

LEWIS COUNTY

Ainslee
Bennett
Brim
Broadbent
Burnt Ridge
Dillenbaugh
Edison
Evaline
Fayette
Fort Henness
Henry
Hopewell
Hopp
Jefferson
Jefferson-Lincoln

Johnson
Kiwanis
Knab
Lincoln
Little Kentucky
Logan
Lum
Mayfield
Noble Field
O.K.
Osceola
Packwood
Riffe
Roosevelt
Ryan
St. Joseph
St. Mary
St. Urban
Smith
Vaness
Washington
West
Western Camp
Zenkner

LINCOLN COUNTY

Jantz
St. Joseph
Stahlville

MASON COUNTY

Ahl
Angle
Bordeaux
Brumbaugh
Callow
Elson
Forbes
Hauptly-Webb

Hawkins
Knight
Lincoln
Loop Field
Miller
Reed
Wivell

OKANOGAN COUNTY

Allen
Ellisforde
Grainger
Liberty Bell
Okanogan
O'Keefe
Sherman
Tonasket

PACIFIC COUNTY

(No school names
submitted)

PEND OREILLE COUNTY

Bailey
Halstead
Herian
Marantha

PIERCE COUNTY

Baker
Ballou
Bates
Bellarmine
Bethel
Birney
Boze
Brookdale
Brouillet
Bryant
Calavan

Centennial
Central Avenue
Challenger
Chambers
Christensen
Collins
Curtis
Cushman
DeLong
Discovery
Dower
Downing
Eatonville Camp
Edgerton
Emerson
Explorer
Fawcett
Ferrucci
Ford
Foss
Franklin
Garfield
GATES
Gault
Geiger
Goodman
Gray
Hawthrone
Hoyt
Hudtloff
Hunt
Irving
Jefferson
Kalles
Karshner
Keithley
Kopachuck
Lee

Chief Leschi
Lincoln
Lister
Lochburn
Logan
Longfellow
Lowell
Lyon
Horace Mann
Iva Alice Mann
Mason
McAlder
McCarver
McIlvaigh
McKinley
Ezra Meeker
Jerry Meeker
Minter
Montessori
Naches Trail
Nelson-Crane
Pierce
Pope
Reed
Rogers
Roosevelt
St. Charles Borromeo
St. Francis Cabrini
St. Joseph
St. Leo
St. Patrick
Sales
Seward
Sheridan
Sherman
Spinning
Stadium
Stanley

Stewart
Mount Tahoma
Tayet
Taylor
Thompson
Tone
Truman
Victor Falls
Voyager
Wainwright
Waller Road
Washington
Weyerhaeuser
Whitman
Whittier
Willard
Wilson
Annie Wright
Charles Wright

SAN JUAN COUNTY

Milton

SKAGIT COUNTY

Centennial
Cleveland
Greene Field
Hickson
Jefferson
Kirkby Field
LaVenture
Lincoln
Madison
Mullen Grandstand
Paxton
Purcell
Roosevelt
Umbarger

Washington
Whitney

SKAMANIA COUNTY

Mill A

SNOHOMISH COUNTY

Bagshaw Field
Bramall
Carver
Cathcart
Challenger
Cicero
Clark
Discovery
Dorrance
Eisenhower
Emerson
Erving
Explorer
Florence
Fobes
Garfield
Hawthorne
Jackson
Jefferson
Kent's Prairie
Lincoln
Little Red Schoolhouse
Longfellow
Madison
Mariner
Monroe
Montessori
Our Lady of Perpetual Help
Our Lady of Seven Dolors
Phoenix
Pilchuck
Rosehill

Sahalee
St. Mary Magdalen
St. Pius X
St. Thomas More
Shorts
Smelter
Stein
Swan's Trail
Trafton
Tualco Valley
Tulalip
Victoria
Wagner
Washington
White
Whittier
Woods
Zion

SPOKANE COUNTY

Adams
Alcott
Argonne
Assumption
Audubon
Balboa
Bancroft
Bemiss
Betz
Blair
Blake
Bowdish
Browne
Bryant
Cataldo
Comstock
Cooper
Cowley
Davis

Edison
Farwell
Ferris
Finch
Franklin
Freeman
Garfield
Garry
Glover
Gonzaga
Grant
Great Northern
Hamblen
Hamilton
Havermale
Hawthorne
Hillyard
Holmes
Hutton
Indian Trail
Irving
Jantsch
Jefferson
Lewis and Clark
Libby
Logan
Longfellow
Lowell
Madison
Mann
McDonald
McKinley
Montessori
Moran Prairie
Mullan Road
Ness
North Wall
Pratt

Regal
Reid
Rogers
Roosevelt
Sacajawea
St. Aloysius
St. Charles
St. Francis Xavier/Assisi
St. George
St. John Vianney
St. Mary
St. Matthew
St. Paschal
St. Patrick
St. Thomas More
Salk
Salnave
Shadle Park
Shaw
Sheridan
Stevens
Trent
Washington
Webster
Whitman
Whittier
Whitworth
Willard
Wilson
Windsor
Woodridge

STEVENS COUNTY

Aster
Eels
Fort Colville
Gess
Hofstetter
Jenkins

Johnson
Angus MacDonald
David Thompson
Sacred Heart
Walker

THURSTON COUNTY

Brown
Bush
Centennial
Chinook
Colvin
Garfield
Griffen
Hawk
Ingersoll Stadium
Jefferson
Knowledge Hill
Knox
Lincoln
Madison
McKinley
McLane
Miller
Nazarene
New Market
Our Redeemer
Reeves
Rogers
Roosevelt
St. Michael
Schmidt
Simmons
Southworth
Wa He Lut
Washington
Woodland

WAHKIAKUM COUNTY

Wendt

WALLA WALLA COUNTY

Assumption
Berney
Davis
DeSales
Edison
Garrison
Hanson Field
Paine
Rogers
St. Patrick
St. Vincent
Sager
Sharpstein

WHATCOM COUNTY

Cozier
Ebenezer
Fisher
Isom
Jones
Larrabee
Lincoln
Lowell
Lummi
Reither
Roeder
Roosevelt
Washington

WHITMAN COUNTY

Adams
Baker
Banner
Beauridell
Belmont
Belshaw

Bishop
Brink
Bryant
Cashup
Cave
Chestnut
Collins
Crabtree
Dial Scoreboard
Fairbanks
Feenan
Fletcher
Ford
Franklin
Gale
Royal Garrison
Gates
Genaro
Gladish
Golding
Goldworthy
Grinnell
Gross
Guardian Angel- St. Boniface
Hamilton
Harlan
Heistuman
Hickman
Horn
Horton
Howard
Hubbard
Hulen
Imbler
Irene
Jefferies
Jefferson
Jennings

Jereta
Jones
Kamiache
Kenova
Knight
Kramer Field
LaDow
Lancaster-Wilada
Lincoln
Lindley
Litzenburger
Lone Star
Lynch
Manchester
Manning
Matlock
Mockonema
Morrow
Moys
O'Dell
Ontario
Pampa
Penewawa
Pitt
Purdy
Reese
Riggs
Robinson Field
Russell
Sain
Schroll
Seats
Small
Squires
Strohn
Sunset
Texas Draw
Turnbow

Turner
Wall Field
Walters
Wawawai
White
Whitlock
Wilma
Wisner Field
Wyer Field
Yoe
Zaring

YAKIMA COUNTY

Adams
Alfalfa
Armstrong
Artz-Fox
Bainter
Barge-Lincoln
Belma
Bethany
Blough
Bradshaw
Campbell
Childs
Columbus
Davis
Denny-Blaine
Eisenhower
Fort Simcoe
Franklin
Garfield
Gilbert
Guyette
Highline Hotel
Hilton
Holy Rosary
Hoover
Jefferson

Johnson
Chief Kamiakin
King
Kirkwood-Mount Adams
Laurence
Leroue
Lewis and Clark
Liberty
Lince
Lincoln
Longmire
Marquette
McAuliffe
McClure
McKinley
Mellis
Monroe
Nile
Orchard Ridges
Outlook
Phillips
Robertson
Roosevelt
St. Joseph
St. Paul
Satus
Shearer
Smith
Stanton
Taylor
Thompson
Waneta
Washington
Wheatland
Whitman-Cowiche
Whitney
Wilson
Woodcock
Yakima